feng shui your life

enhancing energies for home and spirit

feng shui your life

enhancing energies
for home and spirit

700 photographs and
diagrams explain the
ancient art and show
simple ways to
transform and
harmonize your
living environment

By Gill Hale, Stella Martin
and Josephine De Winter

southwater

This edition is published by Southwater, an imprint of
Anness Publishing Ltd, Hermes House, 88–89 Blackfriars Road,
London SE1 8HA; tel. 020 7401 2077; fax 020 7633 9499

www.southwaterbooks.com; www.annesspublishing.com

If you like the images in this book and would like to investigate using
them for publishing, promotions or advertising, please visit our website
www.practicalpictures.com for more information.

UK agent: The Manning Partnership Ltd; tel. 01225 478444;
fax 01225 478440; sales@manning-partnership.co.uk

UK distributor: Grantham Book Services Ltd; tel. 01476 541080;
fax 01476 541061; orders@gbs.tbs-ltd.co.uk

North American agent/distributor: National Book Network;
 tel. 301 459 3366; fax 301 429 5746; www.nbnbooks.com

Australian agent/distributor: Pan Macmillan Australia;
tel. 1300 135 113; fax 1300 135 103;
customer.service@macmillan.com.au

New Zealand agent/distributor: David Bateman Ltd;
tel. (09) 415 7664; fax (09) 415 8892

Publisher: Joanna Lorenz
Editorial Director: Helen Sudell
Executive Editor: Joanne Rippin
Photography: Michelle Garrett and John Freeman
Illustrator: Geoff Ball
Designer: Nigel Partridge
Production Controller: Wendy Lawson

ETHICAL TRADING POLICY
Because of our ongoing ecological investment programme, you, as our
customer, can have the pleasure and reassurance of knowing that a
tree is being cultivated on your behalf to naturally replace the materials
used to make the book you are holding. For further information about
this scheme, go to www.annesspublishing.com/trees

A CIP catalogue record for this book is available from
the British Library.

The author and publishers have made every effort to ensure that all
instructions contained within this book are accurate and safe, and
cannot accept liability for any resulting injury, damage or loss to
persons or property, however it may arise. If you do have any special
needs or problems, consult your doctor or a physiotherapist. This
book cannot replace medical consultation and should be used in
conjunction with professional advice.

Previously published as *The Spiritual Home*

Contents

Introduction

Making a house into a home is an important part of our lives, and when we are successful our houses are places in which we renew ourselves, our family and our friends. This book will enable you to achieve this by combining the ancient principles of Feng Shui, with those of space clearing, and altar making, and offers an entire spectrum of advice on how to create a spiritual home.

Feng Shui is based on an interpretation of the natural world which enabled the Chinese to create efficient agricultural systems, and also the study of the movement of heavenly bodies in order to determine the passage of time. Over the centuries, the interpretation grew more complex and became removed from its original purpose. As its exponents spread out from China across the world, their beliefs altered to fit into local beliefs and customs and, inevitably, folklore and superstition grew up around them. Fortunately, the ancient Chinese preserved the information in written form. In essence, most societies express or interpret in some way the knowledge contained in Feng Shui, but it has become absorbed into different disciplines. In China it underlies all aspects of life, from nutrition and medicine to exercise and the arts.

As practised today, Feng Shui gives us advice on how to create environments in which we feel comfortable and supported. Some of these environments are common sense. Others may not make sense until we understand that by recognizing problem areas in our lives and taking positive steps to improve them, we can connect to the energy of the spaces around us and bring about desired changes.

There is much discussion about which is the correct way to prac- tise Feng Shui in the West. Should we stick strictly to what is now called Traditional Chinese Feng Shui or should we allow for other

interpretations? Is Feng Shui Chinese, or has the West adopted a term which means something else ? This book aims to put Feng Shui in context and, by using modern examples alongside ancient ones, explore what the basic principles are.

Modern lifestyles leave us little time to stop and consider the effect our surroundings have on us. Some aspects of modern technology, the materials we use and the substances we release into the atmosphere can create damage to our health and to the planet. Although this is not Feng Shui in its purest form, concern for our environment and an awareness of our effect on it form part of Feng Shui for the present age.

In much the same way, the ancient art of Space Clearing has come to have more resonance for us in this technological age than it has for many years. Clearing emotional and energetic space is the psychic equivalent of Feng Shui, it is a way of decluttering on a spiritual plane rather than on a physical one, and although the results might not be as dramatic, they have as deep an impact. Space clearing comes from various different cultural and religious traditions, and in this book you will be introduced to several, each one with a particular technique or meaning, so you can find the way that best suits your beliefs.

Once you have altered the physical and the energetic planes of your home you will find that the benefits spread into not only your home life, but also your work and social life. To maintain and nurture this, the third section of the book explores ways in which altars and

shrines can anchor a sacred element in the heart of family and domestic life. Most of us instinctively enshrine what is precious to us, family photographs on the mantelpiece or an arrangement of treasures on a desk, but an altar created with intent takes this further, and creates a spiritual focal point. Creating your own altar brings a sacred tradition into your home and your life, and will enable you to complete the journey you have made with this book, to turn your house into a spiritual home.

Feng Shui

The human race has reached a stage where it is capable of the most amazing feats on the one hand and the most amazing follies on the other. We have the capacity to cure hereditary diseases while the foetus is still in the womb, but we also let genetically engineered organisms loose into the environment in the most dangerous form of warfare humankind has ever known. We send people into space to collect information never dreamed of half a century ago, yet at the same time we allow the planet we inhabit to become increasingly at risk from our pollution, and less able to sustain the life forms we depend on for our own survival. These anomalies of modern life are becoming more and more destructive, and less easy to understand or explain away. More and more people are turning to different approaches to living, in order to attempt to redress the balance. Feng Shui offers us the opportunity to achieve health, happiness and prosperity by living in harmony with our environment, and taking control of our own space so that it becomes more balanced. This section of the book provides an insight into how we can interpret Feng Shui principles to create nurturing and life-enhancing spaces, and begin the process of establishing our own spiritual home.

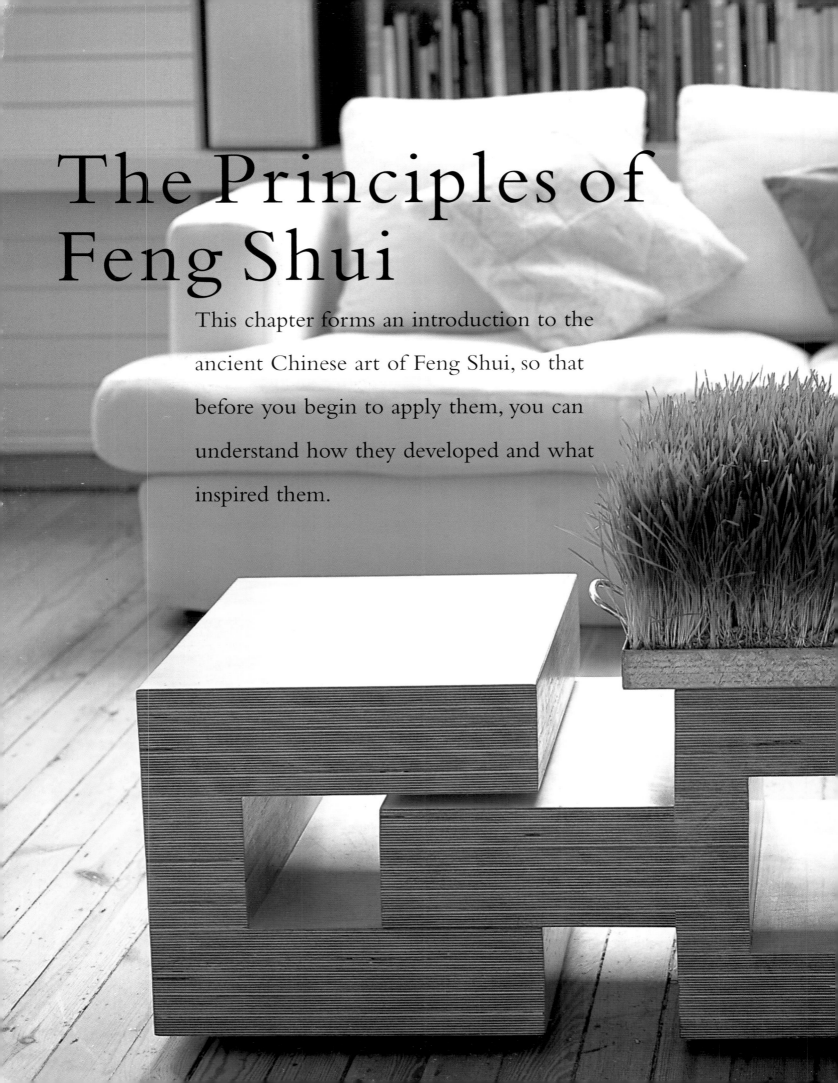

The Principles of Feng Shui

This chapter forms an introduction to the ancient Chinese art of Feng Shui, so that before you begin to apply them, you can understand how they developed and what inspired them.

What is feng shui?

The Chinese have a saying, "First, luck; second, destiny; third, Feng Shui; fourth, virtues; fifth, education": although Feng Shui can be a powerful force in shaping our lives, it is not a cure for all ills. Luck plays a major role, and personality, or karma, is almost as important. What we do with our lives and how we behave towards others will play a part, and education gives us the tools to make sense of the world. Feng Shui is just one part of the complete package.

△ In China the dragon symbolizes good fortune.
Its presence is felt in landforms
and watercourses.

△ The Dragon Hills which protect Hong Kong
are believed to be responsible for its prosperity.

▷ Much of the symbolic imagery in Feng Shui is
taken from landscapes such as this,
in Guilin, southern China.

The single factor which sets Feng Shui apart from other philosophical systems is that it has the capacity for change built into it. Most systems evolved from similar principles; understanding the natural world played a major role and natural phenomena were believed to be imbued with a spirit or deity, recognition of which would give people some benefit in their lives. Where these systems became established as religions, the deities were worshipped, but Feng Shui has remained a philosophy and can be used in any culture and alongside any belief system.

Feng Shui uses formulae which determine the rising and falling energy in a given time span of an individual or a house. Other formulae indicate a person's best location within a home or office, and can suggest the best placing of beds and desks. Many Chinese people consult astrologers annually to further refine this, so that every activity within the year can be pinpointed accurately and undertaken at an auspicious time. This advice can be as precise as the best time to conceive or even when to wash your hair.

The philosophy of Feng Shui is embraced by people who are aware of the impact their surroundings have on them and who feel the need to take action to improve their lives. Using Feng Shui correctly, however, is a skill and its principles cannot be instantly applied, or adapted simply to suit the circumstances of a place or an individual.

▽ **Our surroundings affect us. Fresh air, natural products and a healthy environment enhance our mental and physical well-being.**

Feng Shui enables us to position ourselves within our environment to our best advantage. The positioning of our houses and offices as well as their internal design affects each of us positively or negatively. Feng Shui helps us to determine the most favourable positions for us and the layouts, colours and designs which will support us. In the garden we can determine the best locations for the different activities we intend to pursue there, but we also have to take account of the plants in the garden and their needs, which are equally important if the environment is to thrive.

△ **Water energy plays a significant role in Feng Shui. Here a fountain brings life to an office courtyard.**

The following chapters provide information on those aspects of this complex and fascinating subject that can be utilized by everyone in their own space. When we introduce Feng Shui into our lives we can only benefit, even where we only touch the surface. As we become more aware of our surroundings, and actively begin to change those factors with which we feel uncomfortable, we begin to gain a deeper insight into ourselves and our part in the wider picture.

▽ **The T'ung Shui almanac, produced for centuries, details the best times to move house, change jobs or even bathe.**

Approaches to feng shui

Feng Shui is about interpreting environments. Practitioners use a number of different approaches to connect with the energy or "feel" of a place, and fine-tune it to make it work for those living or working there. Provided the principles are understood, the different approaches will be effective. More often than not, practitioners use a mixture of methods to create the effects they want.

the environmental approach

In ancient times, people lived by their knowledge of local conditions, handed down through the generations. Their needs were basic: food, water and shelter. Observation would tell them from which direction the prevailing winds were coming and they would build their homes in protective sites. They needed water in order to grow and transport their crops so rivers were important, and the direction of the flow and the orientation of the banks would determine the type of crops which could be grown. This branch of Feng Shui is known as the Form or Landform School and was the earliest approach to the subject.

▽ **The Form School regards this as the ideal spot on which to build. The Black Tortoise hill at the rear offers support while the White Tiger and Green Dragon give protection from the wind, with the all-powerful dragon slightly higher than the Tiger. The Red Phoenix marks the front boundary, and the river irrigates the site as well as enabling crops to be transported for trade.**

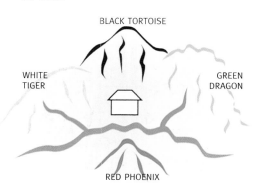

BLACK TORTOISE

WHITE TIGER

GREEN DRAGON

RED PHOENIX

△ **These "Karst" limestone hills in China symbolically protect an area of rich agricultural land.**

▷ **A luo pan or compass, used by geomancers in ancient China. Much of the information it records is regularly used by Feng Shui consultants.**

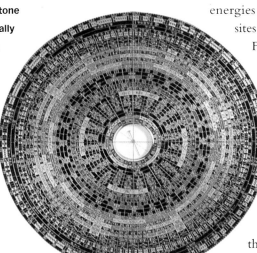

the compass approach

In ancient China, geomancers investigated earth formations and watercourses while astronomers charted the skies. Those who understood the power of the information they possessed recorded their knowledge on an instrument called a luo pan, or compass. The luo pan illustrates not only direction, but also investigates the energy of each direction, depending on the landform or heavenly body to be found there. Interpreting these energies suggests suitable sites for human beings. Feng Shui is based on the *I Ching*, a philosophical book which interprets the energies of the universe. Its 64 images from the yearly nature cycle form the outer ring of the luo pan. With the wisdom of ancient sages added to it over the centuries, the *I Ching* offers us a means to connect to the natural flow of the universe. Its built-in time factor allows us to connect to it in different ways at different times in our lives.

the intuitive approach

Ancient texts illustrate every shape of mountain and watercourse. The names illustrate concepts significant to the Chinese psyche. "Tiger in Waiting" suggests a negative place, where residents will never be able to relax, whereas "Baby Dragon Looking at its Mother" indicates a much more restful environment.

The ancient text of the *Water Dragon Classic* provides more information on the best places to build, showing flow direction and position within the tributaries, with the names again indicating the type of environment. The sensibilities of people living and working on the land were finely tuned and their knowledge of the natural world endowed them with an instinct for suitable sites to grow crops.

▷ **Mountain sites (1 & 2) and river sites (3 & 4); the dots represent buildings. All except for "Tiger in Waiting" are auspicious positions to build a new home.**

▽ **This prime site is protected by mountains, with healthy watercourses.**

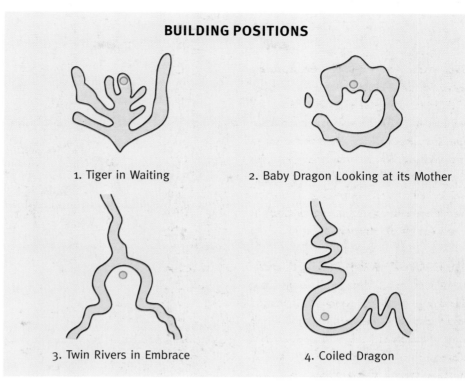

BUILDING POSITIONS

1. Tiger in Waiting

2. Baby Dragon Looking at its Mother

3. Twin Rivers in Embrace

4. Coiled Dragon

The theories of feng shui

Ancient peoples regarded the heavens, the earth and themselves as part of one system. This holistic view of life persists in many cultures, where health and medicine, food and lifestyle, and the route to salvation are all interconnected in one ecological system.

the Way

The Tao, or the Way, the philosophy of which underlies Feng Shui, shows how to order our lives to live in harmony with ourselves, each other and the natural world. We can use Feng Shui to help us work towards achieving this.

▽ "The Dragon Breathing on the Lake" – the lake is a powerful Chinese image, that symbolizes a light-reflective surface harbouring a dark and deep interior.

yin and yang

Positive and negative forces act together in order to create energy – in electricity, for instance. Yin and yang represent these two forces which are in constant movement, each attempting to gain dominance. Where one achieves dominance, an imbalance occurs, so when one

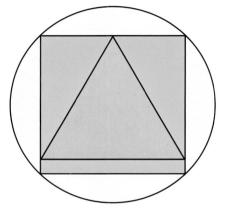

force becomes too strong its influence subsides and the other takes over. Still water, for example, is yin; a raging torrent is yang. Imagine a slow-moving yin river. When it hits rocks and descends, turbulence occurs, it speeds up and becomes yang. When it flows into a lake, it slows down and becomes yin once more. Yin and yang are opposing but interdependent concepts – without the idea of cold we would not be able to describe heat. At their extremes they change into each

△ The T'ai Chi symbol illustrates the concept of yin and yang, the opposite yet interdependent forces that drive the world.

◁ Circle, Square, Triangle – signifying Heaven, Earth, human beings – the universal cosmological symbol.

YIN	YANG
Moon	Sun
Winter	Summer
Dark	Light
Feminine	Masculine
Interior	Exterior
Low	High
Stillness	Movement
Passive	Active
Odd numbers	Even numbers
Earth	Heaven
Cold	Heat
Soft	Hard
Valleys	Hills
Still water	Mountains
Gardens	Houses
Sleep	Wakefulness

other; ice can burn and sunstroke sufferers shiver. The aim is to achieve a balance between them. There are examples throughout the book of how we can achieve this in our own environments. Some of the more common associations are listed left.

chi

The concept of chi is unknown in Western philosophy but figures repeatedly in the philosophies of the East. It is the life force of all animate things, the quality of environments, the power of the sun, the moon and weather systems, and the driving force in human beings. The movements in T'ai Chi, widely practised in China, encourage chi to move through the body. Acupuncture needles are used to unblock its flow when stuck. Chinese herbal medicine uses the special energetic qualities of herbs to correct chi when it becomes unbalanced. Meditation helps to establish a healthy mind: every brush stroke of the Chinese artist or sweep of the calligrapher's pen is the result of trained mental processes and the

▽ **An acupuncturist at work. The needles unblock the energy channels and enable chi to flow round the body.**

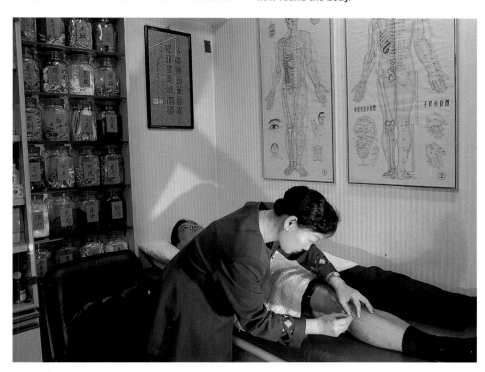

△ **Chinese people practising T'ai Chi. The exercises are designed to aid the flow of chi in the body.**

correct breathing techniques, which ensure that each carefully composed painting or document is infused with chi.

The purpose of Feng Shui is to create environments in which chi flows smoothly to achieve physical and mental health. Where chi flows gently through a house, the occupants will be positive and will have an easy passage through life. Where chi moves sluggishly or becomes stuck, then the chances are that problems will occur in the day-to-day life or long-term prospects of those living there.

Where chi flows smoothly in the garden, the plants will be healthy and the wildlife there will flourish. Animals, birds, insects and the myriad of unseen microorganisms that live there will regulate themselves and create a balanced and supportive environment. Where chi cannot flow unimpeded and becomes sluggish or stuck, an area may become dank or there may be an imbalance which creates, say, a plague of aphids.

In an office where chi flows freely, employees will be happy and supportive, projects will be completed on time and stress levels will be low. Where the chi is stuck, there will be disharmony and the business will not flourish.

Five types of energy

Some of the latest scientific theories enable us to make sense of the ancient formulae on which Feng Shui is based. It is accepted that everything in the universe vibrates. All our senses and everything we encounter are attuned to certain frequencies, which react with us in a positive or negative way. We are all familiar with sound waves, which bring us radio, and electromagnetic waves, which bring us television. Colours, shapes, food, weather conditions – everything in our lives affects us on a vibrational level for good or ill and, in turn, we react in various yet predictable ways, depending on our individual traits.

The concept of elements exists throughout the world. The Chinese recognize five which arise out of the interplay of yin and yang and represent different manifestations of chi. They represent a classification system for everything in the universe, including people, as seen in the Relationships of the Five Elements table.

Ideally, there should be a balance of all the elements. Where one dominates or is lacking, then difficulties occur. Interpreting and balancing the elements plays a major part in the practice of Feng Shui. The elements move in a predetermined way, illustrated as a cycle in which they all support each other. A useful way of remembering this is by looking at the cycle in the following way. Water enables Wood to grow, Wood enables Fire to burn resulting in ashes or Earth, in which forms Metal, which in liquid form resembles Water. Another cycle indicates how the five elements

control each other and can be memorized as follows: Water extinguishes Fire, and in turn is soaked up by the Earth, which is depleted of energy by Wood in the form of trees, which can be destroyed by Metal tools.

The "Relationships of the Five Elements" table shown below introduces another aspect – how in supporting a different element, an element can itself be weakened. The applications of each of the five elements, and the ways they relate to each other, are illustrated throughout this book.

△ Storms are nature's way of restoring a balance. They replenish negative ions in the atmosphere, which improves air quality.

▽ The heavenly bodies are essential to our lives and their movements lie at the heart of Feng Shui theory.

THE RELATIONSHIPS OF THE FIVE ELEMENTS

Element	Helped by	Harmed by	Weakened by	Weakens
Wood	Water	Metal	Fire	Earth
Fire	Wood	Water	Earth	Metal
Earth	Fire	Wood	Metal	Water
Metal	Earth	Fire	Water	Wood
Water	Metal	Earth	Wood	Fire

THE FIVE ELEMENTS

Element	Characteristics	Personalities	Associations
WOOD 	Symbolizes spring, growth and plant life. In its yin form, it is supple and pliable, in its yang form as sturdy as an oak. Positively used, it is a walking stick; negatively used, a spear. Bamboo is cherished in China for its ability to sway in the wind yet be used as scaffolding. Viewed as a tree, Wood energy is expansive, nurturing and versatile.	Wood people are public-spirited and energetic. Ideas people, their outgoing personalities win them support. They visualize rather than committing themselves to plans. *Positively* – they are artistic and undertake tasks with enthusiasm. *Negatively* – they become impatient and angry and often fail to finish the tasks they have begun.	Trees and plants Wooden furniture Paper Green Columns Decking Landscape pictures
FIRE 	Symbolizes summer, fire and heat. It can bring light, warmth and happiness or it can erupt, explode and destroy with great violence. Positively, it stands for honour and fairness. Negatively, it stands for aggression and war.	Fire people are leaders and crave action. They inspire others to follow, often into trouble, as they dislike rules and fail to see consequences. *Positively* – they are innovative, humorous and passionate people. *Negatively* – they are impatient, exploit others and have little thought for their feelings.	Sun symbols Candles, lights and lamps Triangles Red Man-made materials Sun or fire pictures
EARTH 	Symbolizes the nurturing environment that enables seeds to grow, which all living things emanate from and return to. It nurtures, supports and interacts with each of the other elements. Positively, it denotes fairness, wisdom and instinct. Negatively, it can smother or represent the nervous anticipation of non-existent problems.	Earth people are supportive and loyal. Practical and persevering, they are a tower of strength in a crisis. They do not rush anything, but their support is enduring. Patient and steady, they possess inner strength. *Positively* – earth people are loyal, dependable and patient. *Negatively* – they are obsessional and prone to nit-picking.	Clay, brick and terracotta Cement and stone Squares Yellow, orange and brown
METAL 	Symbolizes autumn and strength. Its nature represents solidity and the ability to contain objects. On the other hand, metal is also a conductor. Positively, it represents communication, brilliant ideas and justice. Negatively, it can suggest destruction, danger and sadness. Metal can be a beautiful and precious commodity, or the blade of a weapon.	Metal people are dogmatic and resolute. They pursue their ambitious aims single-mindedly. Good organizers, they are independent and happy in their own company. Faith in their own abilities inclines them towards inflexibility although they thrive on change. They are serious and do not accept help easily. *Positively* – they are strong, intuitive and interesting people. *Negatively* – they are inflexible, melancholic and serious.	All metals Round shapes Domes Metal objects Door furniture and doorsteps Kitchenware White, grey, silver and gold Coins Clocks
WATER 	Symbolizes winter and water itself, gentle rain or a storm. It suggests the inner self, art and beauty. It touches everything. Positively, it nurtures and supports with understanding. Negatively, it can wear down and exhaust. Associated with the emotions, it can suggest fear, nervousness and stress.	Water people communicate well. They are diplomatic and persuasive. Sensitive to the moods of others, they will lend an ear. They are intuitive and make excellent negotiators. Flexible and adaptable, they view things holistically. *Positively* – water people are artistic, sociable and sympathetic. *Negatively* – water people are fickle and intrusive.	Rivers, streams and lakes Blue and black Mirrors and glass Meandering patterns Fountains and ponds Fish tanks Water pictures

Chinese astrology

An analysis of an environment using a luo pan compass looks at the energetic qualities of the various compass points. The Earthly Branches on the compass represent 12 of these points and also correspond to the 12 animals which relate to Chinese astrology. We often find ourselves in situations at home, or at work, when we canot understand how another person can view the same situation so differently from us, or can make us feel uncomfortable, or find different things irritating or amusing. Looking at the animals enables us to explore these differences by allowing us an insight into the make-up of our natures and personalities.

With this knowledge, we can come to know ourselves better and to accept the personalities of others. At home, it may encourage us to think twice, for instance, before launching into a tirade on tidiness or punctuality. It also has an important use in the workplace in keeping warring factions apart and ensuring a harmonious balance between productive output and socializing.

the cycles

The Chinese calendar is based on the cycle of the moon, which determines that each month is approximately 29½ days long, beginning with a new moon. The years progress in cycles of 12 and it is helpful to appreciate the subtleties of Chinese symbology since each year is represented by an animal and the characteristics of each animal and its way of life are used to identify different types of people. Cultural differences are apt to get in the way if we attempt this identification ourselves; whereas Westerners would describe the Rat's character, for example, as sly and crafty, the Chinese respect its quick mind and native cunning.

Each animal is governed by an element which determines its intrinsic nature. The cycle of 12 is repeated five times to form a larger cycle of 60 years and in each of these cycles, the animals are ascribed an element with either a yin or yang characteristic, which determines their characters. Thus in 60 years, no two animals are the same. We begin by investigating the basic animal characteristics.

◁ In the Chinese calendar each year is represented by an animal and each animal is governed by an element.

If we do not get on with someone, it may be that the animals associated with us in the Chinese calendar are not compatible. Alternatively, it may be that the elements that represent the time of our birth are not in harmony with the elements of the other person.

finding your animal

The Chinese year does not begin on 1st January but on a date which corresponds with the second new moon after the winter equinox, so it varies from year to year. Thus someone born on 25th January 1960 according to the Western calendar would actually be born in 1959 according to the Chinese calendar. The "Chinese Animals Table" opposite gives the exact dates when each year begins and ends, as well as its ruling animal and element. Their outer characteristics are identified by the element of the year they were born, as shown in "The Nature of the Animals" box (left). The ways in which the elements affect an animal's personality are described in "The Five Elements" table.

animal cycles

One of the 12 animals represents each lunar month, each with its own element governing its intrinsic nature. Over 60 years, the Five Elements cycle spins so that each animal can be Wood, Fire, Earth, Metal or Water, which determines its character.

In a full analysis by an experienced Feng Shui consultant, each of us will have a collection of eight elements that together make up not only our character, but also our destiny.

THE NATURE OF THE ANIMALS

Rat	Water
Ox	Earth
Tiger	Wood
Rabbit	Wood
Dragon	Earth
Snake	Fire
Horse	Fire
Goat	Earth
Monkey	Metal
Rooster	Metal
Dog	Earth
Pig	Water

CHINESE ANIMALS TABLE

Year	Year Begins	Year Ends	Animal	Element
1920	20 February 1920	7 February 1921	Monkey	Metal +
1921	8 February 1921	27 January 1922	Rooster	Metal −
1922	28 January 1922	15 February 1923	Dog	Water +
1923	16 February 1923	4 February 1924	Pig	Water −
1924	5 February 1924	24 January 1925	Rat	Wood +
1925	25 January 1925	12 February 1926	Ox	Wood −
1926	13 February 1926	1 February 1927	Tiger	Fire +
1927	2 February 1927	22 January 1928	Rabbit	Fire −
1928	23 January 1928	9 February 1929	Dragon	Earth +
1929	10 February 1929	29 January 1930	Snake	Earth −
1930	30 January 1930	16 February 1931	Horse	Metal +
1931	17 February 1931	5 February 1932	Goat	Metal −
1932	6 February 1932	25 January 1933	Monkey	Water +
1933	26 January 1933	13 February 1934	Rooster	Water −
1934	14 February 1934	3 February 1935	Dog	Wood +
1935	4 February 1935	23 January 1936	Pig	Wood −
1936	24 January 1936	10 February 1937	Rat	Fire +
1937	11 February 1937	30 January 1938	Ox	Fire −
1938	31 January 1938	18 February 1939	Tiger	Earth +
1939	19 February 1939	7 February 1940	Rabbit	Earth −
1940	8 February 1940	26 January 1941	Dragon	Metal +
1941	27 January 1941	14 February 1942	Snake	Metal −
1942	15 February 1942	4 February 1943	Horse	Water +
1943	5 February 1943	24 January 1944	Goat	Water −
1944	25 January 1944	12 February 1945	Monkey	Wood +
1945	13 February 1945	1 February 1946	Rooster	Wood −
1946	2 February 1946	21 January 1947	Dog	Fire +
1947	22 January 1947	9 February 1948	Pig	Fire −
1948	10 February 1948	28 January 1949	Rat	Earth +
1949	29 January 1949	16 February 1950	Ox	Earth −
1950	17 February 1950	5 February 1951	Tiger	Metal +
1951	6 February 1951	26 January 1952	Rabbit	Metal −
1952	27 January 1952	13 February 1953	Dragon	Water +
1953	14 February 1953	2 February 1954	Snake	Water −
1954	3 February 1954	23 January 1955	Horse	Wood +
1955	24 January 1955	11 February 1956	Goat	Wood −
1956	12 February 1956	30 January 1957	Monkey	Fire +
1957	31 January 1957	17 February 1958	Rooster	Fire −
1958	18 February 1958	7 February 1959	Dog	Earth +
1959	8 February 1959	27 January 1960	Pig	Earth −
1960	28 January 1960	14 February 1961	Rat	Metal +
1961	15 February 1961	4 February 1962	Ox	Metal −
1962	5 February 1962	24 January 1963	Tiger	Water +
1963	25 January 1963	12 February 1964	Rabbit	Water −
1964	13 February 1964	1 February 1965	Dragon	Wood +
1965	2 February 1965	20 January 1966	Snake	Wood −
1966	21 January 1966	8 February 1967	Horse	Fire +
1967	9 February 1967	29 January 1968	Goat	Fire −
1968	30 January 1968	16 February 1969	Monkey	Earth +
1969	17 February 1969	5 February 1970	Rooster	Earth −
1970	6 February 1970	26 January 1971	Dog	Metal +
1971	27 January 1971	15 February 1972	Pig	Metal −
1972	16 February 1972	2 February 1973	Rat	Water +
1973	3 February 1973	22 January 1974	Ox	Water −
1974	23 January 1974	10 February 1975	Tiger	Wood +
1975	11 February 1975	30 January 1976	Rabbit	Wood −
1976	31 January 1976	17 February 1977	Dragon	Fire +
1977	18 February 1977	6 February 1978	Snake	Fire −
1978	7 February 1978	27 January 1979	Horse	Earth +
1979	28 January 1979	15 February 1980	Goat	Earth −
1980	16 February 1980	4 February 1981	Monkey	Metal +
1981	5 February 1981	24 January 1982	Rooster	Metal −
1982	25 January 1982	12 February 1983	Dog	Water +
1983	13 February 1983	1 February 1984	Pig	Water −
1984	2 February 1984	19 February 1985	Rat	Wood +
1985	20 February 1985	8 February 1986	Ox	Wood −
1986	9 February 1986	28 January 1987	Tiger	Fire +
1987	29 January 1987	16 February 1988	Rabbit	Fire −
1988	17 February 1988	5 February 1989	Dragon	Earth +
1989	6 February 1989	26 January 1990	Snake	Earth −
1990	27 January 1990	14 February 1991	Horse	Metal +
1991	15 February 1991	3 February 1992	Goat	Metal −
1992	4 February 1992	22 January 1993	Monkey	Water +
1993	23 January 1993	9 February 1994	Rooster	Water −
1994	10 February 1994	30 January 1995	Dog	Wood +
1995	31 January 1995	18 February 1996	Pig	Wood −
1996	19 February 1996	6 February 1997	Rat	Fire +
1997	7 February 1997	27 January 1998	Ox	Fire −
1998	28 January 1998	15 February 1999	Tiger	Earth +
1999	16 February 1999	4 February 2000	Rabbit	Earth −
2000	5 February 2000	23 January 2001	Dragon	Metal +
2001	24 January 2001	11 February 2002	Snake	Metal −
2002	12 February 2002	31 January 2003	Horse	Water +
2003	1 February 2003	21 January 2004	Goat	Water −
2004	22 January 2004	8 February 2005	Monkey	Wood +
2005	9 February 2005	28 January 2006	Rooster	Wood −
2006	29 January 2006	17 February 2007	Dog	Fire +
2007	18 February 2007	6 February 2008	Pig	Fire −
2008	7 February 2008	25 January 2009	Rat	Earth +
2009	26 January 2009	13 February 2010	Ox	Earth −
2010	14 February 2010	2 February 2011	Tiger	Metal +
2011	3 February 2011	22 January 2012	Rabbit	Metal −
2012	23 January 2012	9 February 2013	Dragon	Water +
2013	10 February 2013	30 January 2014	Snake	Water −

The animal signs

Using characteristics that are perceived to be an inherent part of the natures of the 12 animals, Chinese astrology attributes certain aspects of these to the characteristics and behaviour of people born at specific times. This system operates in much the same way as Western astrology.

the rat

An opportunist with an eye for a bargain, Rats tend to collect and hoard, but are unwilling to pay too much for anything. They are devoted to their families, particularly their children.

On the surface, Rats are sociable and gregarious yet underneath they can be miserly and petty. Quick-witted and passionate, they are capable of deep emotions despite their cool exteriors. Their nervous energy and ambition may lead them to attempt more tasks than they are able to complete successfully.

Rats will stand by their friends as long as they receive their support in return. However, they are not above using information given to them in confidence in order to advance their own cause.

▽ Sociable and family-minded, Rats are quick witted and opportunistic.

▽ Dependable and loyal, the Ox displays endless patience until pushed too far.

△ Dynamic and generous, Tigers are warm-hearted unless they are crossed.

the ox

Invariably solid and dependable, the Ox is an excellent organizer. Oxen are systematic in their approach to every task they undertake. They are not easily influenced by others' ideas. Loyalty is part of their make-up, but if crossed or deceived they will never forget. Oxen do not appear to be imaginative though they are capable of good ideas. Although not demonstrative or the most exciting people romantically, they are entirely dependable and make devoted parents. They are people of few words but fine understated gestures. Oxen are renowned for their patience, but it has its limits – once roused, their temper is a sight to behold.

the tiger

Dynamic and impulsive Tigers live life to the full. Tigers often leap into projects without planning, but their natural exuberance will carry them through successfully unless boredom creeps in and they do not complete the task. Tigers do not like failure and need to be admired. If their spirits fall, they require a patient ear to listen until they bounce back again. They like excitement in relationships and static situations leave them cold. Tigers are egotistic. They can be generous and warm, but sometimes show their claws.

the rabbit

A born diplomat Rabbits cannot bear conflict. Rabbits can be evasive and will often give the answer they think someone wishes to hear rather than enter into a discussion. This is not to say they give in easily: the docile cover hides a strong will and self-assurance. It is difficult to gauge what Rabbits are thinking and they can often appear to be constantly daydreaming, though in reality they may be planning their next strategy. The calmest of the animal signs, Rabbits are social creatures up to the point when their space is invaded. Good communication skills enable Rabbits to enjoy the company of others and they are good counsellors. They prefer to keep away from the limelight where possible and to enjoy the finer things of life.

△ **Good counsellors and communicators, Rabbits also need their own space.**

the dragon

Posessed of a pioneering spirit, Dragons will launch straight into projects or conversations. Dragons often fail to notice others trying to keep up or indeed those plotting behind their backs. Authority figures, they make their own laws and cannot bear restriction. They prefer to get on with a job themselves and are good at motivating others into action. They are

△ **Powerful leaders, Dragons prefer to follow their own path in life.**

always available to help others, but their pride makes it difficult for them to accept help in return. Although they are always at the centre of things, they tend to be loners and are prone to stress when life becomes difficult. Hardworking and generous, Dragons are entirely trustworthy and are loyal friends. They enjoy excitement and new situations. When upset, they can be explosive, but all is soon forgotten.

the snake

Although a connoisseur of the good things in life, Snakes are also inward-looking and self-reliant, Snakes tend to keep their own counsel and dislike relying on others. They can be ruthless in pursuing their goals. Although very kind and generous, Snakes can be demanding in relationships. They find it hard to forgive and will never forget a slight. Never under-estimate the patience of a snake, who will wait in the wings until the time is right to strike. They are elegant and sophisticated and although they are good at making money, they never spend it on trifles. Only the best is good enough for them. Very intuitive, Snakes can sense the motives of others and sum up situations accurately. If crossed, Snakes will bite with deadly accuracy. They exude mystery, ooze charm and can be deeply passionate.

▽ **Mysterious and passionate, Snakes have endless patience.**

△ **Active and excitable, the Horse's nervous energy often runs away with them.**

the horse

Ever-active, the Horse will work tirelessly until a project is completed, but only if the deadline is their own. Horses have lightning minds and can sum up people and situations in an instant, sometimes too quickly, and they will move on before seeing the whole picture. Capable of undertaking several tasks at once, Horses are constantly on the move and fond of exercise. They may exhaust themselves physically and mentally. Horses are ambitious and confident in their own abilities. They are not interested in the opinions of others and are adept at side-stepping issues. They can be impatient and have explosive tempers although they rarely bear grudges.

the goat

Goats are emotional and compassionate. Peace-lovers, Goats always behave correctly and they are extremely accommodating to others. They tend to be shy and vulnerable to criticism. They worry a lot and appear to be easily put upon, but when they feel strongly about something they will dig their heels in and sulk until they achieve their objectives. Goats are generally popular and are usually well cared for by others. They appreciate the finer things in life and are usually lucky. They find it difficult to deal with difficulties and deprivation. Ardent romantics, Goats can obtain their own way by wearing their partners down and turning every occasion to their advantage. They will do anything to avoid conflict and hate making decisions.

▽ **Peace-loving Goats are kind and popular, they hate conflict and will try to avoid it.**

the monkey

Monkeys are intelligent and capable of using their wits to solve problems. Monkeys often wriggle out of difficult situations and are not above trickery if it will further their own ends. Monkeys tend to be oblivious of other people and of the effect their own actions may have on them. In spite of this, they are usually popular and are able to motivate others by their sheer enthusiasm for new projects. Monkeys are constantly on the look out for new challenges and their innovative approach and excellent memories generally make them successful. They are full of energy and are always active. They have little sympathy for those who are unable to keep up with them, but will soon forget any difficulties.

▽ **Energetic Monkeys use their intelligence to push their own ideas forward.**

△ **The flamboyant Rooster can be easily won over by flattery and admiration**.

the rooster

Highly sociable creatures, Roosters shine in situations where they are able to be the centre of attention. If a Rooster is present, everyone will be aware of the fact because no Rooster can ever take a back seat at a social gathering. They are dignified, confident and extremely strong-willed, yet they may have a negative streak. They excel in arguments and debates. Incapable of underhandedness, Roosters lay all their cards on the table and do not spare others' feelings in their quest to do the right thing. They never weary of getting to the bottom of a problem and are perfectionists in all that they do. Roosters can usually be won over by flattery. Full of energy, Roosters are brave, but they hate criticism and can be puritanical in their approach to life.

the dog

Dogs are entirely dependable and have an inherent sense of justice. Intelligent, Dogs are loyal to their friends and they always listen to others, although they can be critical. In a crisis, Dogs always help and will never betray a friend. They can be hard workers, but are not all that interested in

▽ **Dogs are loyal and hard-working, but enjoy relaxing too**.

accumulating wealth for themselves. They like to spend time relaxing. Dogs take time to get to know people but have a tendency to pigeon-hole them. When they want something badly they can be persistent. If roused they can be obstinate and occasionally they lash out, although their temper is usually short-lived. Some Dogs can be rather nervous and they may be prone to pessimism.

△ **Peace-loving Pigs are sociable and popular and are able to organize others well**.

the pig

The Pig is everybody's friend. Honest and generous, Pigs are always available to bail others out of difficulties. Pigs love the social scene and are popular. They rarely argue and if they do fly off the handle, they bear no grudges afterwards. They abhor conflict and very often will not notice when others are attempting to upset them. They prefer to think well of people. Over-indulgence is their greatest weakness and Pigs will spend heavily in pursuit of pleasure. They always share with their friends and trust that, in return, their friends will make allowances for their own little weaknesses. Great organizers, Pigs like to have a cause and will often rally others to it as well.

Compatibility of signs

The saying, "You can choose your friends but not your family", is often heard from those who do not have harmonious family relationships, and we all find that we are drawn more to some people than to others. Chinese astrology uses the year, month, day and time of birth (each of which is represented by an animal and the yin or yang attributes of its accompanying element) to analyse characters and predict fortunes.

Analyses of relationships depend upon the interaction of the elements on each person's chart. We can gain some insight

△ We function well at work when we are compatible with our colleagues. The man on the right looks uncomfortable.

into our own characters and those of our family and colleagues by using the "Chinese Animals Table" and then looking at the associated elements with their yang (+) (positive characteristics) or yin (−) (negative characteristics) in "The Five Elements" table.

▽ **We are drawn to people for a variety of reasons. Compatibility of animal signs and elements can certainly help.**

▽ **This table shows which of our family, friends and colleagues we relate to best according to Chinese astrology.**

COMPATIBILITY TABLE

	RAT	OX	TIGER	RABBIT	DRAGON	SNAKE	HORSE	GOAT	MONKEY	ROOSTER	DOG	PIG
RAT	+	=	+	−	*	=	−	−	*	−	+	+
OX	=	+	−	=	+	*	−	−	+	*	−	+
TIGER	+	−	+	−	+	−	*	+	−	=	*	=
RABBIT	+	+	−	+	=	+	−	*	−	−	=	*
DRAGON	*	−	+	=	−	+	−	+	*	+	−	=
SNAKE	+	*	−	+	=	+	−	=	−	*	+	−
HORSE	−	−	*	−	=	+	−	=	+	+	*	+
GOAT	−	−	=	*	+	+	=	+	+	−	−	*
MONKEY	*	+	−	−	*	−	−	+	=	+	+	=
ROOSTER	−	*	+	−	=	*	+	=	−	−	+	+
DOG	+	−	*	=	−	+	*	−	+	−	=	+
PIG	=	+	=	*	+	−	−	*	−	+	+	−

KEY: * Excellent = Good + Workable − Difficult

The animal years

As we have seen, each year is ruled by an animal and its character is said to denote the energetic quality of the year.

The animal which rules each year and the date of the Chinese New Year for around a hundred-year period are shown on the "Chinese Animals Table". For ease of reference, 1999–2010 are shown below. Our fortunes in each year are indicated by whether or not we are compatible with the animal ruling that year, which can be checked by referring back to the "Compatibility Table".

1999	Rabbit	2005	Rooster
2000	Dragon	2006	Dog
2001	Snake	2007	Pig
2002	Horse	2008	Rat
2003	Goat	2009	Ox
2004	Monkey	2010	Tiger

year of the rabbit

A respite from the past year and a breather before the next, rest is indicated here. This is a time for negotiations and settlements, but not for new ventures. Women's and family concerns are considered important.

year of the dragon

The time for new business ventures and projects. Euphoric and unpredictable, this is the year for wild schemes and risks. Dragon babies are considered lucky.

year of the snake

Peace returns and allows time to reflect. Care should be taken in business matters as treachery and underhand dealings are indicated. Money is made and communication is good. A fertile year, in which morality becomes an issue.

year of the horse

An energetic and volatile year in which money will be spent and borrowed. Some impulsive behaviour will bring rewards, while some will fail. A year for marriage and divorce.

year of the goat

A quiet year in which family matters are to the fore. A year for consolidating and for diplomatic negotiations, rather than launching new projects.

year of the monkey

An unpredictable year when nothing goes according to plan. Only the quick-witted will prosper. New ideas abound and communication will flourish.

year of the rooster

A year for making feelings known and letting grievances out. This may cause disharmony in families so tact is required.

year of the dog

Worthy causes abound – human and animal rights and environmental issues are in the public eye. Security should be checked, by governments and at home. A year for marriage and the family.

year of the pig

The last year of the cycle and unfinished business should be concluded. Optimism abounds and the pursuit of leisure is indicated. Family concerns will go well.

year of the rat

This is a lucky year, a good time to start a new venture. The rewards will not come without hard work, but with careful planning they will arrive.

year of the ox

Harvest is the symbol for this year so we will reap what we have sown. Decisions should be made now and contracts signed. This is a conservative year so grand or outrageous schemes are not considered appropriate.

year of the tiger

Sudden conflicts and crises arise in this year and will have an impact for some time. The year for grand schemes for the courageous, but underhand activities may suffer from repercussions.

▽ **Family relationships are usually harmonious if the animal signs are compatible and the elements do not clash.**

The Bagua and the magic square

The compass directions and their associations are fundamental to the practice of Feng Shui. Astronomical and geomantic calculations and the place of human beings within them are plotted on a luo pan, an instrument so powerful that it has been likened to a computer. The luo pan can indicate, to those who know how to interpret it, which illness someone in a certain location might be suffering from, or the fortunes of a person living in a certain room in a house.

This vast amount of information has been reduced to a shorthand form incorporated in a "Magic Square". In cultures worldwide, this was used as a talisman. Many formulae based on the magic square are used to discover whether a place is auspicious, in itself and for the people living there, and the simplest of these are introduced in this book. The diagram on the right shows how the energies represented by the Magic Square always move in a fixed pattern. These patterns are repeated over time and can indicate the fortunes of a person or building in a certain year.

the bagua

The information contained in the luo pan is condensed into the Magic Square, which forms the basis of the Bagua, or Pa Kua, a tool we can use to investigate our homes and offices. The Bagua below holds some of the images which describe the energies of the eight directions and the central position. The Bagua represents the journey of life, the Tao, and we can use it to create comfortable living, working and leisure spaces.

When applying Feng Shui principles to your house, garden or office you will need a tracing of the Bagua with the colours, compass points and directions all added on.

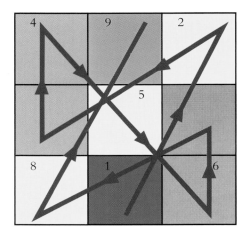

△ **The Magic Square: the "magic" lies in the fact that every line adds up to 15. Magic squares exist all over the world. In ancient cultures, such symbols were a source of power to their initiates. In Hebrew culture, the pattern formed by the movement of energies is known as the seal of Saturn and is used in Western magic. In Islamic cultures, intricate patterns are based on complex magic squares.**

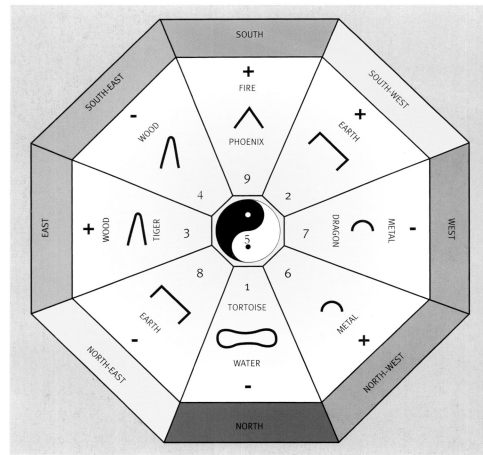

THE BAGUA, OR PA KUA

This shows the energies associated with the eight directions. The outer bar shows the colours and directions associated with the five elements. The symbols indicate the yin (-) or yang (+) quality of the element associated with each direction. Also shown are the shapes associated with each element. The four symbolic animals which represent the energy of each of the four cardinal directions – north, south, east, west – are indicated, and the numbers of the Magic Square are shown in their associated directions. We take on the characteristics of a number and the energies associated with it, which shape we are, where we feel comfortable, and our fortunes. The Chinese compass is always drawn facing south but this does not affect the actual magnetic north-south directions.

Finding your magic number

To complete the picture, it is necessary to discover how human beings fit into the scheme. Each person is allocated a "magic" number that enables them to position themselves to their best advantage. Before finding our number from the tables opposite, we must check the date of the Chinese New Year from the "Chinese Animals Table". The previous year is used if our birthday falls before the start of the new year.

▽ Each of the magic numbers represents a particular type of energy suggested by the annual nature cycle. Find your number on the table and discover your energy below.

ENERGY OF NUMBERS

1: Water. Winter. Independent. Intuitive
2: Earth. Late Summer. Methodical.
3: Thunder. Spring. Progressive
4: Wind. Late Spring. Adaptable.
5: Earth. Central Force. Assertive.
6: Heaven. Late Autumn. Unyielding.
7: Lake. Autumn. Flexible. Nervous.
8: Mountain. Late Winter. Obstinate. Energetic.
9. Fire. Summer. Impulsive. Clever.

USING THE MAGIC NUMBERS

Some Feng Shui consultants use only the male, or yang, numbers in their calculations, some use both male and female, or yin, numbers. Others regard the yin (female) numbers as depicting the inner self, while the yang (male) numbers represent the image a person presents to the world. Modern men and women, with more interchangeable roles, tend to have both yin and yang characteristics, rather than the traditional gender stereotypes.

east-west directions

People tend to fare better in some directions than in others. They fall into two groups, the east group or the west group. Those who fall into the east group should live in a house facing an east group direction, those in the west group a west group direction. If this is not possible, your bed and/or your chair should face an appropriate direction.

▽ Once you have found your magic number, you can identify which group you are in, east or west, which directions suit you, and whether your house is compatible.

GROUP	NUMBERS	DIRECTIONS
East	1, 3, 4, 9	N, E, SE, S
West	2, 5, 6, 7, 8	SW, NW, W, NE, CENTRE

THE MAGIC NUMBERS

YEAR	M	F	YEAR	M	F	YEAR	M	F	YEAR	M	F
1920	8	7	1952	3	3	1984	7	8	2002	7	8
1921	7	8	1953	2	4	1985	6	9	2003	6	9
1922	6	9	1954	1	5	1986	5	1	2004	5	1
1923	5	1	1955	9	6	1987	4	2	2005	4	2
1924	4	2	1956	8	7	1988	3	3	2006	3	3
1925	3	3	1957	7	8	1989	2	4	2007	2	4
1926	2	4	1958	6	9	1990	1	5	2008	1	5
1927	1	5	1959	5	1	1991	9	6	2009	9	6
1928	9	6	1960	4	2	1992	8	7	2010	8	7
1929	8	7	1961	3	3	1993	7	8	2011	7	8
1930	7	8	1962	2	4	1994	6	9	2012	6	9
1931	6	9	1963	1	5	1995	5	1	2013	5	1
1932	5	1	1964	9	6	1996	4	2	2014	4	2
1933	4	2	1965	8	7	1997	3	3	2015	3	3
1934	3	3	1966	7	8	1998	2	4	2016	2	4
1935	2	4	1967	6	9	1999	1	5	2017	1	5
1936	1	5	1968	5	1	2000	9	6	2018	9	6
1937	9	6	1969	4	2	2001	8	7	2019	8	7
1938	8	7	1970	3	3						
1939	7	8	1971	2	4						
1940	6	9	1972	1	5						
1941	5	1	1973	9	6						
1942	4	2	1974	8	7						
1943	3	3	1975	7	8						
1944	2	4	1976	6	9						
1945	1	5	1977	5	1						
1946	9	6	1978	4	2						
1947	8	7	1979	3	3						
1948	7	8	1980	2	4						
1949	6	9	1981	1	5						
1950	5	1	1982	9	6						
1951	4	2	1983	8	7						

Key: M = male F = female

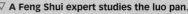

▽ A Feng Shui expert studies the luo pan.

Perception and the symbolic Bagua

Much of the skill in undertaking a Feng Shui survey of our immediate environment is in reading the signals there. If we are healthy and happy, this may prove to be a comparatively easy process. If we are not, our perception may be coloured by our emotional or physical state and we may not be able to see things clearly.

The Chinese phrase "First, luck; second, destiny; third, Feng Shui; fourth, virtues; fifth, education" is worth repeating, as it shows that to some extent our fortunes and personalities are out of our hands. If we embrace Feng Shui, think and act positively, and make use of the knowledge the universe has to offer, then we can begin to take charge of the parts of our lives that we can control and make the best of them, without struggling against the things we can't change.

Part of the process of Feng Shui is to awaken our senses and sensibilities to our environment. Among other things, each of the Five Elements governs different senses, and our aim is to create a balanced environment in which all our senses are satisfied and none is allowed to predominate over the rest to create an imbalance.

We can heighten our perception of the world if we introduce ourselves to different experiences. Take an objective look at your weekly routine and decide on a new experience or activity which will add something different to your life.

a magical template

When Feng Shui began to take off in the West several years ago, the workings of the compass were known only to a handful of scholars. Those early days were distinguished by the creation of, and endless discussions on, the workings of the Bagua. It was used then, as it is now, by the Tibetan Black Hat practitioners, as a magical template that is aligned with a front door, the entrance to a room, the front of a desk or even a face.

This template is then used to supply information which can enable us to understand our energy and make corrections to create balance and harmony. Some Chinese practitioners have since

A HEALTHY LIFESTYLE AND A HEALTHY MIND

Stuck energy in our homes is often a reflection of our lifestyle and state of mind. A healthy daily regime will make us receptive to the powers of Feng Shui. Ideally, we should take time out each day to meditate – or just to escape from stress. Often a short walk, gardening or a few minutes sitting quietly will help us to relax. Chi Kung and T'ai Chi are part of the same system. Their exercise programmes help to keep the energy channels in the body unblocked, while also releasing the mind.

Eating a healthy balanced diet of food-stuffs, produced without chemical interference, is another way of ensuring that harmful energies, or toxins, do not upset our bodily balance.

If we do become ill, acupuncture and acupressure and Chinese herbal medicine can balance the energies in our bodies and help to keep us fit.

◁ Meditation (left), hiking in the mountains (bottom left) or a daily session of T'ai Chi (bottom right) will all benefit our mental energy and help to heighten perceptions.

sought to use the Bagua alongside the compass method. They place it over the plan of a home so that it is positioned with the Career area in the north, irrespective of where the front door lies.

Other traditional Chinese approaches concentrate on interpreting the energies indicated by the Five Elements and by the rings of the luo pan. Such is the "magic" of Feng Shui that, in the right hands, all approaches appear to work.

Newcomers to Feng Shui may find it difficult to connect to a compass. Hopefully, they will use either method to experience for themselves the magic of the early days of discovery, and will be drawn deeper into this amazing philosophy, gaining an insight into its power.

the symbolic bagua

Throughout this book we will see how various images are connected to each of the eight points of the Magic Square or the Bagua, which is based on it. The symbolic Bagua uses the energies of each direction to relate to the journey of life. The journey begins at the entrance to our home – the mouth of chi – and moves in a predetermined way through the home until it reaches its conclusion. By focusing on an aspect of our lives which we want to stimulate or change, we can use the energies of the universe and make them work for us. Psychologically, focusing on an area enables us to create the circumstances to bring about change.

So far, a traditional compass approach has been used, but the diagram to the left allows us to use either approach. From now on readers should feel free to connect with the Bagua as they wish, and through it to the intangible forces which make this such a fascinating subject. Most people who have used Feng Shui have experienced changes in their circumstances. These often correspond to the actual energy around a relationship or situation rather than our desires. The results will ultimately serve our best interests, but the outcome is often unexpected.

△ **Mountains afford protection to the rear and sides of this village, while a lake in front accumulates chi – the perfect situation – all that remains is to arrange the inside of the house to echo and maintain the supportive external environment.**

▽ **The Three Gates Bagua. This may be entered through "Career" (back), "Knowledge" (bottom left) or "Helpful People" (bottom right). The compass Bagua with associated colours is shown inside to help you balance the elements of your home.**

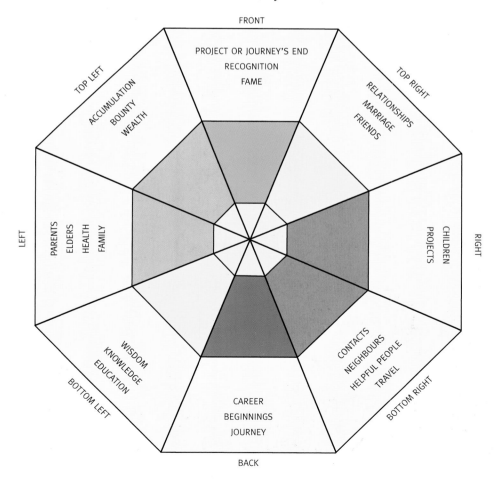

FRONT

PROJECT OR JOURNEY'S END
RECOGNITION
FAME

TOP LEFT

ACCUMULATION
BOUNTY
WEALTH

TOP RIGHT

RELATIONSHIPS
MARRIAGE
FRIENDS

LEFT

PARENTS
ELDERS
HEALTH
FAMILY

RIGHT

CHILDREN
PROJECTS

WISDOM
KNOWLEDGE
EDUCATION

BOTTOM LEFT

CAREER
BEGINNINGS
JOURNEY

CONTACTS
NEIGHBOURS
HELPFUL PEOPLE
TRAVEL

BOTTOM RIGHT

BACK

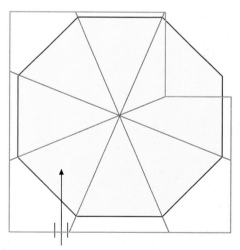

△ **The Three Gates Bagua is flexible. If a home has an irregular shape, the corresponding area of the Bagua is also considered to be missing. In this house, the front entrance is in the "Knowledge" area and the "Relationships" part of the house is missing.**

Feng shui in the modern world

Modern lifestyles are far removed from those of our ancestors. For them, charting the progress of the moon and sun, and interpreting the different weather conditions and other activities occurring in the natural world in relation to the movement of the stars and planets, was vital.

△ **Night-time in Mexico City. The 23 million inhabitants are denied a view of the stars because of neon lighting and pollution.**

▷ **The rice harvest in traditional regions of China has used many of the same processes for the past thousand years.**

▽ **A village in Chad in which ancient skills and lifestyles remain unaffected by the technological development in the West.**

These peoples depended on the land to provide them with the means to survive. The modern city-dweller may never see food growing naturally and may not even be able to view the night sky because of pollution and neon lighting. However, we still depend on the natural world for our well-being. We can be at the mercy of hurricanes, or bask on sun-drenched beaches; mountains may erupt, or provide sustenance for livestock; human beings are able to pollute the air and contaminate the land, while at the same time create sanctuaries for wildlife species.

Ancient peoples regarded the heavens, the earth and themselves as part of one system. This holistic view of life has persisted in many cultures, where health and medicine, food and lifestyle are all interconnected.

In the West, scientific development has created different disciplines which have advanced in isolation from each other. Through recent changes in health and food production, we are now seeking to correct the imbalances caused by this approach. The Tao, or the Way, the philosophy which underlies Feng Shui, shows how it is possible to order our lives to exist in harmony with each other and the natural world. We can use Feng Shui to help us work towards achieving this.

The traditional concept of Gaia, the Greek earth goddess, was used by James Lovelock and Lynne Margulis in the 1970s to encourage us to perceive the world as a biosphere in which each constituent part has a role to play. In order to understand Feng Shui we need to expand this concept of ecosystems further to include human beings and the impact of

△ In 1948 science writer Fred Hoyle predicted: "Once a photograph of the Earth taken from the outside world is available ... a new idea as powerful as any other in history will be let loose." The environmental awareness movement began during the same period that human beings landed on the moon.

WORKING WITH THE NATURAL WORLD

A good example of working with the natural world is provided by an apparently admirable scheme to plant 300 oak forests in Britain. But in the natural world oak trees grow singly and not in rows in large groups, and recent research has indicated that where many oaks grow together there is a higher incidence of Lyme disease, a debilitating illness which attacks the nervous system. The reason for this is that mice and deer feed on acorns and also carry the ticks which transmit the disease. Thus, where there are many oaks, there is also a high incidence of Lyme disease. Mixed planting, which mirrors the natural world, would be preferable.

In order to save money, one forest was planted with Polish oak trees that came into bud two weeks later than the native trees. This meant there were no caterpillars feeding on the buds to provide food for newly-hatched fledglings. These mistakes might have been avoided if Tao principles had been applied.

▽ Native trees act as the Tortoise, Dragon, Tiger formation to protect these buildings.

the cosmos, and to expand our awareness so that we can predict the consequences of our actions.

As we investigate the ideas behind Feng Shui and consider practical ways of introducing them into our lives, we also need to shift our perception. Feng Shui in the modern world incorporates intuition. Maori warriors navigate hundreds of miles by the feel of a place and by observing signs. The Inuit language incorporates many words to describe the complexities of different types of snow. Similarly, we can heighten our awareness of our environment by adopting the principles of Feng Shui.

Until recently navigators used the stars to steer by, and in some parts of the world those who work with the land still use the stars to determine planting times for their crops. These people recognize patterns in the interrelationship between different parts of the natural world, noticing which plants are in flower or when birds return from migration and comparing them to the weather. Many customs are firmly based in natural wisdom.

The Outside World

The primary consideration when beginning to
understand Feng Shui is to assess the world
around us, to take stock of the energies and
influences that surround our living spaces.

Choosing a location

Whether we own our own home or apartment or live in rented accommodation, we can use the principles which follow to create a living space in which we feel comfortable. If we are on the verge of moving, or are in the fortunate position of having acquired a piece of land to design and build our own home upon, there are some important considerations to make. You will probably already have a location in mind, but within the area there will be choices you can make which will affect your well-being in your new home.

When choosing a property we normally investigate the immediate environment. We use certain criteria to judge it according to our individual requirements – the appearance of neighbouring properties, proximity to schools, efficient transport for travel to work, green spaces, sports facilities and so on.

Some moves are dictated by new jobs in different areas, some when people give up their hectic urban lifestyles and relocate to rural areas. Many older people retire to the coast. Young people leaving home for the first time might be attracted by the hurly-burly of city living.

△ **The modern city of Durban in South Africa is full of young energy.**

▷ **A seaside location is very attractive in summer but can be inhospitable in winter.**

The decline of heavy industry in many countries has seen a rise in the regeneration of dockland and riverside areas with large warehouses being developed as spacious apartments for these new city dwellers. Whatever the reason for the move, few people remain where they were born, or retain the extended support networks which prevailed only a generation or two ago. Our choice of home as a nurturing space is therefore important. With a little foresight and a knowledge of Feng Shui principles, we can select prime positions for our homes.

think before you move

There are certain things to consider when selecting an area to which to move before we even consider choosing a house. Ideally we should know the area well. An idyllic bay in summer may be cold and windswept in winter, and a woodland glade at the end of an unmade track may be inaccessible after heavy winter snows. Although it's impossible to see the house in all seasons you can at least try to visualize how it will be.

Neighbours can prove to be a problem. They may resent a new house which spoils

▽ **Living on a remote farm will suit some people perfectly, but not others.**

ASSESSING A LOCATION

NATURAL PHENOMENA	IMMEDIATE ENVIRONMENT	POSITIVE ASPECTS	NEGATIVE ASPECTS
Wind direction	Proposed road developments	Local amenities	Factories
Sun direction	Proposed building developments	Trees	Petrol stations
Rainfall	Land use plans	Street lighting	All-night cafés
Flood areas	Previous land use	Good street maintenance	Pubs and discos
Geological faults	Tree preservation orders	Good schools	Police stations
Soil type	Local architecture	Community spirit	Fire stations
Height above sea level	Neighbours, predecessors	Local shops	Airports
		Clubs and classes	Cemeteries and crematoriums
		Playgroups and nurseries	Motorways and highways
			Electricity sub-stations and pylons

◁ **This sheltered village is a delightful location to return home to after a day in the bustling city.**

▷ **High-rise flats in Hong Kong – financially the sky is the limit and young people are attracted there, but few of them stay to put down roots.**

a view, or may erect screens that maintain their privacy but deprive you of light. It is important to determine the ownership of boundaries. Previous owners are another consideration. Perhaps earlier occupants have tipped chemicals just where you want to grow strawberries, or you may learn that all the previous owners got divorced or mysteriously contracted a similar illness while living in the house. Feng Shui may be able to offer an explanation for any of these negative aspects.

▽ **Pavement cafés are part of metropolitan life in many cities around the world.**

The modern world has problems that did not exist in the ancient world and these must be taken into consideration when we apply Feng Shui today. It is no use selecting a site with the classic Tortoise, Dragon, Tiger formation if the Tortoise is an electricity pylon, which may be linked to childhood leukemia, the Dragon is a chemical factory leaking its waste into the river, and the Tiger is a poorly managed petrol station. In modern times we have to apply the formulae to contemporary life and the ancient sages were wise enough to allow us the leeway to do this by building in formulae for change.

Our environment makes a psychological impact on us: whatever we see, hear or smell will make an impression and have an affect. We also have to look at ourselves and what type of people we are in order to understand our needs in terms of living spaces. There is no point moving to a remote country area if you enjoy street life and love shopping because you will never feel comfortable. Someone whose astro-

logical sign is the Rabbit who retires to the seaside will, at best, be tired and drained and, at worst, become ill. With a new insight into our own natures and increased awareness of the effect our environment has on us, we can use Feng Shui principles to find harmonious spaces.

When you are ready to sell your home and move on, Feng Shui can help to speed up this often lengthy and stressful process. The tip below combines the energy of the Five Elements to give a powerful boost to the progress of the sale.

FENG SHUI TIP FOR SPEEDING UP A HOUSE SALE

If you are having problems, take a red envelope and place in it:

A piece of metal from the kitchen
Some earth from the garden
Some wood from a skirting board

Seal the envelope and throw it into a fast-moving river.

Unseen energies

Before finally deciding on a location, it is wise to check if there are any underground water sources, geological faults or major other earth disturbances. These all create unseen energies which could affect your well-being.

geopathic stress

The word "geopathic" comes from the Greek *geo*, meaning "Earth", and *pathos*, meaning "disease". It covers naturally occurring phenomena that cause problems for us and our homes. The Earth and living organisms vibrate at complementary frequencies, which are negatively affected by geopathic faults. Dowsers are able to detect these problems, which a property surveyor may miss.

underground streams

Just as water erodes rocks on the coastline, underground streams have had the same effect underground, beneath the Earth's surface. This process alters the electromagnetic frequency of the Earth so that it is out of our frequency range. Fast-moving or polluted underground water produces the same effect.

Underground streams produce energy spirals, the effects of which are felt inside

△ **If trees lean for no obvious reason, they may be situated on a geopathic stress line.**

any buildings directly overhead. Where a clockwise spiral meets an anti-clockwise spiral, ill health may be experienced by people situated above them. Where spirals meet other forces, such as leys, the problems are accentuated.

leys

Leys, or ley lines, are a network of energy lines running across the land. Some think that our distant ancestors may have built their churches and standing stones on these lines, performing a kind of "acupuncture of the Earth" as they tapped into its energy. It is believed the leys also provided routes for travellers.

△ **Underground water creates magical places, but it is not desirable near a house as it can undermine the foundations.**

◁ **Stone circles are extremely powerful places. They harness the Earth's energies and respond to those of the Cosmos.**

△ **The Chinese believe that quarrying damages the Dragon – the spirit of a place.**

△ **Nearby railway lines can cause land disturbance and create instability.**

earth is covered by a series of force lines which are activated by the interaction of the Earth's magnetic field and the gravitational pull of the sun and moon. It is thought that these lines shift as a result of their interaction with the movement of charged particles trapped in the atmosphere as the sun blasts the Earth with radiation. The point where these lines cross may adversely affect the human body.

human activity

It is also possible for human beings to disturb the Earth's energies. Quarries, tunnels, mines, polluted water and railways have all been found to contribute negative effects. Before erecting or buying a house, check for any mining or tunnelling that may have taken place in the area.

radon

We are exposed to radiation throughout our lives, mainly from the sun. Exposure over long periods to higher than normal levels may make us ill. Leukemia and birth defects have been linked to exposure to radon, which occurs naturally in uranium in the Earth. As the uranium breaks down, it forms radioactive ions which attach themselves to air particles that become trapped inside houses. Some regions in the world have recorded dreadfully high

levels of radioactivity, in excess of those recorded after the Chernobyl disaster. Pockets of high incidence have been found in Sweden and the United States as well as in Derbyshire and Cornwall in Great Britain. Local authorities are aware of the problem and assistance is available to eradicate it from buildings.

earth grids

Two German doctors, Hartmann and Curry, have advanced the theory that the

STRESS INDICATORS

Leaning trees
Cankers on tree trunks
Elder trees
Illness shortly after moving
Uneasy atmosphere
Tunnelling activity
Cold, damp rooms

CLEARING THE ENERGIES

If there is no apparent reason for feeling unwell for a long period of time, then geopathic stress is a possible cause. Experienced dowsers are able to detect Earth energies and, in some instances, divert negative energies, albeit often only on a temporary basis. Many people can detect water with rods or pendulums, but experience is needed to deal with Earth energies and protection is needed to minimize ill effects. It is best, if possible, to move away from such energies, and it may be a question of simply moving a bed 60 cm–1 m (2–3 ft). The effect of clearing energies can be dramatic, and the work should be done slowly.

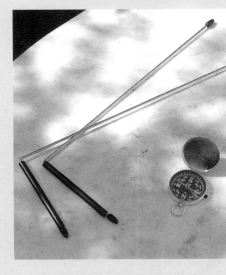

△ **Dowsing rods are part of a Feng Shui consultant's tools. Metal coat hangers also work for dowsing.**

△ **Dowsing rods cross when they detect underground water. They are used to locate landmines and to find pipes.**

The urban environment

Urban environments are very diverse. Living in an apartment above a shop in a city centre throbbing with night-life is quite different to the tranquillity of a house in a leafy suburb or the vast buildings in a redeveloped docklands area.

city and town centres

The centres of large cities, where clubs and restaurants are open through the night, are full of yang energy and lifestyles will reflect this. City centres attract younger people with no roots, who can move about freely. Homes in the inner cities tend to be apartments, and inside we should aim for some yin energy – muted colours, natural floor-ing and a large plant or two to create a quiet haven.

Smaller town centres, particularly where there are shopping precincts, tend to close down at night and the atmosphere is yin and rather spooky. If you live here, make sure you have plenty of lights on the perimeter of your property and bright colours inside to prevent feeling closed in.

parks and spaces

These green oases are somehow apart from the bustling city centre. Homes are usu-ally expensive and sought after, since they

△ **An enticing night scene in Villefranche, Cote d'Azur, France. Summer in the city can be invigorating and exciting.**

provide tranquil spaces and fresh air while still connected to the life of the city. People residing here will have more stable lifestyles as they have the yin-yang balance. Their

▽ **Suburban living at its best in Sag Harbour, New York; well kept, clean, wide streets, mature trees and no parked cars.**

homes should reflect this with a mixture of stimulating shapes, colours and materi-als, plus restful spaces.

urban renewal

The energy of reclaimed industrial areas in inner cities is interesting. The yang energy of the large converted warehouses contrasts with the daytime yin energy when the occupants, usually business exec-utives, are at work in large, highly charged, corporations. At weekends this changes as café life and leisure activities take over. Old dockland areas for example, are usually on main traffic routes, so on weekdays there is often stuck energy. Large trees should be planted to help cope with the pollu-tion, and also to bring yin energy into the area. Rooms in converted industrial build-ings tend to be huge and it is difficult to ground the energy. Cosy yin spaces need to be created within to offer support.

suburbs

The energy in the suburbs is mainly yin, with little nightlife. People tend to hide and become insular in suburbs, and often a yang balance is required. Imaginative use of colour is often all that is required to raise the energy of suburban homes.

roads

It is roads that conduct chi through an environment, and transport patterns can affect the nature of a neighbourhood. Living close to urban highways is an obvious health risk, but so too is living on narrow suburban "rat runs". Chi travels fast on straight urban roads and thus residents will not relax easily. In the United States, where suburban roads are built on a grid system, large gardens compensate and help to maintain a balance. Check the transport patterns before purchasing a new home and visit at different times of the day. Well-designed cul-de-sacs have excellent chi, but those where car movement has not been well planned create stuck energy and danger for children playing there.

The visual impact of a flyover in a residential area can be devastating. The fast-moving traffic conducts chi away from the area and will greatly affect the fortunes of those living at eye level or underneath the flyover.

railways

The effect of a railway is similar to a motorway in that trains carry chi away from an area, particularly if they are at the end of the garden. Trains also create slight unease in the subconscious expectation of their arrival. Underground trains are destabilizing if they pass immediately below houses. If systems are old and poorly maintained the Chinese saying "Angry Dragons waiting to erupt" applies.

▽ Parks and green areas are a very important part of city life. This park, overlooking the city, is located in Adelaide, Australia.

Roads conduct chi. Steadily moving traffic on curving roads near our homes is beneficial. Fast traffic and roads pointing at us are not.

THE CURVING ROAD The road gently curves and appears to "hug" this house. This is a very auspicious Feng Shui position for a dwelling.

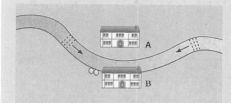

THE BENDING ROAD House B is in an inauspicious position. Traffic from both directions may break suddenly at the bend and could hit the house. At night, car beams will illuminate the rooms. There will always be a negative air of expectancy here. Convex mirrors on the outer bend would deflect and deplete the energy of the auspicious house A. Instead, a better solution would be to have traffic-calming measures in place.

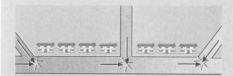

THE FAST ROAD This creates a visual and psychological barrier. Waist-high shrubs and plants on the boundary of the garden and plants on the windowsill inside the houses will slow down the chi. Those living at the junction of such roads are likely to be jumpy. Screeching brakes and even crashes are common at such points.

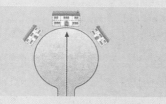

THE DEAD-END ROAD The house facing the entrance is at risk since the chi seems to hurtle towards it, as at a T-junction. Deflection is needed, and a hedge would help, or a porch with the door at the side. Mirrors are often used to return the harmful influence back on itself. If the path to the door faces the road, it would be better to move and curve it. The effect is the same where a bridge points at a house. Residents will feel exhausted in such a location.

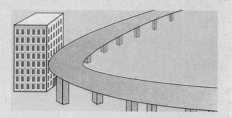

THE KNIFE The road appears to cut into the apartments like a knife. The constant flow past the window will leave residents tetchy. A mirror outside will symbolically deflect the problem. Coloured glass in the windows facing the road would block the unattractive view whilst allowing light in.

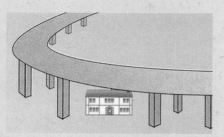

THE FLYOVER Residents here will feel overwhelmed. Lights on the corners of the house will symbolically lift the flyover, but this is not a good house to live in. Residents will feel oppressed and have no energy.

Rural locations

The energies found in the countryside are quite different to those of urban areas, but just as powerful. By carefully positioning our homes within the natural features of the landscape we can draw on their protection to nourish us.

country living

A sheltered position contained by trees or hills is ideal, especially in remote areas where protection from the elements is very important in winter. The classical arrangement of the four animals is the perfect site but if there are no woods or mountains where you wish to live, large trees and buildings can also act as protectors. Road access is vital in rural areas but, as in towns, it is preferable not to live close to major roads or through routes.

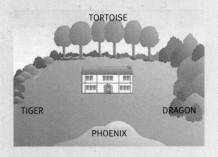

BENEFICIAL LOCATIONS

A tree belt behind acts as the Tortoise, and hedges represent the Dragon and Tiger. The Dragon is higher to keep the unpredictable Tiger in its place. A small hill in the foreground acts as the Phoenix.

A stream feeding a healthy pond is auspicious. Shrubs hide the water's exit from the property.

△ This lovely Mediterranean-style house is positioned in a supportive rural setting.

Even if you live out in the wild, it is important to have a social centre within reach. Out-of-town superstores have knocked the heart out of many country towns and villages, and have made an impact on the chi of these places, but those that continue to thrive usually have an excellent yin-yang balance. They provide sport and leisure facilities for young people and a good community life, which are the yang activities in the yin setting of the countryside.

In the fields and woods, chi is good and there are many opportunities to restore the balance in our busy modern lives. Intensive farming methods can be harmful, however, so look out for telltale signs such as few songbirds or no hedges before purchasing a property.

Positive Aspects	Possible Negative Aspects
Natural smells	Agrochemicals
Leisurely pace of life	Isolation
Walks	Flooding
Trees	Travel distances & access
Wildlife	Limited public transport
Fresh food	Landfill
Air quality	Military training areas
Relaxed lifestyle	Bad weather
Outdoor life	Effluent pipes
Happy people	Amenities closed in winter

rivers and lakes

Energy is usually very good near water, especially near slow-flowing rivers that meander through the countryside. Proportion is important, so if the water is balanced by an undulating landscape and plenty of green vegetation it will feel comfortable. A stream feeding into a healthy pond is ideal as it will accumulate chi and also attract wildlife to visit your garden. The energy near lakes is different, reflecting the breathless movement of the wind across the water and the sudden appearance and disappearance of water sports activities at weekends.

If you decide to live in a flood plain you will need to make enquiries about the likelihood of floods in the area, especially following those of recent years.

coastal areas

Being beside the sea gives most of us a sense of well-being. This is partly due to the beneficial effects of negative ions in the air, which create an invigorating atmosphere. Waves can, however, adversely affect some people, depending on their animal sign – Rabbits, for example, tend to feel uneasy near the sea.

△ A house situated next to a slow-moving river will benefit from good chi flow.

In the summer, the teeming beaches full of holiday-makers are yang. In winter the towering seas are also yang, but the deserted seaside towns and isolated bays are yin. It is a good idea to visit the area in both seasons as they are so different. The elements of wind and water are never so much in evidence as when the storms lash the sea against the rocks. A peninsula is difficult to live on because the chi there dissipates in the winter when it is hammered by the elements.

▷ A tranquil bay in summer looks very different in winter.

ROADS TO HOME

Living in rural areas may mean that you have to commute to work and spend quite some time in the car. The daily journey, and the roads on which you travel, will have a big impact on your life, so check both when considering your new home.

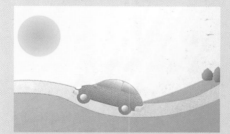

Travelling to work in an easterly direction in the morning and returning in a westerly direction with the sun glaring on the windscreen could affect our moods considerably. This can be particularly dangerous on narrow roads. Wonderful views can make us feel euphoric and energized, although care must be taken not to lose concentration when driving. Scenic roads can be tricky in adverse weather conditions.

Where trees overhang a road they can afford a welcome relief from the glaring sun. However, long stretches may cause nausea and headaches brought on by the dappled light.

Narrow country lanes with high banks or hedges funnel chi and afford no relief for the driver. Where they twist and turn, the driver's vision is extremely limited. Regular use will become a strain.

House styles

The position of our homes within their environment and how they fit in with the surrounding buildings can affect how comfortable we are living there. At a simple level, if our home is a big detached house in a road of smaller terraced houses, then we will be set apart from the rest of the community. Similarly, if the house is very different from its neighbours it may not fit into its environment. Strict planning laws in some areas have preserved the "spirit"

▽ **This painted terraced house is not in sympathy with its neighbours.**

△ **A balance of Metal, suggested by the circular lawn, and Water in the curved path.**

or chi of towns and villages, and such places tend to have a sense of community. Where building has been unrestricted and tall blocks spring up between two-storey houses with no regard for the character of the environment, then the area's chi dissipates and its sense of community is lost.

When we make alterations to our houses or decorate them, we should be mindful of the impact on the neighbourhood. If ours is the only stucco house in a row of brick houses, we isolate ourselves and change the chi of the area. If all the houses in the neighbourhood are of a certain era and we decide to change the style of the windows or substantially alter the architectural detail, we again damage the

BALANCING THE ELEMENTS

Element	Helped by	Harmed by	Weakened by	Weakens
Wood	Water	Metal	Fire	Earth
Fire	Wood	Water	Earth	Metal
Earth	Fire	Wood	Metal	Water
Metal	Earth	Fire	Water	Wood
Water	Metal	Earth	Wood	Fire

45

△ **The intrusive tower blocks have completely changed the nature of this area.**

energy of the environment. Doors, chimney stacks and porches all add to the character and overall proportion not only of our house, but of the neighbourhood.

house shapes

The best-shaped house from a Feng Shui point of view is square. The square is a well proportioned space, and is the symbolic shape for Earth, which gathers, supports and nourishes. Rectangular buildings are also well regarded. An L-shaped building is considered inauspicious since it is said to resemble a meat cleaver and the worst position to have a room is in the "blade". If a teenager has a room in this position, they may feel isolated and may get up to all sorts of things undetected. An older relative with such a room may feel unwanted. Where houses are not a uni-

---

FIVE ELEMENT CURES FOR CORRECTING IMBALANCES

WOOD: Posts, pillars, tower-shaped plant supports, green walls, trees
FIRE: Pyramid-shaped finials, wigwam-shaped plant supports, garden buildings with Fire-shaped roofs, red walls, lights
EARTH: Straight hedges, rectangular garden buildings, flat-topped trellis, terracotta troughs, or terracotta walls
METAL: Round finials, round weather vanes, metal balls, white walls
WATER: Wavy hedges, water features, black or blue walls

BUILDINGS AND THE FIVE ELEMENTS

WOOD: Tall thin apartment blocks and offices are often Wood-shaped.

EARTH: Earth-shaped buildings are long and low such as bungalows.

FIRE: Fire buildings have pyramid-shaped or pointed roofs.

FIRE: Wood-shaped windows and Earth-shaped lines give balance.

METAL: Metal buildings are domed, such as these African huts, and some religious buildings in the west

WATER: Water buildings are those which have had sections randomly added to them over the years.

form shape, we need to make them more regular, in reality or symbolically, as we will investigate later.

orientation

The direction in which a building faces will also affect its chi. North-facing buildings with the main windows at the front will feel cheerless since they will not receive any sun. The energy can become stagnant and it is important to warm the house with colour. Houses which have the main windows facing south and south-west will receive strong yang energy and will need cool colours to compensate. Houses facing east receive early morning sun and vibrant energy. In the west, the energy is falling. Directions determine room placement within the house.

Entrances, paths and front doors

The main entrance to our home is very important. It represents the image we present to the world and can also indicate the view we have of ourselves. When we return to our home, we need to be drawn into our own nurturing space through a pleasant environment, however small. If we live in an apartment, we need to distinguish our own special part of the block and make it unique in some way, by using a colourful doormat, for example, or introducing plants.

entrances

Front gardens can fill up with an accumulation of stagnant energy unless we are careful. In house conversions where the grounds are not managed, the situation can be difficult since no-one is in overall charge of the garden. As a result, packaging, old furniture, chunks of wood and other assorted rubbish can pile up. Often, dustbins are sited in the front garden and can seriously affect how we feel when we return home. Bins should be placed away

△ Tree guardians mark the entrance to this attractive house. The effect that is created is very welcoming.

from the front entrance, preferably behind a hedge or fencing. If one resident clears up, others may follow suit.

paths

These should gently meander through the garden to help us unwind at the end of a long day, or welcome us back from a trip. Straight paths from the street to the front door carry chi too quickly and we do not have time to change gear. Ideally there should be an open space in front of the entrance where chi can gather, but often these are filled with parked cars and there is no distinction between home and work.

▽ A meandering path enables us to shed the cares of the day before arriving home.

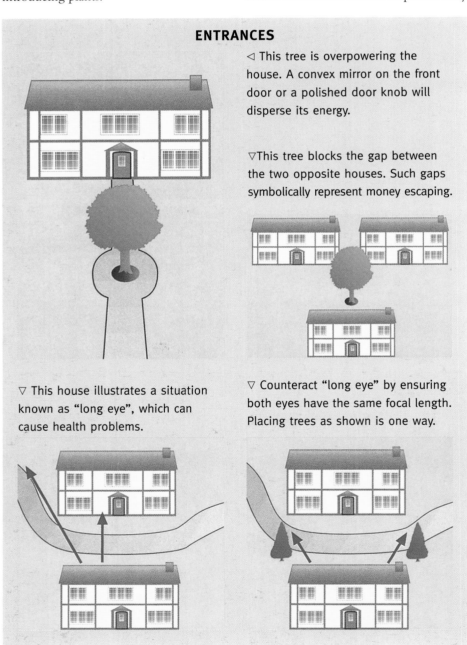

ENTRANCES

◁ This tree is overpowering the house. A convex mirror on the front door or a polished door knob will disperse its energy.

▽This tree blocks the gap between the two opposite houses. Such gaps symbolically represent money escaping.

▽ This house illustrates a situation known as "long eye", which can cause health problems.

▽ Counteract "long eye" by ensuring both eyes have the same focal length. Placing trees as shown is one way.

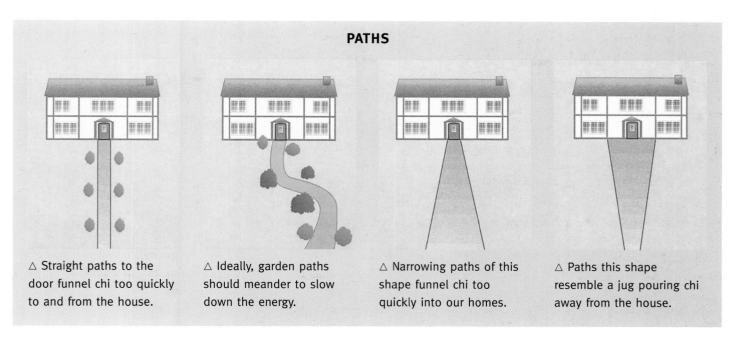

PATHS

△ Straight paths to the door funnel chi too quickly to and from the house.

△ Ideally, garden paths should meander to slow down the energy.

△ Narrowing paths of this shape funnel chi too quickly into our homes.

△ Paths this shape resemble a jug pouring chi away from the house.

Squeezing past a car to enter the house is claustrophobic, as are very small enclosed porches, creating restriction which may be mirrored in our approach to life.

front doors

These should be well-maintained and clean. A tub of plants on either side is welcoming but they should not restrict the space or act as an obstruction. House numbers should be visible by day and night and doorbells should be in working order to maintain harmonious relationships with

callers. The chi of an area can be severely depleted if visitors whistle, shout or use their car horns. The colour the door is painted should reflect the compass direction they face and be balanced according to the Five Elements.

departing

What we see when we leave our homes can also colour our day. Large objects like telegraph poles and trees directly in line with the front door send "poison arrows" of chi at the house, as do the corners of other buildings. If tall hedges or fences restrict our vision from the house we may become insular or feel depressed.

◁ **Plants either side of the poles would improve these well-maintained apartments.**

▽ **A balance of the Five Elements, but taller plants would improve the proportion.**

▽ **A plant pot on the left would help to balance this front entrance.**

▽ **The Metal-shaped pot plants on either side of this door are full of energy.**

Inside the Home

Even if the external environment of your home is less than perfect, you can still use Feng Shui to enhance specific areas of your home and help to improve certain aspects of your life that you are not satisfied with.

Beneficial positions

Having selected a protected site in which to live, it is desirable that the house is orientated in what is considered in Feng Shui to be an auspicious direction, which will support its occupants. Those people who fall into the east category should face their houses toward the east directions; west group people should face the west directions. It is very likely that there will be a mixture of east and west group people within a family or others sharing a house. The people who are compatible with the house will feel most comfortable in it. Others should ensure that principle rooms fall into their favoured directions or at least that their beds, desks and chairs are positioned correctly.

positioning yourself

Once you know your "magic" numbers, it is possible to design the interior of your house so that you position yourself in directions which are beneficial to you. Beds should be orientated so that the top of your head when lying down faces one of the four beneficial locations. In the same way chairs that you sit in should also face one of your beneficial locations.

▷ **We need to relax at the end of the day. A room with windows facing west is good, or a position favoured by our "magic" number.**

▽ **We aim to locate our rooms in good directions and decorate to suit the elements.**

△ The compass direction your house faces is dependent on where the main entrance is, and is the starting point for positioning yourself inside the house.

FIND YOUR BEST AND WORST DIRECTIONS

1. Check your magic number on "The Magic Numbers" table.
2. Check the "Best and Worst Directions" table to determine prime places for you to sit, sleep and work.

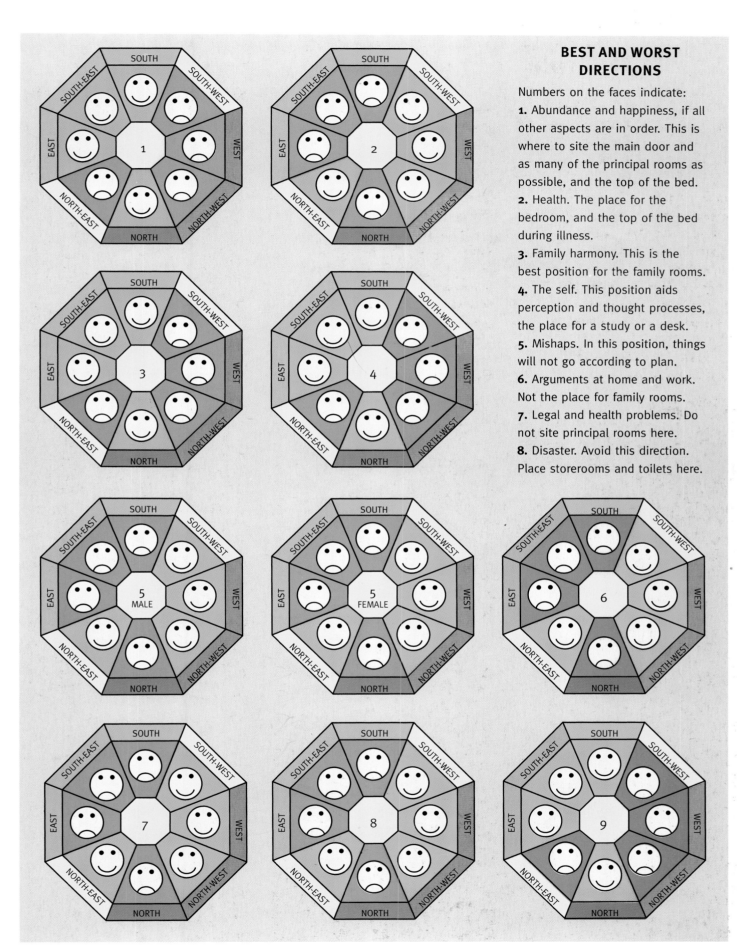

BEST AND WORST DIRECTIONS

Numbers on the faces indicate:

1. Abundance and happiness, if all other aspects are in order. This is where to site the main door and as many of the principal rooms as possible, and the top of the bed.

2. Health. The place for the bedroom, and the top of the bed during illness.

3. Family harmony. This is the best position for the family rooms.

4. The self. This position aids perception and thought processes, the place for a study or a desk.

5. Mishaps. In this position, things will not go according to plan.

6. Arguments at home and work. Not the place for family rooms.

7. Legal and health problems. Do not site principal rooms here.

8. Disaster. Avoid this direction. Place storerooms and toilets here.

Drawing the plan

It is now possible to begin to apply the principles we have learned. In order to position ourselves to our best advantage, we need to determine the compass readings for our homes.

YOU WILL NEED

A compass with the eight directions clearly marked
A protractor – a circular one is best
A scale plan of your home. If you own your home you will already have one. If not, it will be necessary to draw one, in which case you will also need a tape measure and graph paper
A ruler
A lead pencil and five coloured pencils – green, red, yellow, grey, dark blue
A tracing of the Bagua

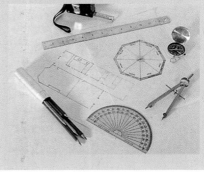

to draw a plan

Using graph paper, take measurements for each floor, marking external and internal walls, alcoves, staircases, doors, windows and permanent fixtures such as baths, toilets, kitchen units and fireplaces.

take a compass reading

1. Take off any watches, jewellery and metal objects and stand clear of cars and metal fixtures.

2. Stand with your back parallel to the front door and note the exact compass reading in degrees.

3. Note the direction, eg 125° SE, on to your plan as shown in the diagram. You are now ready to transfer the compass readings on to your Bagua drawing.

▷ Use this table to double check that your heading in degrees corresponds with the direction your front door faces, since it is possible to misread the protractor.

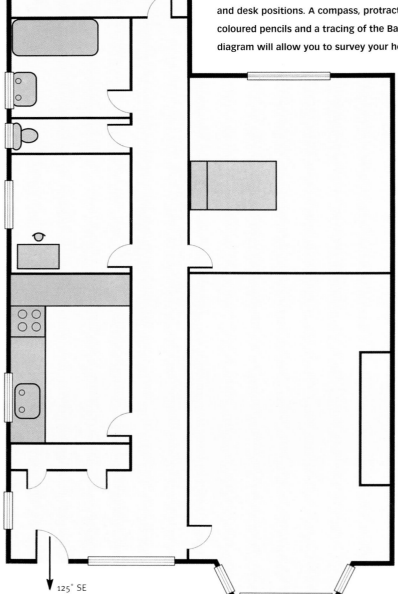

125° SE

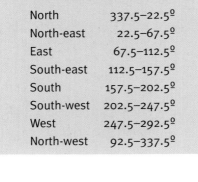

DIRECTIONS AND DEGREES

North	337.5–22.5º
North-east	22.5–67.5º
East	67.5–112.5º
South-east	112.5–157.5º
South	157.5–202.5º
South-west	202.5–247.5º
West	247.5–292.5º
North-west	92.5–337.5º

▽ Draw a scale plan of your home and mark on it the positions of windows, doors, alcoves and all internal fixtures and fittings as well as bed and desk positions. A compass, protractor, ruler, coloured pencils and a tracing of the Bagua diagram will allow you to survey your home.

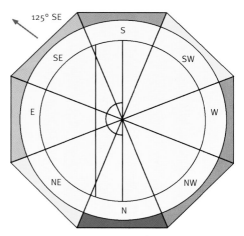

125° SE

△ **When you have worked out the compass reading for your front door, transfer it to the Bagua, as shown.**

▷ **The next step is to find the centre of your home, and then transfer the shape of the bagua to the plan**.

transfer the compass reading to the bagua

1. Place the protractor on the Bagua diagram so that 0° is at the bottom, at north, and mark the eight directions.

2. Having found the compass reading for your home, ie the direction faced by your front door, check it matches the direction; if not you may be reading the wrong ring. Mark the position of your front door.

3. Double-check the direction by looking at the "Directions and Degrees" table. When you have done this you will end up with a Bagua diagram such as the one above, with the front door position marked. You are now almost ready to place this template on to your home plan.

EAST WEST DIRECTIONS

Just as people fit into east or west categories, so too do houses. Determine whether your house belongs to the east or west group of directions by checking the direction in which the front door faces.

EASTERN DIRECTIONS: north-east, south-east, south

WESTERN DIRECTIONS: south-west, north-west, west, north-east.

transfer the directions to the plan

1. Find the centre of the plan. Match the main walls across the length of the plan and crease the paper lengthways.

2. Match the main walls across the width and crease the paper widthways. Where the folds cross is the centre of your home. If your home is not a perfect square or rectangle, treat a protrusion of less than 50% of the width as an extension to the direction. If the protrusion is more than 50% of the width, treat the remainder as a missing part of the direction.

3. Place the centre of the Bagua on the centre point of the plan and line up the front door position.

4. Mark the eight directions on the plan and draw in the sectors.

5. Transfer the colour markings.

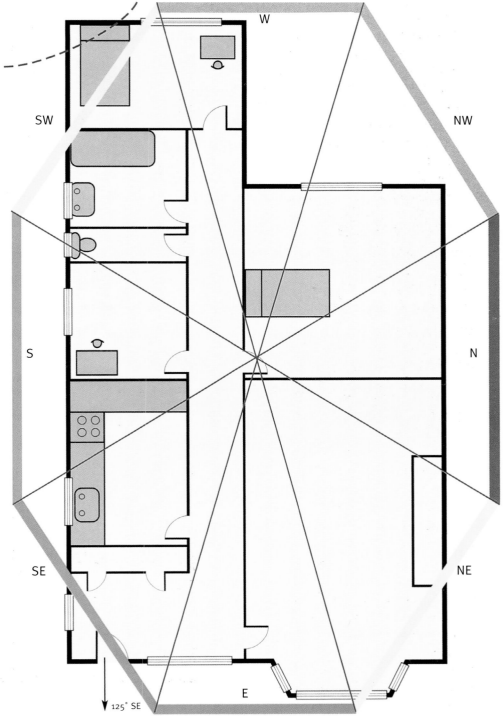

Edges, corners and slanting walls

Certain structural details are problematic in Feng Shui. Often the result of conversions, they affect chi and can cause discomfort for the occupants of the house.

edges

Wherever the chi flow in a room is disrupted, difficulties occur. Anyone who has ever walked down a windy street flanked by high buildings will know that the gusts are always worse at the corners of buildings where the wind whips up into a spiral. Where major structural work has been undertaken and walls have been knocked down, a room is often left with supporting pillars. These are not conducive to the free flow of chi because they are usually square and have four corners which point, knife-like, into the room, and they can also interfere with vision.

If there are edges we should aim to soften them. Plants are one solution and fabrics are another. Wherever possible, make columns rounded as this creates an entirely different feel.

Having the edges of furniture pointing at us when we are relaxing on a chair or sofa, can make us feel uncomfortable, as can the edges of bookshelves and fireplaces. Keeping books in cupboards is a solution, but the pleasure of plucking a book from a shelf would be lost and the cupboards would become harbingers of tired energy. Instead, we can use plants to soften shelf edges near where we sit.

△ Round pillars are less obtrusive than square ones. The plant softens the effect.

corners

The corners of rooms are often dark, so it is a good idea to place something colourful there, like a vase of silk flowers for example. Alternatively, you can use something that moves such as a lava lamp or a water feature. Putting plants in dark corners where stagnant chi accumulates will help the chi to move on. Spiky plants are particularly good for moving on chi, provided they are away from chairs where they could direct "poison arrows" towards the occupants. Uplighters or round tables with lamps on them are other options for dark corners.

Alcoves on either side of a fireplace are often filled with shelves, which help to prevent stagnant areas provided they are not crammed full and some gaps are left.

△ A plant will enliven an awkward corner and move the chi on.

◁ Plants can be used to soften shelf edges near to where we sit.

△ Here, in one place, we have several methods of introducing movement into a dark corner – an octagonal table, a plant, a corner cupboard and a little shelf.

▽ This slanting wall will not adversely affect anyone sleeping in this room as there is plenty of headroom.

THE FLOW OF CHI IN A LIVING ROOM

1. The chairs need to be repositioned as the fireplace corners shoot "poison arrows" at those sitting in them.
2. The edges of these built-in shelves will affect anyone sitting here unless the edges are softened with plants.
3. A round table with a lamp will move the chi on in this dark corner.
4. The corner of this pillar will send a "poison arrow" at the occupant of the chair; the chair can be moved or the edge of the pillar softened.
5. Anybody who chooses to sit in this seat will be unaffected by the pillar as it is a safe distance away.
6. Uplighters in these corners of the room will lift the energy.

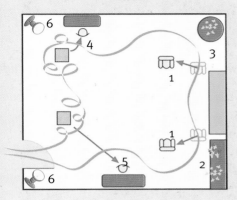

slanting walls

These are becoming increasingly common as expanding families in small houses convert attic space into rooms. Attic rooms with sloping ceilings are often turned into children's bedrooms or home offices. Sleeping or working under a slope depresses personal chi and these areas do nothing to aid the regenerative process of sleep nor creative processes during the day. Sloping ceilings also create a visual imbalance in a room. Mirrors and lights may help to create the illusion of lifting the slope and paint can achieve the same effect. Such rooms are better used as hobby or play rooms or for any short term activity.

If possible, it is preferable to have a smaller room of a conventional shape created instead of a room with sloping walls, even it means sacrificing some of the floor space. A good solution is to fill the sloping walls in with built-in cupboards for storage. Where roof windows are installed to let light into attic conversions, make sure it is possible to see more out of them than just a patch of sky.

▽ Placing storage cupboards under the eaves gives an attic room a more regular shape.

Beams

Not recommended in Feng Shui beams can be oppressive when positioned over a bed, stove or desk and suppress the chi of the people living beneath them. Proportion, however, is everything. In a barn conversion or a self-build eco-house, the ceilings are high and often vaulted so the beams do not seem to press down on the occupants. The reverse problem occurs when people and small-scale furniture rattle around in vast spaces and are unable to gather chi around them. However, beams in normally proportioned houses do tend to upset the flow of chi in a room, especially if we position ourselves in unsuitable places under them. Simply by moving the

▽ **The oppressive effect of these beams is reduced by painting them a light colour.**

dining table, desk or bed, we can often overcome any difficulties.

Many people dream of owning a country cottage, complete with roses round the door, log fires and beams. Traditionally it has been the custom to paint beams black so that they stand out, but when these cottages were built it is highly unlikely that this was their original colour. In the same way that pollution and time turn pale sandstone buildings in cities to a tobacco brown, so cooking and fires down the ages have transformed pale oak beams into charcoal-coloured wood. Interior fashions change, however, and it is now more common for beams to be painted the same colour as the ceiling, a welcome trend which makes all the difference to low-ceilinged rooms.

△ **These beams are unobtrusive because the roof is so high. Avoid sitting under the low crossbeam running across the room.**

Another way of reducing the effect of beams is to use uplighters underneath them, which give the illusion of "lifting" the beam. Small, light-coloured hanging objects will lighten a beam. Do not hang large, dark or heavy objects below a beam, or anything that collects dust. False ceilings can be attached to beams, either the conventional type or translucent ones with light behind. In larger spaces, such as

▽ **Sloping walls and a beam across the bed make this an inauspicious bedroom. The insecurity of the window behind the bed adds to the effect.**

restaurants, beams have been successfully mirrored, but this would not look good in most homes. Muslin or other fabrics will hide them, but these will harbour dust and create stagnant chi unless washed regularly. Traditionally, bamboo flutes tied with red ribbon were hung from the beam to create an auspicious octagon shape.

Beams over a bed are believed to cause illnesses to occupants at the points where they cross. A beam that runs along the length of the bed can cause a rift between

◁ **This modern living room is made inauspicious by the sloping walls and the dark beam running down the centre of the room.**

△ **Exposed beams that are painted the same colour as the ceiling give a lighter airy feel than if they are left in natural dark wood.**

the couple that shares it. When beams are situated over the stove or dining room table, they are thought to hamper the fortunes of the family.

If beams are over a desk, they may hinder the creative flow of the person who works there, and may even be a cause of, or contributory factor to, depression. It is certainly better not to sleep under a beam, and sitting in a chair under a beam or under a gallery, or any length of time, is not a comfortable experience.

Doors and windows

The doors of our home represent freedom and our access to the outside world; but they are also a barrier, acting as a means of protection, supplying support and comfort. Windows act as our eyes on the world. Both play an important role in Feng Shui and if our access or vision through them should not be impeded in any way.

doors

Open doors allow us access to a room or to the outside world. Closed doors shut off a room or our entire home. If either of these functions is impeded, then the chi flow around the house will suffer. Doors

▷ The uplifting view from this window has not been restricted by curtains or blinds.

which squeak, stick, have broken latches, or handles too close to the edge so we scrape our knuckles whenever we open them, should all be repaired or altered. Keep a wedge close to doors that might slam irritatingly in the breeze. Ideally, a door should not open to a restricted view

▽ Stained glass panels in doors permit light and lift the energy in dark spaces.

CURES FOR PROBLEM DOORS

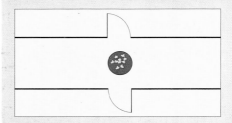

△ If doors are located opposite each other, place an obstruction such as a table to slow down the chi.

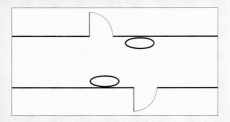

△ Where doors are out of alignment, create a balance by positioning mirrors or pictures on each side.

△ Where there are three or more doors in a row, break up the perspective with low-hanging lights or curved tables to slow down the chi.

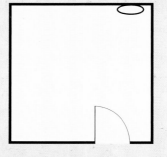

△ Where an opened door restricts the view into a room, position a mirror to correct this. Doors were traditionally hung in this way to prevent draughts. This practice may also have arisen because of the desire to preserve modesty in Victorian times.

of the whole room on entering, but doors in old houses used to be hung in this way to prevent through draughts or, some speculate, to preserve modesty during the decorous Victorian era.

windows

Sash windows which only open halfway restrict the amount of chi that can enter a room. Some double-glazed units only open halfway, with the same result. Ideally, all windows should open fully, and outwards. Beware of windows which have fixed double-glazed panels with only a small opening section at the top. These can cause fatal accidents if fire breaks out; they are usually fitted with safety glass, so it is virtually impossible to smash them. If

△ Adding an attractive stained-glass hanging can offer some privacy while creating a lively energy in the room.

▽ This stencilled decoration allows privacy in a bathroom, while at the same time letting in as much daylight as possible.

△ Tied-back curtains are ideal here as they do not restrict the pleasant view.

these have been fitted in your home, it is advisable to remove them as soon as possible, particularly in children's rooms. Safety is, of course, paramount in children's rooms and measures should be taken to ensure that they cannot open and fall out of windows.

The top of a window should be as tall as the tallest person in the house. Everyone should have a view of the sky through the seasons or they will lose their connection with the natural world. Drooping blinds which prevent this view lower the chi of a room considerably, and slatted blinds send cutting chi into the room.

If you feel the need to keep your curtains closed during the day, the chances are that you are depressed and feel vulnerable. Net curtains, although necessary in some areas, and preferable to curtains, blur the view out of the window. Experiment with other solutions, such as large plants, coloured glass or window stickers to prevent the outside world looking in. The aim should be to see out as much as possible. South-west-facing windows will, however, need some screening in summer, particularly in a study or kitchen.

Too many windows can create excessive yang since they blast the house with chi, while too few windows restrict its flow and are yin. Windows too near the

△ The seating in this room impedes access to the window, and can be easily rearranged.

floor in attic rooms feel unstable and a solid object or low table should be placed in front. It is preferable for bathrooms to have windows with an air flow. If this is not available, a water feature containing aromatic oils should be used and an extraction unit installed.

Too many windows in the dining room are considered to be especially inauspicious since the aim is to gather chi around the dining table and the food prepared for friends and family.

▽ This lovely etched bathroom window allows the occupants privacy, but still permits the maximum amount of light.

Materials

The materials with which we surround ourselves affect us on a physical level by how they feel and what they look like. They also affect us on a psychological level through their energy. Like everything else, materials have elemental qualities that affect

▽ **A wooden floor makes the room look attractive and warm**.

△ **Natural materials such as wood, wicker and cotton fabrics look fresh and inviting.**

the chi of the part of the home in which they are used, and they can also have a profound effect on our health and well-being.

Hard, reflective surfaces such as those used in the kitchen have a yang energy and chi moves across them quickly. Soft materials and those with depth of colour or texture are yin and can be used to slow chi movement down.

materials and health

Our choice of materials for fabrics and soft furnishings, furniture, decorating materials, and cleaning and washing agents can play a part in our health and well-being.

HARMFUL CHEMICALS ARE FOUND IN

Wood preservation treatments: use safe alternatives
Cavity wall foam
Paint: use natural pigments
Vinyl wallpaper and paints: use untreated papers and paints
Synthetic carpets and treated woollen carpets: use natural untreated materials
Plastic floor tiles and coverings: use linoleum or rubber
Adhesives: use non-chemical and acrylic alternatives
Upholstery foam: use natural fibres
Processed wood products: use solid or recycled wood
Cleaning materials: use natural alternatives
Food: Select organic food
Fuels: keep consumption to a minimum
Water supply: dispose of hazardous chemicals safely

PLANTS TO CLEAN THE AIR

Lady Palm – *Rhapis excelsa*
Anthurium – *Anthurium andraeanum* (below right)
Rubber Plant – *Ficus robusta*
Dwarf Banana – *Musa cavendishii*
Peace Lily – *Spathiphyllum*
Ivy – *Hedera helix*
Heart Leaf Philodendron
Croton – *Codiaeum variegatum pictum*
Kalanchoe – *Kalanchoe blossfeldiana* (below left)
Golden Pothos – *Epipremnum aureum Ficus alii*
Boston Fern – *Nephrolepis exaltata* 'Bostoniensis'

Each of us takes responsibility for our own health and that of our families whenever we choose materials for use inside our homes. Many substances present in the products we select can cause life-threatening illnesses over time and many are known to be responsible for allergies.

While investigating the air quality inside spacecraft, scientists at NASA discovered that some plants are useful in extracting harmful substances from the atmosphere. This is a very good reason for introducing plants into our homes, in addition to their other virtues. The list above shows plants which have been found useful in cleaning the air.

◁ **Furniture made out of wicker and natural cotton is strong and comfortable, and because they are natural materials is also biodegradable.**

MATERIALS AND THE FIVE ELEMENTS

Materials and their colours and shapes can be used to enhance, weaken or support an area's energy according to the relationships of the elements.

WOOD

Playing a crucial role in most houses, wood's strength supports the structure of a house, yet its grain suggests fluidity and movement. Polished woods conduct chi quickly but stripped pine seems to absorb it. Wood is ideal for use on floors as it is easy to clean and does not harbour dust mites, which can cause allergies.

BAMBOO, WICKER AND RATTAN

These natural products fall into the Wood element category. In contrast to the yang characteristics of highly polished wood, these materials tend to be yin and thus slow down chi.

COIR, SISAL, SEA GRASS AND RUSH MATTING

These are popular because they are natural products. They make attractive floor coverings but are difficult to clean; this must be done regularly or they will harbour dirt and insects.

FABRICS

These can be made of natural fibres, like cotton and linen which belong to the Wood element, or from man-made fibres. Unless they are treated with chemicals for fire or stain resistance, natural fibres are preferred since man-made fibres create static electricity and deplete beneficial negative ions. Fabrics can encourage stagnant chi if they become faded and dirty.

PLASTICS

Like other man-made materials, plastic falls into the Fire element category as it has been produced using heat. Plastics can block chi and produce harmful vapours and chemicals which may affect health, so they should be kept to a minimum.

METAL

Objects in the house that are made from metal speed up chi flow. The reflective surfaces suggest efficiency and action, and metal is therefore useful in the kitchen and in stagnant areas such as bathrooms. Being smooth and reflective, glass is often classified in the Metal element.

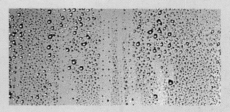

GLASS

Often classified as the Metal element, glass shares some of its qualities. However, glass has depth, and light reflecting on it suggests patterns which flow like Water. Sand is used in the production of glass, so it can also suggest Earth. It depends on the energetic quality of the particular glass and the use to which it is put.

CLAY AND CERAMICS

These two related materials fall into the Earth element category. They can be yin or yang in nature, depending on whether or not their surfaces are shiny. Glazed surfaces are more yang and they conduct chi quickly.

STONE AND MARBLE

Floors and walls made from stone fall into the Earth element category. They tend to be yin since their surfaces are non-reflective and the patterning on them gives them depth. Stone floors are stable and are particularly useful in kitchens. Marble is yang because it is smooth and polished. The natural patterns in marble also suggest the flow of the Water element.

Mirrors

Mirrors have been described as "the aspirin" of Feng Shui and they have many curative uses. They should always reflect something pleasant, such as an attractive view or a landscape, which will bring the vibrant energy of a garden or scene into the house. When placing a mirror to enhance a space or "cure" an area, be aware of what is reflected in it or a problem may be created elsewhere. Mirrors should never distort or cut into the image of a person as this symbolically distorts or cuts their chi. They should always have frames to contain the chi of the image.

Mirrors are useful in small spaces where their affect is to apparently double the size of the area. Don't hang them opposite a door or a window since they merely reflect the chi back at itself and do not allow it to flow around the home. Mirrors opposite each other, with never-ending reflections, indicate restlessness and are not recommended. Other reflective objects can be used in the same way as mirrors; for example, highly polished door furniture, metal pots, glass bowls and shiny surfaces.

△ This hallway is already light but the mirror makes it positively sparkle. Mirrors create an illusion of space and depth.

▽ A mirror will make a small space seem much larger. Do not position it directly opposite a door or window.

irregular spaces

Where part of a house is "missing", in other words irregularly shaped, mirrors can be used to effectively recreate the missing space and make a regular shape.

stagnant areas

Use mirrors in dark corners and at bends in passages to help the chi to circulate around these awkward places.

long corridors

In long corridors where chi moves too fast, mirrors can slow it down. Position several mirrors in a staggered way to reflect pleasant images placed on the opposite wall.

mirrors to deflect

Convex mirrors are used in Feng Shui to deflect fast-moving chi or the influences of uncomfortable features outside the

THE DO'S AND DON'TS OF MIRRORS

Do
Have frames around mirrors
Keep them clean
Replace broken ones
Reflect your whole image

Don't
Have joins or mirror tiles
Hang mirrors opposite each other
Place them opposite the bed
Place them opposite doors
Place them directly opposite windows
Hang Bagua mirrors indoors

THE BAGUA MIRROR

The markings on the Bagua mirror are a kind of shorthand, representing the energies of the Cosmos.

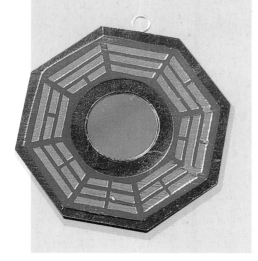

house, for example, corners of buildings, telegraph poles and trees which overpower the front of the house. Convex mirrors will also deflect unwanted influences inside the house, but because they distort images position them in places where they will not reflect people.

bagua mirrors

Bagua mirrors are used to protect a house from malign energies which may attack the occupants. They can often be seen outside Chinese homes and shops. They are used on front doors to deflect the influences of negative energy sources – harsh corners, tall objects and other features. Bagua mirrors represent a yin energy cycle and, as such, should never be hung inside the house or they will affect the energies of the occupants.

△ **If a house is not of a perfect shape, a mirror hung inside will symbolically reflect the missing area.**

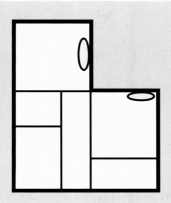

The Wealth area of this house is missing. Place mirrors to symbolically repair the shape and energize the missing space.

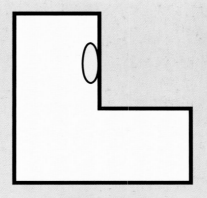

Use a mirror to repair the shape of an L-shaped room by symbolically drawing in the missing area.

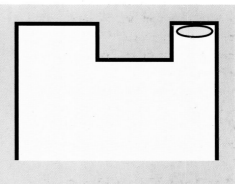

A mirror placed in this gloomy corner, reflecting a view or plant, will enliven a dark space and prevent energy stagnating.

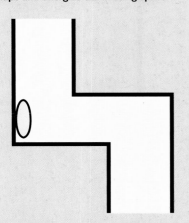

Place a mirror to reflect a bright picture on the opposite wall and thus bring energy to this dark area.

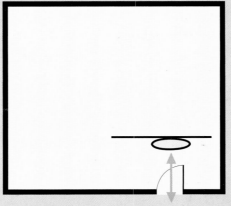

A mirror in this position will not allow the chi into the house or room and will reflect it back through the door.

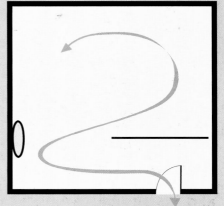

This is a better position as it draws the chi into and through the living area and does not act as a barrier.

Plants

Houseplants play an important role in Feng Shui because they bring a life force into the home and help to keep the air fresh. Depending on their shape, plants create different types of energy. Upright plants with pointed leaves are yang, and are useful in the south and in corners to move energy. Round-leaved and drooping plants are more yin and calming, and best placed in the north. Plants should be healthy – sick, diseased plants, and those which shed leaves and flowers, profusely will create stagnant energy.

colour and shape

Plants with shapes and colours that correspond to the Five Elements are ideal. Care should be taken when siting spiky plants to ensure that they are not directing harmful energy towards a chair where someone may be sitting.

INDOOR BULBS

SPRING: Dwarf tulip, Dwarf narcissus, Crocus, Hyacinth (above)
SUMMER: *Scilla peruviana*, *Albuca humulis*, *Calochortus subalpinus*, *Rocoea humeana*
AUTUMN: Nerine, Autumn crocus, Cyclamen, *Liriope muscari*
WINTER: *Iris reticulata*, *Chionodoxa luciliae*, Muscari, Cymbidium

△ The money plant has been adopted as the Feng Shui plant. Its leaves resemble coins and Metal energy.

▷ This trained ivy plant brings a lively energy to a room. It would look best in the west or north-west areas.

△ Colourful plants will brighten any area and increase Wood energy. Plants in these colours will benefit an Earth area.

PLANTS THAT REPRESENT THE FIVE ELEMENTS

△ **Geraniums are easy to grow on a sunny windowsill and represent Fire.**

FIRE: Geranium, Cordyline, Begonia, Bromeliad, Poinsettia, Aspidistra.
EARTH: Slipper flower, Marigolds, Sunflowers and other yellow plants.
METAL: Money plant, Jasmine, Fittonia, Oleander, Calathea.

△ **All the elements are here, captured in both the colours and the shapes of this attractive pot of lillies.**

△ **Summer jasmine is often grown in an arch shape. Its delicate white flowers have a beautiful scent.**

WATER: The Water element can be introduced by standing plant pots on blue or clear glass nuggets.
WOOD: All plants are representative of the Wood element.

flowers

Cut flowers look beautiful in a vase but, once picked, they are technically dead and often stand forgotten in stagnant water. The cut-flower industry uses vast amounts of energy in heating greenhouses, transportation and the manufacture of chemicals. Although there are occasions when only a beautiful bunch of flowers will do, consider the possibility of choosing a potted plant instead, as it can be planted outside afterwards.

Dried flowers are also technically dead and possess a stagnant energy, particularly when their colours have faded and they are full of dust. As an alternative, pictures of flowers, or brightly painted wooden replicas and well-made silk flowers are all acceptable to symbolize growth and stimulate energy.

the feng shui plant

The money plant (*Crassula ovata*) has been adopted as the Feng Shui plant. The name helps, but the round succulent leaves are representative of Metal energy. Use them in the west and north-west. If used in the south-east (the Wealth area), their Metal energy will be in conflict with the Wood energy of that direction.

▽ **Use a pretty flowering plant in the house like this Cymbidium as an alternative to cut flowers.**

▷ **This bright arrangement would do well in the south-west – an Earth area.**

USE PLANTS TO:

Hide a jutting corner
Move energy in a recessed corner
Harmonize Fire and Water energy in kitchens
Slow down chi in corridors
Drain excess Water energy in the bathroom
Bring life into the house
Enhance the east and south-east, and support the south

Lighting

△ **Our bodies need plenty of sunlight in order to stay healthy.**

▷ **Muslin filters the light in rooms where the sun's glare is too strong, or offers privacy.**

Life on Earth depends directly or indirectly on the sun. Our bodies are attuned to its cycles and in every culture the daily rhythms of light and dark are built into the mythology. In China, the yin-yang or T'ai Chi symbol reflects the cycles of the sun: the white yang side representing daytime and the dark yin side night-time. In the

▽ **Stained glass is very decorative and provides privacy in a room which is overlooked.**

modern world, many of us spend a lot of time inside buildings and our rhythms become out-of-tune with the natural cycle of the sun. In northern countries, which have little sunlight, a condition known as SAD (Seasonal Affective Disorder) is prevalent. It is treated with light that imitates the ultraviolet and infra-red rays of the sun.

The correct type and level of light is very important to our general health and well-being. In our homes, natural light is essential, but its quality varies throughout the day according to the way our houses face. Natural light can cause glare or create shadows and we often have to subdue it or enhance it by artificial means. Light can be reflected off shiny surfaces or blocked by curtains or filtered by net or

muslin curtains, blinds or frosted or tinted glass. Being aware of how natural light comes into our homes enables us to position our furniture and arrange our activities to make the best use of it, and control it as much as possible.

artificial lighting

In rooms where we are active, such as kitchens, offices and workrooms, and where safety is important, for example on staircases, direct lighting is necessary. In rooms we relax in – living rooms and bedrooms – we can use softer lighting which can be reflected or diffused. To highlight particular areas, such as a picture, chopping board or desk, task lighting can be used.

The position of lighting has a profound effect on the occupants of a house. If shadows are cast where we read or prepare food, or the lights flicker, or light glares on to the computer or TV screen, we will constantly be irritated. Harsh lighting can also affect our moods.

The quality of light is important. Ordinary light bulbs produce light which veers towards the red end of the spectrum, with little blue or green light. Fluorescent light is the opposite; it emits higher electromagnetic fields than other sources and its constant subtle flicker can cause headaches. Full spectrum lighting was designed to copy natural daylight as much as possible, but unfortunately contains slightly higher levels of ultraviolet radiation than ordinary light sources.

Energy production is a drain on the world's natural resources. Recent developments designed to reduce this include CFL (compact fluorescent lamp) bulbs, which not only last longer but also use less

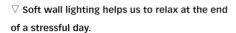
▽ **Soft wall lighting helps us to relax at the end of a stressful day.**

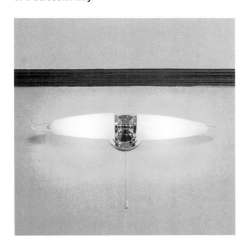

△ **Glass bricks have been used here instead of a solid wall. They can be very useful if you want to open up dark areas.**

▷ **Use uplighters to transform dark corners. Placed under heavy beams, they serve to lighten their negative effect.**

electricity, and are useful for halls and landings. Tungsten-halogen lamps give a bright, white light that is close to daylight, high-voltage varieties are too bright for task lighting but useful as uplighters; the low-voltage varieties can be used for spotlights. These bulbs are also energy-efficient.

Electrostress

We are becoming increasingly aware of the negative effects of electromagnetic radiation on the human body. The effects of exposure to ionizing radiation in X-rays and ultraviolet rays in sunlight are now well-known. The low-frequency radiation which surrounds power lines has also been linked to childhood illness. Such radiation also exists around electrical appliances. Non-ionizing radiation emitted by household appliances can be equally harmful over time. Cathode ray tubes in televisions and computer monitors are particularly harmful because both adults and children now spend so much time in front of them. It is wise to sit as far away as possible from the screen. Lap-top computers should not be used on our laps as we would then be connected to an electric circuit. The electromagnetic field around ionizers has a particularly large range so it is not a good idea to place them in bedrooms.

We live in an electrical "soup". Radio, TV and microwave emissions pass around

△ Placing a Boston fern next to the television screen has been shown to absorb some of the radiation it emits.

◁ Round-the-clock working and satellite links to the rest of the world have resulted in Hong Kong having higher-than-average electromagnetic activity.

▽ Mobile phones are convenient and allow us to conduct business outside, but pose a health risk if used constantly. A laptop computer should not be used on our laps.

◁ **Microwave ovens can damage your health if they leak. Have them checked annually as you would other household fixtures. They are not well regarded in Feng Shui.**

▷ **A gadget-free bedroom is essential for a healthy body and peace of mind. While we sleep, our body cells can regenerate naturally, a process which works best if unimpeded by any harmful external influences.**

and through us wherever we live. There are few places left on Earth where this is not the case. Satellites connect continents instantly and we can communicate with people across the world, but at a price. Recent research into the use of mobile telephones indicates that frequent use can affect us. The radiation from the appliances we use every day of our lives has been linked to various cancers, allergies, Parkinson's disease, Alzheimer's disease, cataracts, ME and even the total breakdown of the immune system.

Despite our awareness of the effects of radiation, we are so dependent on appliances and communication technology that we are unwilling, or unable, to live without them. We should therefore take precautions. At night, electric blankets should never be left on when we are in bed; if we must use them, they should be unplugged from the mains before we get into bed. Water beds are connected to the electricity supply, so in Feng Shui terms they display the conflict of Fire (electricity) and Water. We need to feel secure when we sleep and the constant motion of a water bed is not a natural way to rest.

Microwave ovens are potentially the most dangerous of all household appliances. If you must have one in your kitchen, it should be used with great care. They have been found to emit low-frequency radiation far in excess of that known to cause lymphatic cancer in children, and are also thought to corrupt the molecular structure of food.

Apartments that have under-floor or overhead heating systems should be avoided as they can create the effect of living in an electromagnetic box.

PRECAUTIONS

Use mobile phones as little as possible and make lengthy social calls from a land phone

Fit screen filters to VDUs

Sit, and make sure children sit, at least 2 m (6 ft) away from the television screen

Sit as far away from the computer as possible when not working

Limit children's use of the computer

Do not use the computer and television as substitute babysitters

Do not stand near a microwave when it is on

Dry your hair naturally instead of using electrical appliances

Choose gas or wood-burning stoves and heaters rather than electric

Keep all electrical appliances away from the bed

Do not have wiring under the bed

Do not use storage heaters in bedrooms

▽ **Storing electrical equipment out of sight will help us to relax.**

△ **Children sleep better if they are not surrounded by stimulating equipment.**

▽ **A wood-burning stove lends an attractive focus to a room.**

The senses: sight

What we see affects us positively or negatively, or even subconsciously so we may not even be aware of the effect. If we surround ourselves with wonderful views, bright colours, interesting food and a clean and clear environment we are more likely to lead full and happy lives, because our surroundings will reflect a positive attitude to life, and will stimulate all our senses. The reverse is equally true.

Most homes have problem areas – dark corners which would benefit from light, rooms with columns or L-shaped rooms where the corners point at us – but we can disguise them with plants and materials to soften the edges. There may be things outside which affect us and we may want to keep their influence out.

△ **Skyscapes are so beautiful that we should make sure we can capture a view of them in our homes if possible**.

We can attempt to deflect the problem with mirrors and other reflective objects, or create a barrier, such as a hedge or shrub, to keep it at bay. There is a difference between this type of positive, or yang, barrier designed to keep the negative exterior forces out and a yin barrier which we sometimes create to keep our own negative energies in – tall hedges and walls and drawn curtains. Wherever the ancient Chinese had a wall, there would be a window, or "Moon Gate", in it through which to see the world beyond and open up future possibilities. Think of this as a good principle to try and follow.

◁ **"Moon Gates" were built into walls in China to afford a glimpse of the world outside.**

△ This intricately decorated window can be found in a temple in China.

▽ Crystals are used to bring a sparkle to stuck energy. Suspend one in a window and the light will shine through it, creating a rainbow effect on a wall or ceiling.

crystals

Colour resonates with us on both a conscious and a subconscious level, and can affect our moods. The combination of crystal and light gives a lively dancing pattern which will enliven a dark room if the crystal is hung in a window. Where energy is stuck, crystals can help to move it on.

Crystals should be used with care. They have many facets which break light up into tiny segments and can do the same to other energies. If the energy of an area is not working, do not hang up a crystal to repair it − or the problem will be exacerbated. A small crystal is adequate for the average home, but larger ones would be needed for a large area.

▷ Coloured glass panels in a window add life to a colourless room. They also provide privacy and so are ideal for a bathroom or for ground floor rooms.

▽ This lovely room has been transformed by the balanced pairs of stained glass windows. Little extra decoration is needed.

coloured glass

Glass, when painted or stained, makes a bolder statement than crystal and its effects can be stunning. Many urban houses have side doors which look out on to a wall and there is a temptation, if they are overlooked by a window from a neighbouring house, to keep a blind permanently down. Replacing the blind, or the plain glass in a door, with coloured glass that supports the elements of the area will bring a wonderful, transforming energy into a dark room. Stained glass is suitable for most rooms.

SIGHT ENHANCERS

Natural light, Lamps, Candles, Glass and crystal, Colour, Still water, Moon Gates, Reflective metals, Windows, Mirrors

The senses: sound

Each of the Five Elements governs a different musical quality and sound. We all connect to a particular sound and in Chinese medicine the tone of our voice is categorized according to the elements and used in diagnosis. We each have our own favourite sounds. Gentle background music, the rustle of leaves, bird songs – all have a therapeutic effect. Where noise is rhythmic – a dripping tap, music from a neighbour's party, even someone sneezing at regular intervals – it can grate on our nerves.

Pleasant sounds in the right place and at the right time can soothe and refresh. Bubbling water will create a peaceful ambience and slow us down. If we want to bring life to a place, honky-tonk music, drums and cymbals will fulfil the purpose. Background sounds are comforting and the sound of passing traffic or a ticking clock can be reassuring.

wind chimes

Feng Shui sees wind chimes as an enhancer and it is interesting to note how people respond differently to the noise they make, and their various tones. Take care when

▽ **The vibrations from Tibetan bells will energize a room.**

using wind chimes near fences in a build up area, since your neighbours may not enjoy their sound as much as you do.

Wind chimes are used to slow energy down, for example, where a staircase faces the front door, but only if they are activated as the door opens. Chimes are very effective in the kitchen where people often stand at the sink or stove with their backs to the door, because it is comforting to know that the chimes will sound if anyone enters.

Chimes should be hollow to allow the chi in. They can be used to enhance the Metal area of a building, particularly if placed outside the door of a west-facing house, until the year 2003, when they should be removed. Do not use them in a Wood area (east or south-east) because in that position they are detrimental to the energy of the area.

▽ **The deep-toned, soothing ticking of a grandfather clock is a reassuring sound.**

△ **Here wind chimes help to balance the negative effect of a sloping ceiling.**

water

The sound of gently bubbling water can be relaxing and there are many delightful indoor water features available. Water should be placed in the north, the east, where it is particularly auspicious until 2003, and in the south-east. From 2004 until 2023, the south-west is auspicious. Fish tanks are recommended, but must be clean, and contain living plants and natural features. Neglected tanks and unhealthy fish will have a negative effect. The preferred number of fish is nine, one being black to absorb negative chi.

SOUND ENHANCERS

Wind chimes, Moving water, Music, Clocks, Rustling leaves

The senses: touch

Too often disregarded, touch is as vital as the other senses and is linked to our primeval desire to be in contact with the Earth. No mother can forget her first contact with a new baby – skin on skin is the most basic yet the most magical feeling there is. The tactile sensations in our homes affect our feelings of comfort and security. A scratchy plant that brushes our ankles as we return home will colour our evening, and a cold or harsh feel underfoot as we step out of bed affects the start of our day.

People who have impaired vision develop their other senses and touch becomes much more important. Guide dogs provide physical contact as well as being their owner's eyes. Isolated elderly people are said to live longer if they have pets to stroke.

When we are depressed, physical contact such as a hug from a relative or partner plays an important part in the healing process. Those who are deprived of physical affection as children often have difficulty making relationships.

△ No mother ever forgets her first skin-to-skin contact with her new baby.

The materials with which we surround ourselves in our homes make a considerable impact on us. Few people can resist the urge to stroke a beautiful wooden bowl, although they might pass by a steel sculpture without touching it. Visitors to stately homes are asked to refrain from stroking fabrics and priceless furniture, but it is an irresistible urge, especially if the furnishings are particularly sumptuous. If we clothe ourselves and cover our furniture in fabrics which feel soft and luxurious, it will positively affect the way we feel. The yin-yang balance in our homes is revealed in the sense of touch. Yang rooms like the kitchen and study are full of yang metal objects which are utilitarian, we would never dream of connecting with these except on a working basis. In yin rooms (bedrooms and other rooms for relaxation) we put on warm and comfortable clothing and snuggle into soft beds and sofas.

△ Velvet furnishings and accessories feel wonderfully luxurious.

◁ Different textures provide sensual appeal and give a room character.

TOUCH ENHANCERS
Plants, Wooden objects, Fabrics, Pets, People, Fruit, Smooth objects

The senses: taste

This is not as easy as the other senses to describe in terms of Feng Shui yet it forms as great a part of our well-being as any sense. The Chinese see the tastes affiliated to the Five Elements as an integral part of life. If we are to change our perceptions and lifestyles, part of the process includes how we treat our bodies. If the chi is to flow unblocked, then we need to live in a holistic way in every aspect of our lives.

"We are what we eat" expresses the view that our diet directly affects our health. The frantic lifestyles that many of us lead mean that we often grab what we can, and eat it on the run, without taking nutritional balance, or proper digestion, into account. Modern medicine may come up with the cures, but if we eat healthy balanced diets then we are less likely to become ill in the first place.

△ **Spend time preparing home-cooked meals rather than resorting to store-bought foods**.

Using yin and yang and the Five Elements in the kitchen is a science in itself. Chinese herbal medicine balances the constitution using the same techniques as Feng Shui does to balance an environment. (Chaucer's red-faced, lecherous Summoner in *The Canterbury Tales*, a lover of onions and leeks, is a classic case of an excess of the Fire element.) Being aware of the balance of elements in our food, and the poor nutritional value of the

◁ **Using fresh natural ingredients keeps us healthy – and tastes wonderful**.

pre-cooked fast food products which we now consume, enables us to take charge of all aspects of our lives. The benefits and disadvantages of genetically engineered food products are currently being debated, but we do not need scientific reports to tell us that we should make time in our lives to use natural ingredients. It is unwise to rely on packaged food when we do not know the accumulative effects on our bodies of the chemicals they contain.

SUPPORTIVE FOODS

Once we have consulted the "Chinese Animals" Table and discovered which element governs our sign, we can see below which food types support us. Using "The Relationships of the Five Elements" table, we will then be able to see which of the elements are beneficial to us and which are not, and adjust our eating habits accordingly.

Wood	sour
Fire	bitter
Earth	sweet
Metal	pungent
Water	salt

The senses: smell

Large stores know only too well the power of the sense of smell. Who can fail to be tempted by the aroma of freshly baked bread at the supermarket entrance, pumped through grills to lure us into the store where the bakery is almost always in the farthest corner?

Animals excrete pheromones to attract their mates and to mark their territory. Our homes also have a unique smell and most of us, if blindfolded, could tell which of our friends' homes we were entering. First impressions make an impact and if

△ A herb path by the back door will smell wonderful and give us pleasure.

△ The smell of freshly-baked bread and natural foods heighten our senses.

▽ Scented oils give pleasant aromas and can make a colour statement too.

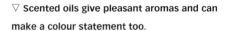

our homes smell less than fresh, this can affect how comfortable we and our visitors feel there.

There is something very different about the subtle smell of lavender as we brush past it in the garden on a warm evening after rain and the artificial lavender-scented air-fresheners sold commercially. Natural smells affect us in a way that manufactured scents never can, with the added advantage of not causing us respiratory problems or polluting the atmosphere. There is nothing to beat the flower-perfumed fresh air which wafts through an open window from a garden, balcony or window box. Many cultures use incense to sweeten the air, and we are now beginning to rediscover the long-lost knowledge of the benefits to health and well-being of certain aromatic oils.

SMELL ENHANCERS

Fresh air, Aromatic oils, Plants, Fresh potpourri, Fruit

Colour

The Tao teaches that out of the interplay of yin and yang all things come. Yin is the blackness which absorbs all colours and yang the whiteness which reflects them. They give rise to the Five Elements and their associated colour representations, from which arise the whole spectrum of colours. Colour is vibration and we each respond to it on many levels, consciously and unconsciously. Colour affects how comfortable we are in different environments and can affect our moods. Our use of colour also affects how others perceive us. Colour is used to cure physical ailments and can be used symbolically to enhance spaces or evoke emotions.

When we use colour we are also working with light since light contains all colours, each with its own frequency. Every light situation is different – each home and each room within it. The light

△ **This room works wonderfully well. All the elements are there but not contrived.**

quality depends on the aspect, the size of the windows and how they are decorated, artificial light sources and the size of the rooms. The materials we use on floors and in decorations and furnishings have the ability to reflect and transmit light or to absorb it. We can use colour to create illusions – of size (dark colours absorb more light than lighter ones); of depth (natural pigments draw light in or reflect it according to the time of day and the season); and of movement (spots of colour around a room create movement and energy there).

Light quality varies around the world. In Africa, where the sun beats down under a bright blue sky, pigments, fabrics and skins in earth colours such as browns, beiges and terracottas are used to great effect. In Britain, where the climate dictates more of a seasonal, indoor life and the light is much less vibrant, the same colours signify a closing in and, used to excess, can lead to a level of withdrawal

and depression. Similarly, the intense colours of Indian silks and the warm tones of the Mediterranean palette have to be used with care when they are introduced in countries where light quality differs. However, they can play a useful role in moving the energy and, with thought, can be effective.

▽ **African colours – browns, beiges and terracottas – predominate here.**

BEWARE PEACH

Using the colour peach in your bedroom is asking for trouble if you are married. "Peach-Blossom Luck" is a well-known concept in China, meaning a husband or wife with a roving eye. A married person may be drawn into adultery. A single person, however, will have an active social life but will probably be unable to find a life partner.

▽ **Mediterranean colours make us think of sunshine and holidays.**

◁ In this conservatory, the Metal and Wood elements are in conflict.

▷ The colours green (Wood), red (Fire) and yellow (Earth) balance the Five Elements.

the five elements

The five colours associated with the elements evoke the quality of the energy of each one. We use them to highlight areas of our lives we wish to concentrate on, and the Bagua diagram gives us the associated colours for each direction. In Feng Shui, balance and harmony have prime consideration, but we should decorate our homes according to our personal tastes or we will never be comfortable there. We should also remember the purpose of the room and the element associated with the direction it is in. Then we can achieve true balance and harmony. It would be treating the subject superficially to ensure that a room has, say, a cushion in each of the Five Elemental colours. A more subtle approach would be to put a single red tulip in a glass vase in the south of an all-white room, this would bring in the Wood element in the green stem, and Fire in the red flower. The Metal element is represented by the white room, the Water element by the light moving through the glass vase and the Earth element in the sand used to make the glass, and as the medium the flower grew in.

THE COLOURS

White represents a fresh canvas, and black symbolizes a clean slate, upon both of which we can create a picture with the colours below.

RED: Red is stimulating and dominant, it reduces the size of rooms and increases the size of objects. It is useful as an accent colour. Unsuitable for dining rooms, children's rooms, or kitchens, it is associated with warmth, prosperity and stimulation, but also anger, shame and hatred.

YELLOW: Yellow is associated with enlightenment and intellect, it stimulates the brain and aids digestion. Its positive qualities are optimism, reason and decisiveness, its negative qualities are craftiness, exaggeration and rigidity. Suitable for hallways and kitchens, but not bathrooms.

GREEN: Green symbolizes growth, fertility and harmony; it is restful and refreshing. Its positive associations are optimism, freedom and balance, and its negatives envy and deceit. Good in therapy rooms, conservatories and bathrooms but not in family rooms, playrooms or studies.

BLUE: Blue is peaceful and soothing. Linked with spirituality, contemplation, mystery and patience, its positive associations are trust, faithfulness and stability. Negatives are suspicion and melancholia. Use blue in meditation rooms and bedrooms, but not in family rooms or studies.

PURPLE: Encouraging vitality, purple is dignified and spiritual. Positive associations: excitement, motivation and passion, negatives: mournfulness and force. Use in bedrooms and meditation rooms but not bathrooms or kitchens.

PINK: Pink is linked with purity of thought and has no negatives. Suitable for adults' and children's bedrooms but not kitchens or bathrooms.

ORANGE: A powerful and cheerful colour, orange encourages communication. Positive qualities are happiness, intellect and concentration, negative is rebelliousness. Use in living rooms and hallways, but not in a small space or bedrooms.

BROWN: Brown suggests stability and weight. Its positives are safety and elegance, while its negatives are dinginess, and aging. Good for studies but not for bedrooms.

WHITE: White symbolizes new beginnings, purity and innocence. its positive qualities are cleanliness and freshness, its negatives cold, lifelessness, starkness. Use for bathrooms and kitchens, not suitable for children's rooms.

BLACK: Black is mysterious and independent. Its positive qualities are intrigue, and strength, while its negatives are death and evil. It should not be used in children's rooms, studies or living rooms.

Clutter

Not merely items or belongings, clutter is also a state of mind. It can be the things we haven't done that prey on our minds, like unreturned telephone calls and appointments not made, or the ideas and perceptions we hoard which prevent us from doing the things we really want to do. Everything we do not use or wear, or which we are keeping in case it comes in handy one day, constitutes clutter. Inherited objects, and those given to us as presents which we do not like but feel guilty about parting with, are also clutter.

For one reason or another, perhaps due to our upbringing or past experiences, or because we doubt our own abilities, we hang on to situations and ideas which do not let us move on. We may stay in a job thinking we are indispensable or we are

△ This low-beamed cottage room looks oppressive, with its fussy decoration and too many disparate ornaments.

▽ A similar room but far less cluttered gives a lighter, more airy feel.

△ Any extraneous objects would look out of place in this cool, clutter-free bedroom, a perfect place to unwind.

doing it out of a sense of loyalty, but often it is because we are afraid to take the leap and change direction. We may stay in a relationship through fear of emotional upheaval, or not accept a job away from a familiar area through fear of the unknown. All these attitudes clutter our thought processes but by clearing out our physical clutter we see the benefits of "letting go", which will help us to clear out the mental clutter restricting our development.

clearing out

"Things" or "stuff" constitute a major problem in most homes, and it accumulates by the day. Useless kitchen gadgets, empty gift boxes to recycle, presents we hate or have outgrown, inherited objects which fear of embarrassment or guilt will not let us part with, and an endless list of other items. We do not need these things in our lives if we are to open up and let

new experiences in. Give them to charity shops or sell them at car-boot sales and buy something you really want.

Most of us hold on to clothes "in case" we might need them, grow back into them or our children might like them one day. It is far better to live for today and create space for something new which we will enjoy wearing now.

Books are difficult to get rid of as many people believe it is a sacrilege to throw them out. If books sit and gather dust for years on end, unread and not referred to, they too constitute clutter and stuck energy and we should move them on. The world is changing fast and information becomes out of date almost before it is in print. Should we require a fact in ten years'

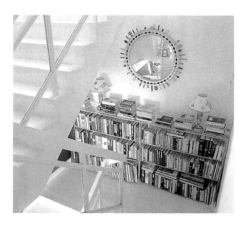

△ **If these overladen shelves are thinned out, there will be room for new books.**

time, the information will be accessible elsewhere. Magazines and newspapers also constitute clutter. We are unlikely to read last week's, or even yesterday's, paper and we can always extract any information we require from magazines provided we file it immediately in a place where we are likely to find it again.

Clutter represents stagnant energy and isn't just made up of unstored belongings, the list is endless – blown light bulbs we keep forgetting to replace, dead wasps and dropped leaves on the window ledge, scum marks round the bath, the unfilled pepper grinder in the kitchen, a squeaking cupboard door. Separately, each of these requires only a few minute's attention, but put together, their effect can make years of difference to the quality of our lives.

Do not attempt to rid the whole house of clutter in one go. Start in a small way with a drawer, and complete the whole task of clearing out, tidying and getting rid of unwanted items before moving on to the next.

△ **There is no clutter here, but enough objects and colours to make the space interesting.**

ENERGIZING OUR HOMES

When we move into a new house, or have had an unpleasant experience in our home, the energy there can become stuck and feel heavy. We can lighten it to some extent by clearing out all the clutter and by cleaning everywhere thoroughly.

Vibrations are important and we resonate at a level which is in harmony with the natural vibrations of the Earth. The senses also work at a vibrational level and if we can improve their quality in our homes we will feel the benefit. Often the

▽ **Candles represent Fire. Use with care in the South and to support the West.**

△ **Burning aromatic oils or incense raises the energy in a room.**

vibrations which have caused the previous owner to behave in a certain way will have the same effect on us and we should take note of any problems before moving to a new home.

There are various methods we can use to improve the vibrations in our homes. Having cleaned and rid the house of clutter, open the windows and

make a noise in every room. Bells, gongs and clapping all raise the vibrational level. Take particular care to go into the corners, where energy is likely to be stuck. Natural light can be represented by candles placed in each corner of the room and in the centre. Smell can be introduced in the form of incense or aromatic oils. Spring water, charged by the vibrations of the moon, can be sprayed around to introduce negative ions back into the air.

▽ **Candles in the corners and centre of a room will help move any stuck energy.**

Using the symbolic Bagua

We all wish at certain times in our lives that some aspect was working better. By focusing on a particular aspect of our lives, we can often stimulate the energy to make things work well for us. Used as a template that we can place on the plans of our home, the Symbolic Bagua gives us a tool for focus with its division into eight life sections. The eight life sections of the Bagua are: Career, Relationships, Family, Wealth, Helpful People, Children, Knowledge and Fame and each area has its own enhancers. By using some of the methods described on the following pages we can hopefully harness some of the "magic" of Feng Shui for ourselves.

The enhancements used in Feng Shui are designed to focus the mind. For example, we can create the belief that it is possible to stabilize something in our lives by using heavy objects such as stones or pictures of mountains. We can move on a "stuck" situation by creating or alluding to movement, for instance, using water or wind-blown items. Whatever image we use must have meaning for us in that we can see it physically and relate to its symbolism. Thus we should use images from our own cultures and experiences. Whatever we use, it should not clash with the element of the direction but if possible should strengthen it.

career

This concerns itself with where we are going in life, either in our jobs or in our journeys through life. It can also mark the beginning of a project. ENHANCERS INCLUDE: moving images, a photograph of an aspiration such as a university, or a company brochure if applying for a job.

relationships

These play an important part in our lives. Getting on well with people and having the support of partners, family or friends play a major role in a happy life. ENHANCERS INCLUDE: double images for

△ **A perfect arrangement for a table in the Relationships area of a room.**

romance, two vases or candlesticks, a photograph of yourself with your partner or group images of friends, a poster or photograph, or a collection of something. Plants are useful to improve the chi, and ribbons or wind-activated objects will energize it as they move, provided there is a breeze blowing. Do not use them if there is no breeze.

family

Our families, past as well as present, will have coloured who we are, how we relate to the world around us and will have contributed to our health and well-being.

▽ **Framed photographs can be placed in the Family area of a room.**

ENHANCERS INCLUDE: Family photographs and documents, and heirlooms.

wealth

This is often taken to be monetary wealth, but it also covers the richness of our lives, fulfilment and the accumulation of beneficial energies around us. Feng Shui cannot help you to win the lottery but if you have worked hard and followed an honest and ethical path towards self-fulfilment, then the magic

△ **Chinese coins for the Wealth area – the circle symbolizes Heaven, the square Earth.**

may work for you. If this happens, you will probably not want to win the lottery anyway and other, more rewarding bounty may come your way.

ENHANCERS INCLUDE: coins, plants, empty bowls and movement, for example, an indoor water feature.

helpful people

Interaction with others is an essential part of life, and this area is a very important one. If you are willing to help others and need some help in return, this is the area to focus on. ENHANCERS INCLUDE: telephones and telephone directories, and business cards.

children

Not quite the same as family, since children are the future rather than part of the past. This area also covers personal

△ **Family photographs can be placed in the Children area.**

projects – the tasks and jobs you nurture from their conception to their conclusion. ENHANCERS INCLUDE: photographs of children, project details, and your artistic and other achievements.

knowledge

This is the area for wisdom and education that is sought after and which can enrich our lives. ENHANCERS INCLUDE: books, framed words of wisdom and pictures of mentors.

HOME ENHANCER

To nurture supportive energy, create a feature that represents all five elements. Fill a glass or crystal bowl (Earth) with blue glass nuggets (Earth and Water), top up with water and a floating candle (Fire) and some flowers or petals (Wood). Add coins (Metal) to the bowl to complete the cycle.

THE POWER OF FENG SHUI

Feng Shui works in mysterious ways and the results of any action taken may not be quite as expected. Our actions trigger the energy required to achieve the outcomes we seek. This may not correspond to what we think we need or offer a quick fix. A consultant will offer solutions having ensured that everything is balanced. If we decide to undertake some of the recommendations and not others there will be no balance. Instigate one change at a time and wait before introducing the next. The following case study illustrates the unpredictable nature of Feng Shui.

Richard and Anne had lived in their house for ten years and had never settled. Through lethargy they had let it run down and now could not sell it. The electric lights blew regularly and there was evidence of a water leak outside the house. The only decorating they had done was to paint the living room walls a deep pink which, together with the red carpet laid throughout the house, resulted in Fire overload.

Richard and Anne did not want to spend money on a new carpet, so they were advised to paint the walls white to drain the Fire. They had already installed a large fish tank in the Wealth area since they wanted their money to move. They put several recommendations into practice, but not the major one – the walls. The result was that the energies took over. Within a week, the washing machine flooded the ground floor, ruining the carpet and forcing out the Fire energy, the overloaded electrical system finally blew and the fish in the tank died. The Chinese use fish as a sacrifice to human bad luck, believing they soak it up on behalf of the people.

Thus Feng Shui achieved its objectives and moved the energy on. Richard and Anne were left with no choice but to fix the electrics and change the carpet, and this time they chose more wisely. The changes made the house sellable and they were able to move.

fame

Not notoriety for its own sake, but recognition of an undertaking well done. ENHANCERS INCLUDE: certificates, newspaper cuttings, products of achievement.

the centre of the bagua

The centre is a special place. In a house it is where the occupants meet and where the energies accumulate and flow on. It should be treated well, be bright and welcoming, and not be cluttered. Do not introduce a light fitting with five bulbs here; glass and crystal light fittings will stimulate the area far better. A round rug often works well.

the right time

Most of us will have heard or read of people who have used Feng Shui and received rewards – a job, a long-awaited child, or a partner. We may be tempted to take Feng Shui on board and tweak every area of our homes in order to achieve perfection. Life is not perfect, however, and it is constantly changing. Essentially, the energies of the various directions change over time. Thus if we activate a particular area when the energies are good, things will be fine. If we leave whatever we have done when the energies are inauspicious, then we will create problems.

The adage, "If it ain't broke, don't fix it" applies, only make changes where they are necessary. Remember also that when using these symbolic measures the compass directions and their related elements are still important, and need to be kept in balance with any changes made.

Investigating your home

The following Feng Shui case study can only offer a glimpse into the kind of analysis which takes place when investigating a home, but gives a good example of the process, and its outcomes.

William and Julia and their son Steven moved into their apartment a year ago. Julia feels comfortable there but William and Steven do not, and Steven has gradually become very run down and cannot concentrate on his schoolwork. William does some freelance work at home to supplement his income, but has not been getting many clients lately. There is tension and the couple's relationship is suffering. A Feng Shui consultant investigates the birthday of each person, their animal, the corresponding element and the compatibility of the animals.

William is a Fire – Rooster, Julia is a Metal + Rat and Steven a Water – Pig. This indicates that while William and Julia have a workable relationship with Steven, William and Julia's relationship can be difficult. According to the Five Elements relationships, Fire (William) is weakened by Metal (Julia), who in turn is weakened by Water (Steven). Being a Metal Rat with yang characteristics, Julia is quite strong and domineering so can hold her own. As a Fire Rooster, William can be inflexible and is not easily swayed by others' emo-

△ The position of the bed is crucial. It should be protected behind and face an auspicious direction for the occupants.

tions so may not be sympathetic to Steven. Fortunately, as a Water Pig, Steven accepts that things are difficult and is perceptive enough to steer clear when necessary.

Next, the consultant looked at the magic numbers, the corresponding east

and west directions, each person's favourable and unfavourable directions, and the compass direction of the house.

William is a 7 and belongs to the west group. Julia, a 4, belongs to the east group and Steven, an 8, belongs to the west group. The house faces south-east, an east group direction, and is therefore most supportive of Julia. William's best direction is north-west, which is missing from the house. His office falls between the south and south-west sectors. The south-west is his second-best direction and the south his sixth. Steven's room has geopathic stress by the head of his bed. His best direction is south-west and his second is north-west. Julia's best direction is north and the second south. The consultant then looked at the shape of the house, Steven's room, William's desk position and William and Julia's bed. He made recommendations listed below.

▽ This bed is well balanced by the matching tables and lamps on either side.

KEY TO DIAGRAM

1. A mirror symbolically completes the house shape. A metal frame represents the element of the area.
2. The head of the bed was re-positioned to face south-west, Steven's best direction, and to remove him from the stressed area.
3. Steven's desk now faces north-west, his second-best direction. This also enables him to see the door and protects him from the fast-moving chi along the long passage. The bookcase and plant also protect him from the chi in the passage.
4. Semi-circular tables with silk flowers slow the chi further. The passage was too dark for live plants.
5. William's desk now faces north-west, his best position. A plant behind him prevents stagnant energy from building up in the corner. A plant on the desk deflects fast-moving chi through the door and hides the point which would symbolically stab him as he enters.
6. The "mouth of chi" to the stove, the point of entry of the energy source, and symbolic of wealth, comes from the south, Julia's second-best position.
7. In this room the bed is best in Julia's best position, north. A mirror should not reflect the bed, so a small mirror has been used here (see 1).
8. Two square tables, signifying containment, are placed on either side of the bed.
9. A picture of a couple is placed here to symbolize togetherness in the symbolic Relationships area.
10. Stones have been placed on the bathroom and toilet windowsills.
11. A plant supports William's personal Fire element.

▽ **A floor plan of William and Julia's room after the changes were made. The numbers correspond with the captions in the box, left.**

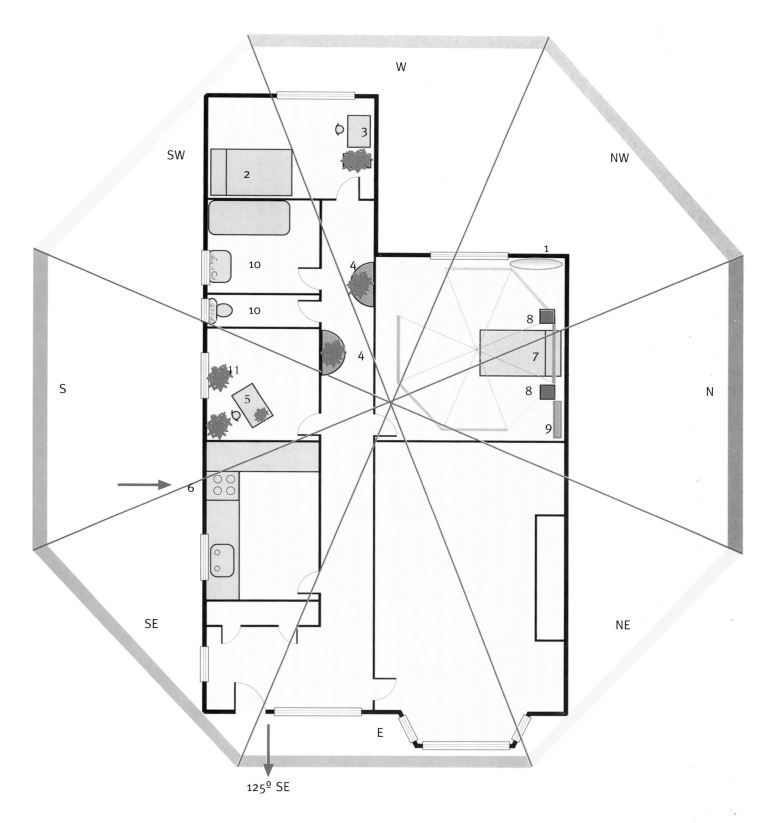

W

SW

NW

S

N

SE

NE

E

125° SE

1

2

3

4

4

5

6

7

8

8

9

10

10

11

Putting the Principles into Practice

Now that you are familiar with the basic principles of
Feng Shui, it is time to look at your home, room by
room, and see if it is possible to arrange them
differently to create spaces that will nourish you.

Halls, lobbies and staircases

When we step though the front door, the first impression we have of a house is the hall. If it is light and spacious with a pleasant, fresh smell, and is clean and tidy, then our spirits will rise. A long dark corridor, the smell of last night's cooking and a stack of newspapers in the corner will set the tone for the whole house. If the energy channels of the house are restricted or blocked, this can have a knock-on effect. Those who live with narrow, dark hallways may suffer restriction mentally or as a blockage in one of their body channels. Psychologically such a place is depressing. It is possible to deal with this by using bright colours and mirrors, and banning clutter. Coat hooks and shoe cupboards or racks make our homecoming easier. If the first thing we see on returning is a mess we will not look forward to coming home.

▽ In this spacious hall, natural finishes, and a variety of shapes, colours and textures create an energetic space.

the view from the door

If a door opens immediately on to a wall, people will feel overwhelmed and they will feel life is a struggle. A landscape picture hung on the wall will attract the eye will help overcome this, and give the illusion that we are being drawn on into the main part of the home. An entrance opposite the back door or window will funnel chi straight out. Keep doors closed, place

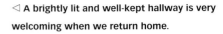

◁ A brightly lit and well-kept hallway is very welcoming when we return home.

▽ Plenty of coat hooks and storage space prevent the hall from becoming cluttered.

plants on windowsills or install coloured glass into the back door window to reflect chi back into the room.

If the first room seen from the door is the kitchen, it will inevitably be the first port of call on returning home. Food will be on our minds before we do anything else. Children will tumble in on returning from school with outdoor clothes and school bags to raid the fridge. An office opposite the door will encourage us to make it a priority to go in and check the answerphone or for emails. Work will be on our minds and we will not be able to relax into the homecoming.

Toilet doors should be kept closed at all times, according to Chinese wisdom, so that we do not watch our wealth being flushed away, and a closed toilet lid is an extra precaution.

HALL CLUTTER
Coats, Shoes, Bags, Junk mail, Free papers, Laundry, Items to take upstairs

communal lobbies

In buildings which were once large houses but are now small flats, or in badly managed apartment blocks, the communal entrance lobby is often a problem. There are two ways of approaching a dirty, messy, badly decorated lobby: negatively, by blaming others, or by taking positive action. Stuck personal chi is often a contributory factor to stuck energy in a house so it is in the interests of all the occupants to move it.

▽ **Plants either side of the entrance welcome the residents of this apartment block.**

CASE STUDY

Nancy lived in a house that had been converted into four flats, with a communal hallway and staircase. The turnover of residents was high and the communal areas were a mess. Approaches to the landlord and other tenants failed, so Nancy painted the hall herself and put up a shelf with a box for each flat into which she sorted the mail and free papers. A bright poster and a plant completed the project. Almost immediately, the neighbours became more friendly. The turnover of tenants slowed down and within two years Nancy and her neighbours bought the property and set about renovating it. The house was transformed into a desirable place to live.

△ **The front door of this house opens directly on to the stairs. There is no barrier against the chi, which enters through the door and rushes through the house too quickly.**

staircases

Often the front door of a house or apartment opens straight on to the staircase. Again the chi will be funnelled without having the chance to circulate so it is a good idea to block the view of the stairs by using a plant, a bookcase or other piece of furniture. If this is not possible, a round rug or a crystal chandelier will gather the chi in the hall. A wind chime which sounds as the door opens will also help to slow down the chi.

Some attention should be paid to how staircases and hallways are lit and decorated. Low ceilings can feel restricting and make the moving of furniture difficult, and a steep stairwell causes problems when decorating, but overcoming these difficulties and making the best of your hall and staircase will pay off.

The staircase should be in proportion to the dimensions of the rest of the house. Steep stairs conduct chi too quickly. Modern conversions often have spiral staircases leading to the bedroom area. These are considered inauspicious in Feng Shui because they resemble a corkscrew through the home. Wrap some ivy or green silk around the staircase and make sure a light shines from top to bottom. Stairs with open treads allow the chi to escape. Place plants, real or symbolic, representing Wood energy underneath.

△ **A large plant placed in this position makes all the difference to the flow of energy. It masks the corner of the stairs from view of the front door and slows down the chi.**

CHI FLOW IMPROVEMENT IN A HALLWAY

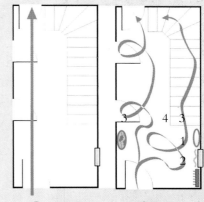

BEFORE   AFTER

1. Muslin curtains create a pause between the outside and the house.
2. Hooks and racks for coats and umbrellas block the view of the stairs from the door and hide outer garments from the inside.
3. At the foot of the stairs a mirror reflects a plaster plate with a painted landscape, which has the effect of drawing visitors deeper into the house.
4. The bottom of the stairs becomes part of the energy flow, instead of being bypassed, so there isn't an inevitable rush to the kitchen by people coming in.

Living rooms

A living room is used for a number of activities – for relaxation, as a family room where games are played, and an entertainment room for watching television and playing music. In some homes, particularly in apartments, the living room may have a dining area attached, or part of it may be used as a study or office space. The arrangement of the room is therefore important if these diverse functions are to be supported successfully.

▽ **Natural materials, lots of colour and a pleasant view give this living room an energetic feeling**.

Living areas should be welcoming, and the colour scheme can help this. Proportion is also important. In barn or warehouse conversions with large open-plan spaces and high ceilings, it is preferable to create small groupings of furniture rather than attempt to create a single room within the space. In small rooms, try to keep bookcases and built-in wall units low, otherwise the room will feel top-heavy and appear to close in.

It is especially important to be able to screen off study or office areas so that work is not constantly preying on the mind when we are trying to relax.

seating

Living rooms are inevitably yin spaces full of comfortable, fabric-covered seats which also represent yin. Chairs and sofas with high backs and arms are protective and represent the Tortoise, Dragon, Tiger formation offering support to those who sit in them. A footstool nearby marks the Phoenix position.

Those sitting in the room should, where possible, not sit with their backs to the door. Guests should feel welcome when they come, so offer them the prime positions facing the door. In rooms where chairs and sofas are not backed by a wall,

▷ **All these chairs are supportive, adding to the peaceful energy of this elegant room.**

create stability behind the seating by placing a table or bookcase there. It is always best if furniture has round edges rather than pointed. If the bedroom leads off the main living area, make sure that the furniture is not sending a "poison arrow" into the room from a corner. Keep doors from a living room closed.

BACKS TO THE DOOR

If you have a visitor who does more than their fair share of the talking, position them with their back to the door to reduce their dominance. Uninvited guests who you would like to leave as soon as possible should also be placed outside the main group.

△ **In this living room the yellow Earth colour on the walls and lamps is welcoming, but the blue Water energy drains it.**

▽ **Plenty of Earth colours on the walls and in the furnishing fabrics make this a nurturing and cosy living room.**

SEATING ARRANGEMENTS

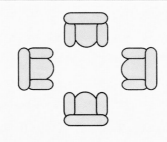

△ **This seating arrangement is suitable for a harmonious family or social gathering. The "circle" is used in all cultures for community gatherings.**

▷ **In this arrangement the table is sending a "poison arrow" into the bedroom. Re-position the furniture to prevent this.**

▽ **The television arrangement spells death to social chat and family unity.**

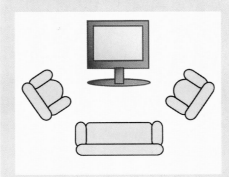

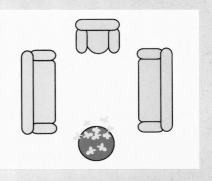

△ **This arrangement is useful for a meeting or important discussion, as it focuses people on whatever is taking place, but also has space to allow the energy in.**

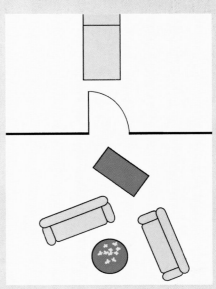

fireplaces

In previous centuries fires were used for cooking, warmth and protection, and were carefully tended. The communal fire was the focal point of family life. These days a real fire is less common, and when it is present it is often a secondary heat source, lit only at festival times or at weekends, rather than a vital source of life. A coal or wood fire, however, always makes a room feel welcoming and draws family and friends toward it.

Since a fireplace is an opening into the room, a mirror above it is beneficial to symbolically prevent the chi from escaping. A fireguard will be necessary, especially where there are children. Plants positioned on either side of the fireplace represent Wood energy, which will symbolically feed the fire and enhance its gathering qualities.

The chimney wall often juts into the living room, creating alcoves on either side. Be aware of this when placing chairs as people sitting in them may be the recipients of harmful chi from the corners. Soften any jutting angles on the mantelpiece with hanging plants.

lighting

A variety of lighting is necessary, particularly if the room is used for a number of purposes. Bright lighting is required for family activities and for children playing, and also in north-facing rooms which get

▽ A larger sofa would give more support in this well-proportioned room.

△ **A cosy living area has been created in the middle of this vast space**.

little natural light. In addition, there should be softer lights; uplighters in the corners or wall lights, and task lighting if there is a desk in the room.

screens

Ideally, kitchens and dining rooms should be separated in some way from the living room. Where they are linked, screen them off with sliding doors, or a curtain, or food will become too important and grazing habits will be encouraged.

A BALANCE OF LIGHT

△ **Here the blue (Water) energy is overpowering the green (Wood) energy and the red (Fire) energy.**

△ **The red lamp makes an enormous difference, restoring the balance of the various energies in the room.**

△ **The additional colours and the mixture of whites turn this into a warm room.**

televisions and stereos

Always arrange the seating so that it does not allow the television to be the main focus of the room. Where the TV is the focal point, instead of a warm, gathering fire, the family will sit in rows and communication will be negligible. (However, this is better than each child having a television in their bedroom, which can result in a total breakdown of the social aspects of family life.) Position stereos as far away from seating as possible to avoid electromagnetic radiation.

accessories

If the living room is painted in a single colour, small areas of stimulation are necessary to keep the energy moving. Too much fabric can harbour dust and fade, creating stagnant energy, but curtains do help to create a cosy feeling. Undressed windows or windows with blinds can be harsh and, being rectangular, add to the Earth energy of the room. In rooms that have many rectangular features and are also decorated in Earth colours the energy will feel sluggish and can make the occupants feel depressed. Keep family rooms well-ventilated and allow in as much natural light as possible.

◁ **A small television set is far better for the family's social interaction than a large set that will dominate the room.**

▷ **Natural materials and fresh colour give this room a good feel.**

paintings and objects

We should always be aware of the effect of the images with which we surround ourselves, since they reflect our inner selves. Gruesome images and spiky objects can reflect inner turmoil, whereas bells, rainbows and pictures of the seasons will reflect inner peace. If we live alone our living rooms will reflect our desire for a peaceful haven or our need for companionship and we can use the space to create positive atmospheres.

Images and artwork displayed in family spaces should be cheerful and reflect pleasant and harmonious themes. Ideally, photographs of the family should be displayed in this room. If one child is more artistically talented than the others, in the interests of family harmony, his/her achievements should not be spread all round the room or the other children will feel that they are failures by comparison. Guns, swords and other weapons have no place in the living room.

It is important that the contents of the home, especially the communal areas, should be balanced and reflect the lives of all the occupants. If our working lives are hectic, our living rooms will reflect our desire for a peaceful haven. Lonely people should, however, use this room to reflect their need for companionship and remove all single images – such as pictures of lone figures; ornaments should be grouped in

△ This is a room designed for sitting and chatting. The round table ensures the conversation will not get too serious.

▽ We should surround ourselves with positive images. The clean lines of this carved wooden bird make the energy soar.

▽ This oval urn prevents stagnation in an otherwise gloomy corner.

LIVING ROOM CLUTTER

Newspapers and magazines
Full ashtrays
Used cups
Children's toys after bedtime
Fallen plant leaves
Unpaid bills and unanswered letters on the mantelpiece

pairs, and the room should be used to create a positive energy.

Where we share our homes with friends, with a partner, or as part of a family, we need to create personal spaces within which we feel comfortable and where we can express ourselves. Relationships with those whose horoscopes or numbers conflict with our own are common and we will be familiar with the phrase "opposites attract". Formulae may suggest, however, that one partner should live in an east group house and the other a west group house. We have to be practical. Where the energies of a house favour one occupant more than the other, it is important to take this into account and enable the other to express themselves within the house and to position themselves in favourable directions in bed and when working and relaxing.

▷ **We should position ourselves in favourable directions surrounded by supportive images.**

CASE STUDY

When David and Sarah retired to the coast from their family house in the country, they left behind a large garden which Sarah had lovingly tended for 20 years. David, a keen angler, purchased a share in a boat and joined the local fishing club, and soon had a full and active social life. Photographs of his boat and his prize catch preserved in a glass case along with accompanying trophies appeared around the house. Sarah was bored and felt unfulfilled in her new life, but since David was so happy she kept to herself the fact that she had preferred their life in the country. As David had an office and a workshop, it was agreed that Sarah should have the living room as her personal area.
1. Sarah, a Water Rooster, was being overwhelmed by too much water. A large plant in the North symbolically drained some of the Water energy.

2. Born in 1934, Sarah's magic number is 3, making her best direction south, so the seating was arranged accordingly.
3. David's fishing trophies and photographs were placed in his study and, since she did not want to hurt his feelings but did not like having dead animals in the house, Sarah compromised and suggested that the prize fish could go into the bathroom and not be banished to the workshop. Sarah framed some watercolours she had painted at their former home and hung them on the wall instead.
4. To dispel the idea that this was to be Sarah's lot for the rest of her retirement, and particularly since the windows faced west and the setting sun, the growth energy of the east was stimulated with a picture of the rising sun.
5. A mirror placed in the south-east, also representing Wood, reflected the garden and drew it into the house to

support Sarah's love of and affinity to the countryside.
6. After reading a Feng Shui book, Sarah decided to try to activate the Relationships area to see if she could find new friends. Using the Symbolic Bagua, she put up a poster of a group of people chatting, which was also reflected in the mirror, thus doubling the effect.

When the changes had been made, a neighbour visited and admired Sarah's watercolours and suggested she should sell them. With the money Sarah bought a greenhouse where she now grows exotic plants which she paints portraits of and sells. Interestingly, the picture of the rising sun is, according to the Symbolic Bagua, in Sarah's Offspring or Projects area. She has made lots of friends and has a full and busy life.

Dining rooms

The dining room is a social area where family and friends can meet, talk and enjoy good food together. As snacking and "grazing" typify modern eating habits, the dining room has diminished in importance. For the Chinese it is a centre of wealth, where a full table, often mirrored to apparently double the quantity, is indicative of the financial standing of the family.

Dining room colours should be bright and stimulating to whet the appetite. Dull,

▷ **If there is a window behind the dining table, it is important that the chairs have backs to them for support.**

△ **This wonderful dining room has a lovely view of the garden. Small shelves would protect diners from the axe-like glass overhead.**

lifeless colours should be avoided as they suppress the appetite. Lighting should be chosen with care to complement the food and not cast shadows over the table. Candles can be romantic, but may get in the way when people are serving themselves or become irritating if they are too tall or flicker. Beware of pictures and ornaments that conjure up inappropriate images – hunting scenes or a china pig collection are not suitable if you have vegetarian

△ A lovely setting for a meal. The candles are low enough not to get in the way or prevent people seeing each other properly.

▽ An excellent dining room – the chairs are backed by a wall and the mirror reflects the table, doubling its apparent size.

△ Kitchen diners make a good setting for an informal meal, and round tables are ideal as they encourage lively conversation.

▷ Low candles such as these pretty shell candles are safer than tall ones at the table.

friends. The best images to display are ones of fruit, landscapes, or of peope dining. If mirrors are used, position them so that diners will not feel uncomfortable.

High-backed solid chairs, preferably with arms, represent the supportive Tortoise, Tiger, Dragon formation. Sitting positions are considered to be very important. The prime positions in the room have a solid wall behind them and a view of the door. The most vulnerable positions are those with a door behind them, followed by seats with their backs to a window.

Table shapes are also important and can affect the quality of the meal. Round tables tend to make your guests leave early because the chi spins round them, while square tables allow more stability. Rectangular tables are difficult as those at either end tend to feel left out. The best

putting the principles into practice

shaped tables are octagonal, which not only enable guests to interact with everyone else on the table, but also represent the Cosmos as reflected in the Bagua.

balanced eating

Much has been made of balanced eating recently but this is not a new concept. Since ancient times, diet has formed part of the same philosophy as Feng Shui. Meals are planned to create a yin-yang balance and with the nature of the Five Elements in mind. Some foods are regarded as having yin qualities and some yang, and different tastes are associated with the Five Elements.

We should learn to recognize the signals that our bodies and our state of mind give out and recognize whether we are becoming yin (feeling tired and slowing down) or yang (unable to relax and stressed). Once we have developed our awareness we can concentrate on maintaining a balance in our diets by ensuring we eat the same proportion of yin foods – such as alcohol, citrus fruits, chocolate,

△ With proper ventilation and heating, conservatory dining rooms can create light, spacious areas for eating in all the year round.

◁ In such a large area as this your guests might feel slightly ill-at-ease. High-backed chairs would help dispel any nervousness. A round table is a good shape for this room.

coffee and sugar – and yang foods – such as cheese, eggs, meat, pulses and salt.

Yin and yang attributes are attached to each of the Five Elements, and in Chinese medicine herbs and other remedies, including food, are recommended in order to maintain a healthy and balanced body. In northern countries (yin) there is a tendency and need to consume more cooked foods (yang) while in southerly areas (yang) more raw foods are consumed. Eating native products in season is highly recommended in Chinese medicine.

TASTES AND THE ELEMENTS

Wood	Fire	Earth	Metal	Water
spring	summer	late summer	autumn	winter
sour	bitter	sweet	pungent	salt
yin	yang	yin	yin	yang

THE BAGUA AND FAMILY SEATING

We have seen that each sector of the Bagua can represent several things. The sectors are associated with particular manifestations of the energy of one of the Five Elements – in its yin or yang form. Each also represents a certain type of energy reflecting a direction, season or time period. The Symbolic Bagua suggests the journey of life, with each sector representing a particular aspect – career, wealth, relationships and so on.

Here we look at the energies of each sector in terms of the family, using the Bagua in seating plans at the dining table. The diagram (right) shows the arrangement of family members around the Bagua. Each represents the energy of the direction they fall within, and this can add further insight into the qualities of the energy in that location. Bear in mind that we are looking at

centuries-old imagery; house-husbands and executive mothers should appreciate that this is an energetic quality, not stereotyping.

FATHER: Representative of solidity, the leader and the head of the household. Sometimes called the Creative energy.
MOTHER: Complements the Father. A nurturing, supporting energy. Also

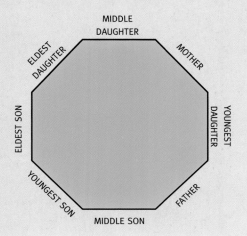

known as Receptive energy.
ELDEST SON: Also known as the energy of Thunder and the Dragon, whose energy erupts from below and soars upwards.
ELDEST DAUGHTER: Called the Gentle energy, this energy is perceptive and supportive and represents growth.
MIDDLE SON: Sometimes called the Abysmal energy, which suggests hard work without much reward.
MIDDLE DAUGHTER: A Clinging energy, representing a fire, bright and impenetrable outside but burning-out and weakness within.
YOUNGEST SON: Also called the Mountain energy, suggesting a firm stillness and waiting.
YOUNGEST DAUGHTER: Also known as the Joyful, or the Lake, which suggests a deep inward energy or stubbornness and a weak, excitable exterior.

THE DINNER PARTY

Imagine that an executive is retiring from your company and you and a rival are in the running for the job. You arrange a dinner party and invite your boss, your rival and a young employee who you have taken under your wing. Using the Bagua to seat everyone will ensure that it is you that gets the job.

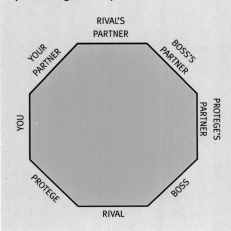

Out of respect, the boss and his/her partner are in the prime positions. When the boss is not giving any attention to the spouse of your protégé (with his back thus turned to your rival) and is concentrating on eating, the people he/she sees when they look up are you, your partner, and your protégé. Your rival, seated in the worst position, representing hard toil for no reward, and his partner, are too far apart to support each other. The attention of the boss's spouse is taken up by the protégé's spouse, and your partner

◁ **Manipulate situations by using ancient interpretations of the energies of the Bagua.**

▷ **Whatever the occasion or intention a decorated table with well-presented, nourishing food will be supportive.**

opposite. After several attempts at conversation, with no support, your rival's spouse gives up. The result is that you get the job, and your protégé moves into your shoes.

Kitchens

The kitchen, perhaps the most important room in the house, is multi-functional, and therefore often the most difficult room to deal with. Apart from its primary purpose for storing, preparing and consuming food, it is a meeting place for family and friends, a children's play area and occasionally even an office. More than any other room, the kitchen holds clues to a person's lifestyle. As our health centre of our lives, and our home, it is important that it functions well and supports us.

The direction a kitchen faces has a powerful effect on its function. In ancient China, kitchens were open to the south-east to catch the breezes that would help ignite the cooking stove. This practical application of Feng Shui reflects the principle of living in harmony with nature. When we have discovered in which direction our kitchen lies, we can use "The Relationships of the Five Elements" table to help us create balance.

A red kitchen facing south will be overloaded with yang Fire energy which needs to be drained. "The Relationships of the Five Elements" table shows that Earth drains Fire, so incorporating a stone floor or some stone pots would be appropriate. As the Fire element is far too dominant, representation of the Water element in the form of a picture of water or a blue blind or tablecloth would also considerably lessen the effect. Plants would not be advisable here since they belong to the Wood element, which feeds

△ Task lighting is ideal in kitchens. Here it gives focus in a high-ceilinged room, where other lights would cast shadows.

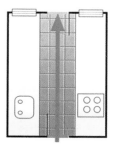 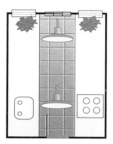

△ Left: Chi rushes through this kitchen, creating a feeling of discomfort.
Right: Ceiling lights and plants by the window low down the chi and contain it.

Fire and makes it stronger. In the case of all kitchens, the Fire element, represented by the cooker and electrical cooking appliances, is in conflict with Water, represented by actual water and the fridge. A delicate balance has to be maintained.

Some modern kitchens are so streamlined that everything is tucked away out of sight and nothing is on display. Since the major features consist of only one or two colours or materials, the kitchen can appear lifeless. Sometimes a dash of red, or a green plant can bring a room to life. Ideally, kitchens should contain something from each of the elements.

the stove

The cooker, or stove, is considered to be of great importance. Where possible, the energy source which flows into it, the electric socket or the gas pipe, should be in your most auspicious location. It is important not to feel vulnerable while standing at the stove. The reasoning behind this is that, since food is the prime source of nourishment and health for the family, it is important that the cook should not feel jumpy or the food will be spoiled through lack of concentration.

A reflective surface positioned behind the cooker, or a well positioned chrome cake tin or toaster nearby, will enable the cook to be aware of anyone entering the room. A wind chime or other sound device activated by the door opening will also serve the same purpose.

△ The kitchen stove is the heart of the home and should face in an auspicious direction.

△ If you cook with your back to the door, shiny objects can reflect the space behind you.

△ Keep your cooking area as clutter-free as possible.

chi flow in the kitchen

As elsewhere in the house, chi should be able to circulate freely round the kitchen. It cannot do this if the kitchen door is in direct line with the outside doors and windows since it is channelled straight through. If this is the case, you should aim to slow it down by physical or psychological barriers. The simplest method is to keep the door closed. Barriers could include freestanding shelves, vegetable trolleys or large plants. More subtle methods such as mobiles or lampshades hung from the ceiling, and colour can be used to create visual and psychological barriers. Barriers can be detrimental, however, and a tall fridge or cupboard by the door will block the flow of chi into the room.

Fast-moving chi is not the only problem. Stagnant chi is particularly harmful in a kitchen. It can occur in a room with

△ Smooth, rounded lines allow the chi to move gently around this lovely kitchen.

◁ In a kitchen where the chi flows straight out of the window, try placing some red glass bottles or ornaments, plants or another barrier on the windowsill to slow it down.

▽ Eye-level cupboards over the cooking area are oppressive; open shelves would be better.

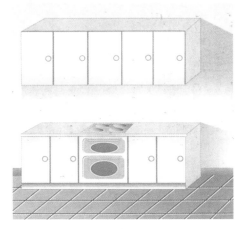

CASE STUDY

This typical modern kitchen has both good and bad points.

1. The cooker, sink and fridge are in an excellent triangle formation.

2. The corner of this work surface has been rounded off so there are no "poison arrows" which otherwise would have pointed at the chairs.

3. The energy is not moving in this corner. A plant or mirror here will help to move the chi along.

4. The chairs have their backs to the door and are vulnerable. A large plant or vegetable basket would act as a barrier. Alternatively, the table and chairs could move out of the corner so the door is visible from each chair.

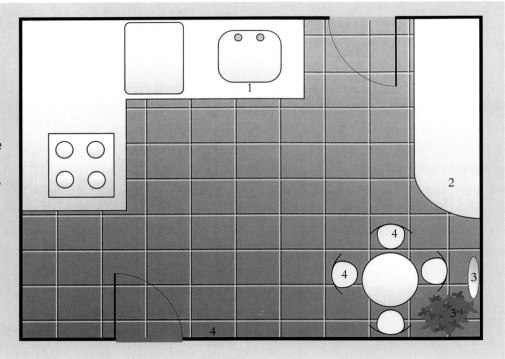

no window and poor circulation, or in a room with dark inaccessible corners. One cause of this is having too much furniture in the room, which impedes movement. If we catch our hip on the corner of a

KITCHEN CLUTTER

Rotting fruit and vegetables
Out-of-date packets and jars
Unlabelled boxes in the freezer
Unused gadgets
Rarely used electrical appliances
Over-full waste bins
Odd pieces of crockery
Plastic bags
Bits of string
Laundry
Crumbs
Fallen plant leaves
Things which "might come in handy"

table each time we need to get to the fridge our body chi will not flow as it should because we are forever twisting to avoid it. At the end of a long day, a ready-made meal may seem an easier option than dodging the furniture to obtain fresh

ingredients from the fridge. Rather than put things away, we may leave out milk bottles and food, which can have health risks as well as cluttering up the kitchen.

Piles of newspapers, overflowing rubbish bins, crumbs and stains on work surfaces all represent stagnant chi. Another undesirable feature of many apartment kitchens is the cat-litter tray. Bathrooms and toilets are not desirable near a kitchen because of the antipathy of the Water element to the Fire element of the kitchen, as well as for more obvious reasons. If we take trouble with the location of our own toilets and bathrooms, we should also give serious thought to those of our pets.

Pointed corners are a feature of most kitchens – the edges of appliances, the corners of work surfaces, knives, shelf edges and the edges of slatted blinds all send out chi that makes us feel uncomfortable. Knives should be kept out of sight in a drawer, and work surfaces should have rounded edges, if possible. Among the worst sources of this inauspicious chi, known as "poison arrows", are wall cupboards, which even when shut can be oppressive. There is a tendency to store far too much in the kitchen – out-of-date jars,

gadgets we never use taking up valuable surface space, a dinner service we only bring out on special occasions or when the person who gave it to us visits. If we examine the contents of the kitchen, we will probably be able to throw out or relocate many items to give us more space and enable the chi to flow. There are many useful storage systems available which help us to make optimum use of the space.

▽ **Efficient storage systems reduce kitchen clutter; review the contents regularly.**

△ **Waist-high cupboards by a work surface are preferable to overhead ones, which can be oppressive, especially in a small kitchen. Keep any frequently used equipment to hand and store cooking equipment, rather than crockery or food, inside cupboards that are adjacent to an oven.**

the healthy kitchen

Kitchens appeal to all our senses. Magazine pictures tantalizingly portray them as rooms featuring bowls of fresh fruit and views over lawns and flower beds. Healthy, freshly prepared meals can be seen on tables where friends and family gather to socialize. Delicious smells, tastes, merry sounds, abundance and happiness radiate from these pages but the reality is often different. Modern kitchens, far from supporting and stimulating us, can unbalance and affect us negatively. The noise from kitchen gadgets, the contamination of food by substances used in packaging, dangers posed by the cleaning agents we use on our work surfaces, the chemicals used in food production, all serve to assault our senses and diminish our well-being.

△ **There is plenty of Wood element in this country-style kitchen, which provides excellent levels of energy.**

CASE STUDY

Mary's kitchen was dark and oppressive. The small area in front was a particular problem because the staircase formed a deep slope, and the space on the left was too narrow for conventional units. The main area felt claustrophobic, with work surfaces and wall cupboards sending out chi in the form of "poison arrows". The cooker could not be moved to face Mary's best direction but this was considered secondary to getting the chi flow right.

1. Red, yellow and green opaque glass was used in the south-facing door and window overlooking a brick wall to stimulate the south Fire element. The light coming through the glass sent a rainbow effect into the room which stimulated the chi there.

2. The plants on the windowsill were placed to stimulate the Wood element of the East.

3. The work triangle is in place, so there is no conflict between the Fire and Water elements.

4. Pale yellow cupboards and a terracotta container in the north-east introduced the Earth element.

5. Stainless steel pans hung in the north-west stimulate the Metal area.

6. Cupboards were used to make the oddly shaped room regular. The one on the right was built over and around the washing machine and drier. Glass doors were put in front of the window to enable the coloured light to shine in. Mary placed her china collection on glass shelves here.

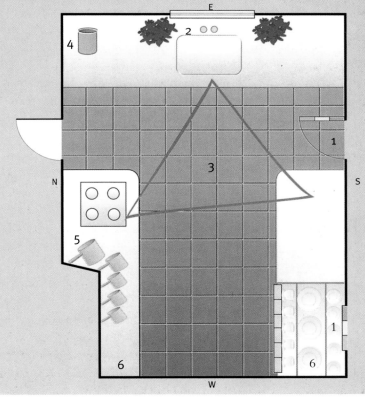

Bedrooms

The bedroom is considered to be one of the most important rooms of the house in Feng Shui. Adults spend a third of their lives in bed, while children and teenagers often spend even more than this. We must therefore be certain that the rooms we sleep in are suitable for relaxing and regenerating us, as well as for encouraging romance in our lives.

beds

A bed should face in one of our auspicious directions, which means that the top of our heads should point that way when we are lying down. Where partners have different auspicious directions, there has to be a compromise; for example, if the house is a West group house and favours one partner, then the bed direction should favour the other.

The best bed position is diagonally opposite the door. The element of surprise is never recommended in the bedroom. If the occupants of the bed do not have a reasonable view of the door, a mirror should be placed to reflect anyone entering. Having the foot of the bed in direct line with the door is known as the "mortuary position" in China because coffins are placed in that position when awaiting collection.

Doors and windows situated opposite each other are not considered auspicious. If a line of chi between two windows – or a door and a window – crosses the bed, it is thought to cause illness.

△ Four-poster beds can be claustrophobic if they have heavy wood and elaborate fabric canopies and drapes, but this elegant bamboo bed without any excess curtaining gives a very light effect.

▽ The symmetry of the tables and lamps at each side of this bed is perfect. Each side of the bed should have identical furnishings.

▽ Here the view of the garden is auspicious, but less spiky ornaments behind the bed would be better for relaxation.

▽ This soft, dreamy room is very restful. Do not have too many books in the bedroom as they are mentally stimulating.

Ideally, beds should be raised off the floor with enough space for air to circulate underneath. Storage drawers full of old clothes and crates of old magazines and other items stored beneath them create a stagnant chi which is not desirable.

Beds should be made of natural materials which can breathe. Wood is the usual choice although bamboo is also used. People belonging to the Metal element often favour metal beds. Since metal conducts heat and electricity, be very careful to keep electrical equipment and heaters away from the bed. Water beds are not recommended because they cause conflict between Fire and Water, as well as creating instability while we sleep.

Headboards offer support but should always be tightly secured. They represent the Tortoise position, and as such, should be higher than the Phoenix, or the footboard. Beds should be backed by a wall, not a window, which feels insecure and can let in draughts.

Where a double bed is in a confined space and one occupant has to climb over the other to get in or out, harmony will not prevail. The best position for a bed is with a wall behind and enough room on either side for a small table or cupboard. These bedside tables or cabinets should always be symetrically balanced at either side; one will not do.

△ **Headboards offer support and this magnificent carved wooden headboard is a particularly fine example.**

furnishings

Images in the bedroom should be in pairs, particularly in the Relationships corner of the room. Images of a solitary figure in a single person's bedroom indicate loneliness, as does a single bed. It is possible to feel isolated and insecure within a marriage. If this is the case, hang a picture of a couple on the wall and display pairs of objects. Photographs of parents, children or friends have no place in a couple's bedroom.

Mirrors in the bedroom should not face the bed. The Chinese believe that the soul leaves the body as we sleep and will be disconcerted to come across itself in the

▽ **This is an attractive bedroom but the mirror should not reflect the bed. En suite bathrooms are not recommended either.**

putting the principles into practice

CASE STUDY

Although Joe and Amy had a comfortable house, lovely children and were blessed in all aspects of their lives, they revealed separately that they felt lonely and isolated. A look at their bedroom revealed all. On a shelf opposite the bed sat a TV, video and stereo system. Joe enjoyed watching videos in bed and waking up to his favourite rock bands. Amy disliked Joe's choice of videos and her collection of self-improvement books on relationships and stress sat on the next shelf. On the top shelf were photos of the children, and a box of toys for when they came in early in the morning was on the bottom shelf. On the walls to either side of Joe and Amy's bed were wistful images of a solitary man and a solitary woman. Following the Feng Shui consultation, the toys were removed to the children's rooms, where they were encouraged to play on waking. The two pictures were placed side by side, where the wistful gaze could turn into a lustful glance, and the TV, video and stereo were relocated. Joe is no longer worried that Amy is miserable and unfulfilled as she no longer has need of her books.

△ **A dressing room is ideal as it frees the bedroom for rest and romance.**

mirror. A modern interpretation might be that most of us are not at our best in the mornings and would not want our tousled image to be the first thing we see on waking. It would be much better to see a picture of the sun rising or a fresh green landscape. Street lights outside the room can also create reflective images in a mirror, which may disturb us when we are half-asleep. In contrast, strategically placed mirrors facing a wonderful view will draw it into the room.

The bedroom should not become a storage area or an office, nor serve any function other than romance and sleep. If you have space in your house, dressing rooms are ideal since they remove most extraneous things from the bedroom. Most bedrooms, however, contain wardrobes and drawer space. Keeping these clear of clutter means we can close them easily and make sure we have plenty of room to hang up our clothes. Garments strewn over chairs constitute clutter, and worry us as we know we will have to deal with them eventually. The worst form of storage is an overhead cupboard linking wardrobes on either side of the bed. This acts in the same way as a beam and can leave those under it feeling vulnerable. The same applies to anything hanging over the bed.

electrical equipment

Electrical equipment in the bedroom is not desirable for two reasons. First, it detracts from the main functions of the room.

▽ **The beam over this double bed symbolically divides the couple occupying the bed.**

CLUTTER IN THE BEDROOM

Pill bottles
Cosmetics
Used tissues
Piles of clothes
Old unworn clothes and shoes
Full waste bins
Piles of unread books
Notebooks and work
Mobile phones
TVs and music systems

morning and are more punctual for work when they are forced to get out of bed to turn off the alarm.

It is surprising how many people have telephones sitting on bed-side tables. They should not be there, they have no place in a bedroom as they prevent relaxation, especially if late night social calls are common. The best place for mobile phones outside office hours is in a briefcase, switched off; everyone is entitled to some time for themselves.

▷ A harp has been placed in the Wealth corner of this room to counteract the sloping wall and lift the energy of the room.

Secondly, the harmful electromagnetic waves that are generated can have an adverse effect on those sleeping there. Ionizers positioned close to a bed present the most serious threat, but even clock radios send out waves over a considerable distance.

Electric blankets are a real problem because they encase the bed in an electromagnetic field. They should be unplugged from the wall before anyone gets into bed. All electrical items should be on the opposite side of the room from the bed, and this includes electrical clocks. One advantage of this is that it makes the snooze button redundant. People find more time to eat a proper breakfast in the

▽ Cramped spaces under slanting walls are not recommended in Feng Shui as they restrict the flow of chi.

BED POSITIONS

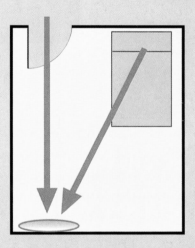

1. If the bed is positioned so that the occupant cannot see who is entering, place a mirror opposite the door.

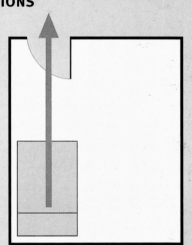

2. When the foot of the bed is in direct line with the door, it is known in China as the "mortuary position".

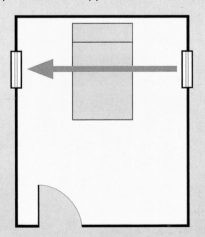

3. A line of harmful chi crosses this bed from two facing windows.

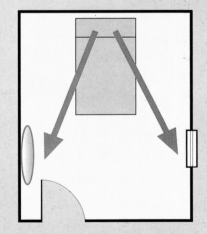

4. A mirror opposite a window can draw in wonderful views.

The nursery

Medical research has shown that pollutants in decorating materials and furniture may be responsible for breathing difficulties and cot deaths in susceptible babies. Decorate the room for a new baby as long as possible before it is due and air the room thoroughly. If this cannot be done, put the baby in the parents' room until the smell of fresh paint has disappeared. Decorating materials should be manufactured from natural products and cot bedding preferably made from natural untreated fibres.

stimulating the senses

We can help small children to distinguish colours and shapes by providing them with suitable stimulation. A mobile hung above the foot of a baby's cot will keep it fascinated for a long time and provide comfort before it falls asleep. Do not place one directly over the head of the baby as this can be threatening.

Very small children could be suffocated if furry toy animals fall on their faces so keep these out of the cot but place them where the baby can see them, perhaps on

▷ **This is a bright, cheerful room with plenty of stimulation for a baby.**

▽ **Bright colours and shapes give lots of visual appeal during the day.**

▽ **A chalkboard gives a child scope for freedom of expression**.

▽ **This large chest will take many toys and keep the room free from clutter.**

△ This first bed for a young child has a canopy to keep it cosy.

a nearby shelf. A bright wall frieze can also occupy a baby's attention, as can a large colourful poster.

Sound can be introduced in a number of ways. Fractious babies who do not sleep well may be soothed by taped music, and the sound of voices from a radio may help the insecure to fall asleep. Musical mobiles can be useful in lulling a baby to sleep, but they might be disturbed if you have to keep rewinding the mobile. Babies soon learn to do things themselves and the look of wonder on its face as a child discovers it can make something happen is magical. By tying bells and rattles to the bars of the cot we help the child on its way to independence, but these are best not left in the cot at night or they will disturb its sleep.

The sense of touch is stimulated by numerous textures – furry, soft, hard and smooth. Allow your child access to a variety of experiences but secure playthings to the cot or you will be forever picking them up from the floor. Do not be tempted to introduce manufactured smells to small children as they are too strong. The familiar smell of a mother or well-loved teddy is far better. At teething time, ensure that all materials which can be put into the mouth conform to safety standards and that cot paint is lead-free.

possible hazards

Pets can be a problem if they snuggle up to the baby for warmth or become jealous of the attention it receives from the parents. Suitable safety precautions should be taken inside the home as soon as the baby

is born. As children begin to crawl, and later to walk and climb, parents need to ensure that all fires and electrical sockets are securely covered, that windows are secure and that stairs have barriers at the top and the bottom.

△ Brightly decorated furnishings in this bedroom lift the energy in a dark corner.

▽ Wood energy, symbolized by the frieze of trees, suits the growing child, who needs to be allowed freedom of expression.

Children's rooms

Bedrooms for children can be a challenge as they often need to fulfil two functions – sleep and play. Although parents aim to ensure that sleep takes place at night and play during the day, a look at some children's rooms indicates why they do not always get it the right way round as there is no division between the two. Children's rooms should also support them and their needs as they grow. Where a room is shared, each child should have a private space within it that they feel is their own.

The energy of the east with the rising sun in the morning is ideal for children. The west with the setting sun at night is good for hyperactive children who cannot settle, although this direction is normally better for elderly people to sleep in.

▽ **Plenty of storage space means that toys can be neatly stacked away.**

The heads of beds should face their supportive directions, although this is not always possible when there is more than one child in the room. It is more important that they should feel safe, and a view of the door is essential for children. Rooms with dark corners which house strange shapes and cast shadows on the walls can prove disturbing for young children with vivid imaginations.

beds

Wooden beds are preferable because they do not pick up electromagnetic radiation. Bunk beds are not considered suitable since they depress the chi, both of the child on top who is close to the ceiling and the one underneath who has a body above, often a fidgety one. Canopies over the bed have the same effect and can also harbour dust. Cupboards and beams can also have a

△ **A stark, but restful child's room. The bed would be better backed by the wall.**

debilitating effect. Children's beds should have a headboard and should not back on to a window or a door.

decoration

As children grow, mentally as well as physically, part of the learning process is to be able to make choices. Children instinctively know the type of energy they require to support them and should be

CLUTTER IN CHILDREN'S ROOMS

Broken, irreparable toys
Outgrown toys
Books they never look at
Outgrown clothes
Dry felt-tip pens
Games and jigsaw puzzles with pieces missing

△ **A reassuring first bed for a young child, as the canopy offers protection**.

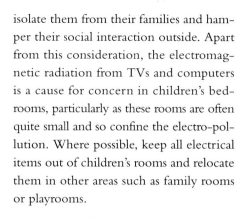

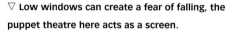

isolate them from their families and hamper their social interaction outside. Apart from this consideration, the electromagnetic radiation from TVs and computers is a cause for concern in children's bedrooms, particularly as these rooms are often quite small and so confine the electro-pollution. Where possible, keep all electrical items out of children's rooms and relocate them in other areas such as family rooms or playrooms.

▽ **Low windows can create a fear of falling, the puppet theatre here acts as a screen**.

allowed to design their own bedrooms and have a major say in the decoration and colours, even if it is not to the parents' taste. We can always shut the door and we should respect it when it is shut. Children need their privacy as we do and if we set an example by knocking and asking permission to enter, then we can expect the same in return.

If there is a family room or playroom elsewhere, then excessive stimulation in the form of toys should not be a problem in the bedroom. Where the room serves a dual purpose, create a separate sleeping area and provide storage for toys to be put away out of sight at night.

furnishings

If the floor is hard, a soft rug by the bed is welcoming in the morning and will give a gentle start to the day. Furniture with curved corners helps to prevent minor accidents. If your child has chosen the colours themselves, you can select shades and hues to suit the child's personality – cooler ones to balance an active child and brighter ones to stimulate a more reticent personality.

It is disturbing how many children, even very small ones, have their own television sets in their rooms as this must inevitably

▽ **A child's room should give her or him the space and facility to read and be creative**.

Teenagers' rooms

putting the principles into practice

△ **The high, sloping ceilings in this attic room do not impinge on this modern room.**

▽ **This is a pretty room for a young teenage girl beginning to move away from childhood.**

Teenagers' rooms are evolving places where children who are growing into adults can express themselves – their happiness, their loves, their hurts and their anger. The latter may be directed against us if we attempt to curb their individuality and try to impose our personalities and values on the private space that will nurture them through to adulthood.

The needs and the tastes of a 13-year-old are very different from those of a 17- or 18-year-old, and some aspects of the room may be changed on almost an annual basis to reflect this. Some principles will remain constant, however. We can introduce our child to the basic principles of Feng Shui and persuade them to place their beds in an auspicious position and think about colour and the flow of chi in their rooms. These principles may help them as they grow into some of the trials of teenage life.

Older teenagers' rooms are multi-functional and usually act as bedroom, study, sitting room and entertainment area for them and their friends. It is no wonder that their occupants sometimes become

TEENAGE CLUTTER
Sweet wrappings and crisp packets
Unwashed clothes
Over-flowing wastebins
Do not touch anything else
in a teenager's private space

△ **Black and white – a bold colour choice – is popular with teenagers.**

confused. Teenagers need our support when they ask for it, even though they do not welcome unsolicited advice. They require their own space, physically and intellectually, but they also need positive affirmation from adults. Hold out against a television in the bedroom and encourage the use of family rooms. A computer in the study will draw teenagers out of their bedrooms and preserve this space for sleep and relaxation.

▽ **The bright decor and pretty feel of this room might not suit an older teenager.**

CASE STUDY

Marie, aged sixteen, was going through an "awkward" phase. Her mother, Ella, struggled to get her out of bed in the mornings to catch the one bus guaranteed to get her to school on time. Every morning was a battle, and resentment festered throughout the day and affected family harmony in the evening. Homework was left undone and Marie's studies were suffering.

A Metal Ox, Marie could be stubborn and, although a girl of few words, she occasionally exploded. Her arrogant manner irritated her father, a Fire Ox, who didn't take kindly to being opposed or to Marie's surliness. He became impatient with his wife, an Earth Goat, who knew Marie needed support and was torn between them in arguments.

Ella decided to take action and offered to redecorate Marie's bedroom and let her choose the decor. Marie chose purple for her room and Ella, who knew purple to be stimulating for the mind and good for raising self-esteem, agreed.

1. Marie chose a multi-coloured bead curtain for the window.

2. They turned her bed around so that she could see the curtain.

3. Ella removed the old square bedside table, since the square shape symbolizes containment, and bought a round one.

4. The alarm clock was placed on Marie's desk so she no longer had access to the snooze button and had to get up to turn it off.

5. To go on the new round table Ella gave Marie a framed photograph showing the family boarding a plane to go on holiday; this energized the "Family" area of the Bagua.

6. Taking a chance, Ella purchased two huge silk sunflowers and suggested they would look lovely in the top right-hand corner of the room – the Earth "Relationships" area of the Bagua represented by the magic number 2.

Now when Ella calls Marie in the morning, she draws the blind and opens the window slightly so the bead curtain moves and tinkles, stimulating the chi. When the alarm rings later Marie has to get out of bed to turn it off, but she is already awake. Family harmony has been restored and they meet on friendly terms more often. Feng Shui is a mixture of common sense and psychology as well as harnessing unseen forces of the universe.

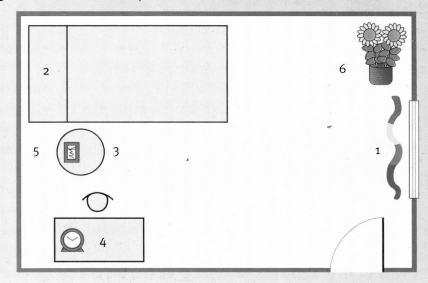

Bathrooms

The position of the bathroom is considered to be important in Feng Shui because water is synonymous with wealth, and thus the disposal of waste water symbolizes the dispersal of the family fortune. Changing climatic conditions have highlighted how precious a commodity water is, and that measures should be taken not to waste it. Conservationists recommend saving water from baths and sinks to water gardens. Dripping taps are symbolic of wealth running away. When we consider that a dripping tap, leaking at a rate of one drip per second, wastes 1,000 litres (264 gallons) per year, we can see the sense in applying ancient rules to modern problems. Baths and sinks that have clogged up plugholes and waste outlets, apart from being a constant source of irritation, can also be a health risk so it is important that we fix them as soon as possible.

▽ **There won't be any need for morning queues for the family that enjoys this large, well-equipped, and airy bathroom.**

△ **This spacious and opulently decorated bathroom, although well-appointed, is free from any unnecessary clutter.**

position

Bathrooms should be positioned well away from the front door as this is not an image we want visitors to our homes to subconsciously take away. It is most important not to have bathrooms close to kitchens for health reasons, but they should also be away from dining and sitting areas so that guests won't be embarrassed to use them.

toilets

It is not desirable to see the toilet on entering the bathroom and, if possible, it should be situated where it is hidden from view. Screens can be utilized or the toilet positioned behind the door. Toilet doors should be closed and the seat closed.

Bathrooms are considered to be linked to the body's plumbing system, so a large bathroom using too much water can lead to health problems concerned with evacuation, while cramped bathrooms are connected with restriction in bodily functions. Large bathrooms are also associated with vanity and perhaps an excessive obsession with cleanliness, whereas small

bathrooms are restricting and can cause accidents as people manoeuvre round.

mirrors and cabinets

The use of mirrors can give the illusion of more space. Generally, mirrors opposite each other are not considered to be auspicious in Feng Shui because they conjure up an image of constant movement away from the self, with no grounding influences. However, unless we spend a vast amount of time in front of the bathroom

▽ Use plants and coloured towels to balance the Water element in a bathroom.

△ Screens can be used to hide the bathroom from an entrance or en suite bedroom.

▷ The reflective materials in this bathroom help to counteract its heavy ceiling. A large plant or dash of colour would also help.

▽ Curvy, watery lines and Metal shapes work well in this unusual bathroom.

mirror, this is acceptable if it improves the suggestion of space. Mirror tiles are not recommended, or those which in any way cut the image. Fixed mirrors are preferred to those which jut out from walls and normal mirrors are preferred to magnifying mirrors that distort the image.

Bathroom cabinets are places where stagnant chi can easily accumulate. Most cosmetics have a limited shelf life and many cabinets contain items dating back years. There is a limit to the number of eye baths, tweezers and combs that are required in a lifetime.

en suite bathrooms

The growing trend to have en suite bathrooms attached to bedrooms is not in accordance with Feng Shui rules. Where possible, create a separate room for the toilet or else make sure the bathroom area in the bedroom has an efficient and well-maintained ventilation system. En suite bathrooms that have been built into the bedroom often leave the room in an L-shape with a corner of the bathroom jutting into the bedroom, so action needs to be taken to ensure that this does not point at the bed.

CLUTTER IN THE BATHROOM

Full waste bins
Empty bottles and toothpaste tubes
Unnecessary soap dishes
Unpolished mirrors
Out-of-date medication
Untried cosmetic samples
Bath oils and perfumes that
are never used

△ **A good balance of natural materials with the right colours, elements and plants raises the energy in this bathroom.**

▷ **Keep any clutter in the bathroom down to its absolute minimum, and keep any soap dishes or holders clean and unclogged.**

relaxation

Very few of us find the time to relax sufficiently and this often affects our health, both physical and mental. The bathroom is one of the few places where we can escape from the world and be alone. Bathrooms should be decorated so as to enable us to wind down at the end of a busy day, or allow us some peaceful moments in the morning.

△ An ideal bathroom – it would be difficult to resist rushing home to relax in this at the end of a hard day.

▷ The huge mirror doubles the space in this elegant bathroom. A frame to the top and bottom would contain the chi.

The colours we use to decorate the bathroom affect how we feel there. Blue is a soothing colour, associated with serenity and contemplation. Colour therapists believe that it lowers the blood pressure, promotes deeper exhalation and induces sleep. Green, on the other hand, rests the eyes and calms the nerves. Whatever colours we choose, we can create a space to relax and soothe ourselves by playing gentle music and by adding a few drops of essential oils to the bathwater. Bergamot, lavender and geranium alleviate stress and anxiety, while camomile, rose, lemon balm and ylang ylang are used to alleviate

irritability and to create a peaceful mood. The bath is an ideal place for self-massage while taking a bath or having just had one. Try stroking one of these oils towards the heart to stimulate the circulation.

Taoists consider that the nutrition we receive from the air when we breathe is more valuable to us than food and water. As we inhale we draw in energy, which provides energy; when we exhale, we cleanse and detoxify our bodies. The art of breathing properly has been part of the Chinese health regime for centuries, and is based on internally balancing yin and yang and creating the correct chi flow within the body. It is thought that illness occurs when the correct chi flow is not maintained. Use your time in the bathroom, especially during long baths, to practise controlled breathing.

Meditation is another very effective relaxation technique. The Chinese call it "sitting still and doing nothing", which is a deceptively simple description of an art that can take years of practice to perfect. Whether our aim is to reflect on the day or to let our minds wander freely and wind down, the bathroom is the ideal place.

Conservatories

Building a conservatory is a popular way of extending our homes and it acts as a mediating space between the garden and the house. Ancient Chinese architects designed homes and gardens to interconnect and regarded each as being essential to balance the other. Glimpses through windows and latticed grilles gave views over lakes and vistas, and gardens were planted right up to the house.

Some conservatories are used for plants or as garden rooms, and are places to sit in to relax. Others have become an integral part of the home, taking on the role of dining room, sitting room and in some cases kitchen. Depending on its purpose and aspect, the conservatory can be decorated in various ways.

the conservatory kitchen

A conservatory that is designated as a kitchen can become very warm in the summer and adequate ventilation will be necessary. It is not considered auspicious to have a glass roof in the kitchen because the symbolic wealth, the food, will evaporate away. Practically speaking, it is not comfortable to work with the sun, or with the rain, beating down above, and a blind or fabric should be put up to block the

△ **A conservatory is a glorious place to relax in all weathers.**

▷ **An indoor garden which opens into a family kitchen, the conservatory provides an ideal outlook when eating or preparing meals.**

▽ **This conservatory opens into the kitchen, enabling the cook to join in the conversation.**

sky. Choose fabrics that are easy to clean and ensure that they do not hang too low and are not highly flammable. The same conditions apply to conservatory kitchens as to conventional ones. If working with the door behind you, place a sheet of metal or a large shiny object so that you can see anyone entering the room.

the conservatory dining room

The conservatory dining room should be treated in the same way as a conventional diner, but there are difficulties. The conservatory room often opens directly into

the kitchen and occasionally also into the main living area. There will be doors to the garden and two or three of the walls will be glass. This makes it very difficult to sit with support from behind, so it is important that chairs have high backs, and preferably arms, to provide this. Depending on the aspect, the evening sun may cause glare so protective measures, such as blinds, should be available. Conservatories can be very warm and fans can help to move the air around. A water feature in the conservatory is not conducive to good digestion and should be turned off during meals.

the conservatory living room

Whether it is used as a living room or simply a small space that faces the setting sun that you use for enjoying an apéritif at the end of the day, the conservatory will be a tranquil spot so long as adequate shade and ventilation are provided.

A water feature works well in the kind of space that is simply for sitting in, it will cool the air when necessary, and add a soothing sound. You do need to make sure that it is placed in an auspicious spot according to the Five Elements. North is

◁ **What a healthy way to dine – absorbing energy from the landscape as much as the food and company.**

▽ **Curtains are not really necessary when you have a wonderful view like this.**

△ **A wide variety of different foliage plants adds interest to this small conservatory area.**

auspicious as it is the Water position. If the conservatory sits in the east or south-west, then this is the spot for a water feature, as in this position it will symbolize present and future prosperity.

Balconies and window-boxes

Many apartments have balconies which are purely cosmetic and act as barriers between neighbouring apartments when the doors are opened. Others are larger but do not really enable outdoor living as such, having no room for tables and seating. Some apartments have neither but may have an external windowsill on which to put plants or window-boxes. All these small spaces bring the natural world inside our homes.

The outlook in many urban apartments is bleak. The most auspicious sites overlook a park or a river, but most overlook a busy road or even a brick wall. Many apartments overlook the windows of other

▷ **Flowers in a window-box are guaranteed to lift the spirits**.

▽ **Even in a small space there is usually room for a windowsill display**.

CASE STUDY

A flower-lover who lived on the seventh floor was so troubled by pigeons nibbling his plants that he decided to give up trying to grow them. He purchased lots of green silk plants and ivy strands, and a collection of flowers to represent the seasons. Set in the original planters these lasted several years, and few people could tell the difference.

▷ **Silk plants are very effective in awkward sites and don't need watering**.

WINDOWSILLS

A kitchen windowsill, inside or outside, is a useful place to have a herb collection and bring not only the sight of the natural world into your home but also the smell and the taste.

The window box on the far left contains nasturtiums, pansies and marigolds, all of which are edible. The window box in the picture on the near left contains chervil, coriander, fennel, garlic, purple sage, French tarragon, savory, oregano and basil – an entire herb garden in a box.

apartments and we can be overlooked by dozens of eyes as we wash up or stand on our balconies. The Four Animals formation suggests that we need to define our space. By placing a window-box on our windowsill we not only define the Phoenix position, we also fill our homes with the Wood energy of growing plants. Recent studies have shown that hospital patients who overlook a garden or green fields recover more quickly than patients who look out onto other buildings or busy urban streets. A healthy display of green plants to greet us in the morning will spur us on for the day ahead and welcome us home in the evening.

Growing plants on a balcony can be problematic. Compost (soil mix) is heavy and can be difficult to transport to the apartment and also to dispose of later.

△ **This green oasis in a bustling city is shaded by an awning which, with the well-maintained plants, creates a protected space.**

◁ **Even a small outdoor space such as this will provide plenty of energy.**

Cosmetic balconies, those that are built for decoration rather than purpose, may not be able to cope with heavy weights and we must be mindful of this when choosing containers and plants. Bulbs can be a useful solution since they require a comparatively small amount of compost. A succession of bulbs throughout the year

will connect us to the seasons, which is auspicious in Feng Shui. Providing we keep them watered until the foliage has died down, we can lift the bulbs and store them for the following year. Depending on the direction in which the balcony faces, the colours of the bulbs may be chosen to correspond to the direction or to focus on a life aspiration, using the Bagua, but this is not essential.

It is preferable to plant shrubs and miniature trees and to use annual plants as spots of additional colour, rather than attempting to uproot plants and dispose of them several times a year.

The home office

Home offices differ from studies in that they are more yang because they have more contact with the outside world. For this reason, they are better placed close to the entrance so that work does not impinge on the whole house and visitors do not have to walk through the living accommodation. Home offices can be difficult places, particularly when situated in the main body of the house. There is always a temptation to take time out to do household tasks, or for the family to drop in. Although home working allows flexibility, it demands a high level of self-discipline in order to work for long enough but not too long, to allow time

▽ **A garden studio or office, removed from the main house, is an excellent idea.**

△ **This luxurious office space is obviously designed for meetings with clients.**

▷ **If the chair and desk positions in this study were to be reversed it would open up a view of the outside world.**

for social activities. A balance has to be maintained. Ideally, home offices should be placed where visitors have access via a separate door and apart from the main house, in a wing or even in a separate building in the garden.

office position

The ideal position for the office is in your best direction or in one of the other three favoured positions. The south-west is not propitious for office locations since the energy levels are falling there. Wherever it is situated, some care in the north will be advantageous.

Any "poison arrows" should be deflected or hidden, using mirrors or screens. Metal supports Water, so hollow metal wind chimes would be helpful. Water is also auspicious in an office but do not use the area for large displays of plants as they will drain the energy.

desk positions

Desk locations are the same as those for the study but if there is a colleague or some other person working in the home office the desks should not face each other. If there is a secretary, he or she should sit nearer to the door to protect the employer from having to deal with mundane matters. Both desks should have the support of a wall behind, and suitably supportive chairs that follow the favourable Four Animals formation. If a desk is close to a door, use a plant to protect the occupant from unfavourable chi.

When visiting clients are received in the office, the owner's chair should always be backed by the wall facing the door and the clients should be seated in the subordinate position in a smaller chair,

THE BAGUA AND DESKS

Use the Bagua to arrange your desk according to Feng Shui principles.

1. This represents Career or the start of the day and should always be clear to open up possibilities.

2. The Relationships area is suitable for brochures and details of people with whom you will come into contact in the course of your project.

3. A plant here in the Elders area will help to freshen the air and symbolize longevity and stability.

4. Accounts and paying-in books should be placed here in the Wealth area, but not cheque books, which represent money going out.

5. Use this central area for the task in hand and then clear it away. Do not leave things to pile up here.

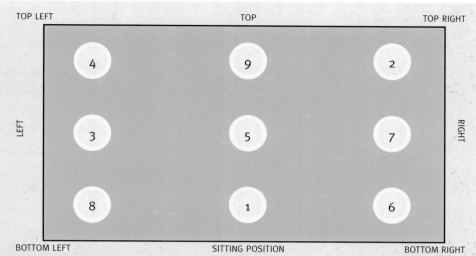

TOP LEFT   TOP   TOP RIGHT

LEFT   RIGHT

4   9   2

3   5   7

8   1   6

BOTTOM LEFT   SITTING POSITION   BOTTOM RIGHT

6. The Helpful People area is the place for the telephone and address book.

7. The Children or Projects position is ideal for putting the current project files.

8. Knowledge and Wisdom – the place to store reference books.

9. The Fame area and the Phoenix position. A crystal object here will denote the boundary of your desk, and of the current project. An uplifting image on the wall in front will represent future possibilities.

△ **This studio's view would be improved if the foliage outside wasn't so dense**.

with their backs to the door. Having sorted out the best location for the furniture in the office, focus on the contents of the desk, either using compass directions or symbolically.

Take care that any measures taken are not in conflict with the element of the area. Task lighting should always be diagonally opposite the writing hand to prevent shadows.

the office environment

Be aware of the approach to the office from outside and check for dustbins and other obstacles, overhanging branches and anything which will detract from your entrance. Inside the house, the same attention is necessary. Clients who come to visit you will not want to clamber over toys or other paraphernalia, which present an unprofessional approach.

It is important, particularly when the office is a section of a room that is used at other times for another purpose, to mark the boundaries – by a screen, piece of furniture or even a rug. Inside the space, aspirational images, landscapes, good task

▽ **This uncluttered desk is arranged following Feng Shui principles**.

FINANCIAL TIP

Tie three Chinese coins together with red thread or ribbon and place them in the back of your accounts book for good luck.

lighting and bright colours all make a psychological contribution to success.

A clutter-free office environment is essential and work spaces should be clear of everything but the task in hand. Do not have stacked filing trays which, symbolically and literally, allow the work to mount up. Deal with letters, emails and telephone calls the same day, note conversations and dates meticulously, and file as you go. Discard catalogues as new ones arrive as well as all out-of-date paperwork.

Home study or studio

The home study may be used by one or more members of the family to study for school or college examinations, for continuing education later in life or for pursuing a hobby or interest. It should be situated in a quiet part of the home, if possible. If study areas form part of another room – the bedroom, sitting room or even the kitchen – care should be taken to ensure that the activities of the two areas are kept quite separate, for example, by screening. It is not a good idea to use a bedroom as a home study, because it will no longer be a place to relax in.

▷ Screens can be used to conceal work equipment in bedrooms and living rooms.

DESK LOCATIONS

The three desk positions below have the support of a wall. You can also see the door and anyone entering. The desk on the right is directly opposite the door. The three desks below right are vulnerable from behind and would make the worker feel nervous.

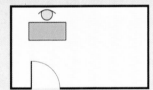

Good: facing the door

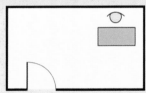

Good: diagonally opposite the door

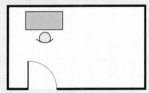

Bad: back to the door

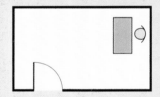

Good: with a view of the door

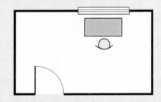

Bad: facing a window

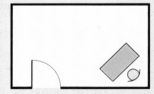

Good: you can see who is entering

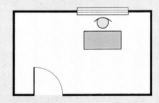

Bad: back to a window

desk positions

The position of the desk is crucial if maximum benefits are to be gained from studying and it should be placed to avoid any areas of damaging chi.

The view from a study window should be pleasant but not detract from work. A view of the neighbours' swimming pool and barbecue area will not be conducive to work. Sitting opposite the windows of a neighbouring house is not recommended since it can cause discomfort, as can facing telephone wires or having roof points

▽ An ideal solution – the folding doors allow light and air in during the day, and you can close down the office at night.

aimed at the office. If there are distractions outside, the window should be covered by muslin, or something similar, to admit light but keep distractions out. Plants placed on the windowsill might serve the same purpose. Studies should have a good supply of fresh air in order to prevent tiredness.

When a considerable amount of time is spent in one position, the furniture should be ergonomically correct. Chairs should fit comfortably under desks and the seat should be at the correct height for writing and using a keyboard. If a conventional computer is used, it should be placed as far away as possible from the chair to reduce the radiation from the screen. Where possible, use a laptop computer. Trailing wires are dangerous and cause irritation, so tie them together and tape them

CLUTTER IN THE STUDY

Piles of used paper
Piles of unread journals
Out-of-date books
Cluttered hard drive
Noticeboards with out-of-date information
More than two adhesive notes
Broken equipment
Run-down batteries

△ It would be difficult to work in this room. The stacked bookshelves are also reflected in the mirror and are overwhelming.

◁ A Mayan chime ball hung in the window deflects the "poison arrow" created by the roof of one of the buildings outside.

out of the way. Printers should be positioned to ensure the paper can eject easily. Plants in the study help to improve the air quality and also add some yin balance to the yang machines.

order in the study

The study should be as streamlined as possible and there should be a place for everything. Cupboards, shelves and bookcases will keep books and equipment off the desk surface. Coloured files and filing boxes store information and prevent paper mountains appearing on the desk and floor. Coloured adhesive bookmarkers avoid piles of open books and journals stacking up on the desk, but the marked items should be read in a day or two otherwise the stickers will be a constant reminder of things left undone.

Journals can pile up. You should try to read them immediately and discard them if they contain nothing of interest. If it is necessary to keep them, a small card index in subject order with the journal title, date, article title and page number will help you to quickly locate the items you want.

Once a piece of work has been completed and recognition has been received for it, it is unlikely that it will ever be referred to again. Consider whether a paper copy is really necessary. If not, store all completed work on floppy disks, which take up considerably less space. Remove past work from the computer hard drive to free up space, clear your mind, and improve performance.

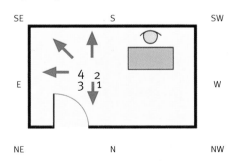

△ Ensure you face your best direction (or one of your other three favoured directions).

Space Clearing

The principles of space clearing are based on the belief that all locations have a spirit of place. When acknowledged and cared for, this spirit can have a positive effect on the place and all those who occupy it. But environments can also be adversely affected by the build-up of negative vibrations. They therefore require regular clearing. Just as physical housework clears dust and debris from a home, so spiritual housework lifts the atmosphere of a place to a higher level of peace.

In early times it was recognized that the home was a very spiritual place. The Romans believed that each home had its resident *genius loci* – the individual deity of the place. The same idea occurs in ancient Chinese and Indian thought, and similar spiritual belief systems can be found all over the world and in all ages. In modern society, a growing awareness of the importance of sacred space is now rekindling this need to sanctify our homes and environments. Space clearing is an important factor in our rediscovery of the spiritual aspect of life.

This section explores different cultural approaches to space clearing and explains how we can keep our own environments clean and clear, and benefit from an atmosphere full of harmony, clarity and peace.

The Ancient Art of Space Clearing

Every human spirit requires peace and quiet, and home is the place, above all others, where we should be able to shut out the bustle and anxieties of the world. The spiritual integrity of the home was revered by our ancestors, and the rituals they observed to protect and maintain it hold valuable lessons for the modern world.

Spirit of place

It is one of the primal urges of animal life to seek out a location in which it can feel safe: a lair, a nest, a den, a shell, a tree or a cave. Human beings share that basic impulse with other animals, and we need to feel instinctively that we are secure.

We cannot be completely at ease in our surroundings unless our spiritual side is also comfortable. The human species may be technologically advanced, but within us there still resides a vestige of that mysterious "sixth sense" that is possessed by all creatures. We can find many instances of its influence in the natural world. There are trees, seemingly indistinguishable from others, in which no birds will nest. There are corners of a house where no cat will linger to sleep. We humans, too, receive and react to this kind of subliminal input, and throughout history there have been those who have understood this and have recognized its importance to our wellbeing.

We choose our carpets because we like their colour or pattern, but the traditional designs from the Far East, Turkey and North Africa were woven to attract good fortune and domestic tranquillity to the places in which they were laid. This tradition has roots in even older cultures: the mosaic floors of the Romans and Greeks served the same purpose. We hang pictures on our walls because we like to look at them, but their origin also lies with the murals of ancient civilizations. For the Egyptians, Minoans, Greeks and Romans, wall paintings often served a spiritual purpose in placating and invoking local deities, who would thus be more inclined to favour the dwelling with their blessing. Further back still, this kind of spiritually enhancing decoration can be seen in the prehistoric cave paintings of France and Spain and their more recent equivalents executed by the Bushmen of Africa and the native Australians.

All these devices were originally intended to drive away bad vibrations or evil spirits and attract good, harmonious ones in their place. They were for clearing negativity and encouraging good vibrations. They were for space clearing.

psychology and intuition

As humankind grew more scientific in outlook, society tended to dismiss the ways of our forebears, but now there is a growing realization that we should not divorce ourselves from our ancient spiritual heritage. An appreciation of the power of the old ways is beginning to return.

All the traditional belief systems of the world include the principle of space clearing. The tribal witch doctor is conducting space clearing when he dresses

△ **We need the comfort and security of a place where we feel at home, and instinctively surround ourselves with things we hold dear.**

▷ **When our home environment is balanced and harmonious, it is easier to relax and unwind there.**

▷ The simplest of altars – such as an arrangement of beautiful natural objects on a windowsill – can restore the spirit.

in a mask and feathers and dances with rattles inside a hut. Whatever we may think of his particular method, it is a means to an end, and that end is to make the occupants of the dwelling feel good about their home because something magical has been done to drive away evil spirits. We may prefer to speak of negative vibrations rather than evil spirits, but the principle remains the same.

Psychology relates to the psyche, the deepest subconscious level of the mind. If we are not feeling comfortable at a subconscious level, we may not be able to put that feeling into words; we may not even realize that we are feeling ill at ease. Nevertheless, our ability to be happy and relaxed will be subtly impaired, and our whole outlook on life is liable to be adversely affected.

Our perception of the atmosphere of a space operates at a subconscious level. The positive changes felt by those who ask the witch doctor to make a house call are certainly psychological, but this does not mean the benefits are any less real.

creating positive space

Space clearing is the art of making a home or workplace feel good as an environment in which we can live at ease and go about our daily lives. Some people, thinking in purely material terms, may believe that if they spend enough money on a house they will automatically be happy there, but experience often shows this is not the case. Most of us have visited what seems like a "perfect" residence that has been expensively decorated, only to feel somehow alienated and uncomfortable. Our psyche, or unconscious sixth sense, is at work again.

There is no doubt that some places feel cold or watchful while others, while they may not seem different in any obvious way, make us feel warm and welcome. Space clearing is the art of introducing the change from one condition to the other. It can be carried out wherever it is needed – in a

house, flat, room, office or even in a factory or workshop. It can be extended to the garden and to places we stay in temporarily when travelling, such as hotel rooms.

Today, we often hear of problems such as "sick building syndrome" and "geopathic stress". These terms are used to describe the dysfunctional energy in a place that seems to have an adverse effect on the people who live or work there. Multinational companies are fully aware of the existence of these phenomena, and employ feng shui experts or architects cognizant with sacred geometry to correct the problem and restore the free flow of their businesses.

Even though techniques like space clearing may at times have been dismissed by the "scientific" way of thought and pushed into the background of modern belief, our need for such traditions has never entirely gone away, and our lives and humanity have been impoverished whenever they are not acknowledged. Such things may be categorized by some people as superstitious magic and therefore not

worthy of serious consideration – but of how much value is a life that has no room for magic in it? It has often been said that it is impossible to draw a line between magic and psychology. Perhaps if we were to allow more magic into our lives, there would be less need for psychologists to heal our troubled minds.

▷ Fresh flowers, plants and crystals not only bring interest and colour into an interior, but lift the atmosphere with their natural energy.

The power of the spirits

As well as acknowledging the nameless spirits that sanctified and safeguarded a place, many traditions sought the protection and goodwill of the major deities. Symbols and depictions of gods and goddesses, and acts of devotion at the domestic altar, were a means of engaging in communication with the spiritual world. They honoured the powers that it was hoped would in turn confer blessings on the home and bring good fortune to its inhabitants. Some deities came to be particularly associated with the protection of the home, such as the Roman god Janus, who guarded the entrances, and the goddess Vesta, who presided over the hearth at the centre of domestic life.

Prayers are one method of focusing the thoughts in order to engage with the higher realm of the spirits, but there are other ways

▽ **Prayer has been used in many cultures to engage with a higher realm of consciousness.**

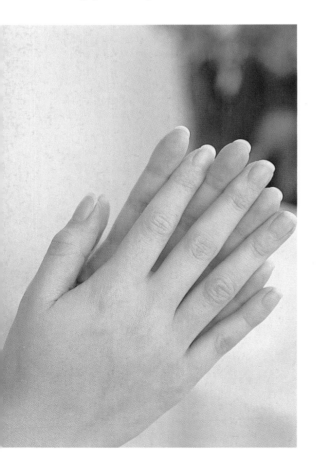

that this state of mind can be approached, such as meditation and the use of rituals and invocations. Specific scents and sounds can also serve to point the mind in a particular spiritual direction.

invoking the spirits

The higher, or astral, realms are usually described in terms that mirror human existence, because that is the only way in which we can comprehend them. It is natural that the energies of our lives should have been personified in the forms of gods and goddesses and various other spiritual entities, each of which embodies particular characteristics. In the ancient Greek pantheon, for instance, Aphrodite is recognized as the goddess of love, while Hermes is the patron of messages, healing and teaching.

Every astral entity has its own area of "speciality", and we can put ourselves in tune with that particular energy by meditating upon the astral form that personifies it. By communing with these spiritual powers we can enhance the side of our own nature that corresponds to their individual energies. This is the basis of invoking the power of the spirits. By so doing, we allow the subconscious mind to achieve communion with astral forms.

Every culture has produced its own names and ideas for picturing these entities, sometimes with sub-cultural variations. As just one example, the Anglo-Saxon sky-god Tiw (from whose name we derive Tuesday – "Tiw's day") can be identified with Tyr in Scandinavia, Tiwaz in northern Europe, Ziu in Germany and Dyaus in ancient India. The Sanskrit name Dyaus is related to the Aryan Djevs ("sky" or "light") or Deivos, and to the Greek Zeus and the Roman Jove. Likewise, the spiritual embodiment of the love-energy appears in many pantheons, with many names other than Aphrodite or Venus, and is always represented by a female form. The great psychologist Carl Jung

△ **Aphrodite, the Ancient Greek goddess of love, can be invoked if you are seeking aid with an issue concerning love or the emotions. She and the other ancient gods are aspects of archetypes that are, in a sense, patterns for self-change.**

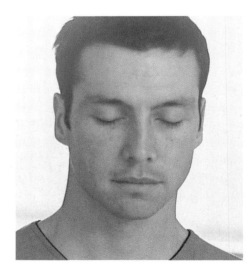

△ **Everyone can benefit from taking a few moments to themselves to calm and focus their thoughts and feelings.**

PROTECTIVE DEITIES

You can dedicate an altar to a protective deity such as those listed here, at any time when protection or blessings are required in your life.

Shiva, the Hindu Lord of the Cosmic Dance, and a powerful protective force for justice, healing and strength. When invoking Shiva, always light a candle to honour his presence. Serpents, elephants and the white bull are sacred to him. Use white candles on his altar.

Kali, the Hindu triple goddess and consort to Lord Shiva. She protects from all negative forces, and helps to reveal the truth. Marigolds are her sacred flower. Offerings to Kali of pleasing foods should be displayed on fresh green leaves. Use black candles on her altar.

Anubis, the ancient Egyptian jackal-headed deity and protector from psychic forces. Burn myrrh grains in a charcoal burner before a statue of Anubis or pictures of the jackal. Use indigo blue candles on his altar.

Innana, the Sumerian goddess of victory. She is highly venerated as the defender of peace, justice and the law. Lion and dog iconography can be placed on her altar, together with a wand strung with ribbons that is twirled when calling to her. Use red candles on her altar.

Hecate, the Greek goddess of the moon. She wards off evil and purifies and transforms negativity. A woven willow basket, fairy icons, dogs and frogs can be displayed. Use black candles on this altar.

Isis, the ancient Egyptian lunar goddess and protector of women. She brings healing and protection to the home. You can display a basket of figs, a small bowl of cow's milk, and hold a piece of carnelian or lapis lazuli while invoking her. Use turquoise blue candles in her honour.

called such deities archetypal beings. The power of the spirits is very real, not least because it has been reinforced by belief through the generations. By communing with them we enhance the side of our nature that corresponds with their energies.

▷ Creating time to meditate will allow your subconscious to commune with higher realms.

△ Lord Shiva, the Hindu creator deity, can be called upon whenever you are seeking transformation or clarity.

The folklore tradition

Many ancient space clearing ceremonies have persisted into the modern age as part of the folklore tradition. The spiritual beliefs and practices of our forebears gave rise to numerous local rituals that play an important part in the continuity of the community.

traditional forms of space clearing

"Beating the bounds" is an old custom whose original purpose was the spiritual protection of the community. The village boundary line was beaten with birch wands to ensure the safekeeping of the village and establish a magical barrier around it so that no evil spirit could enter. In later times, the ceremony also had a secondary purpose: to teach the young boys who accompanied the parish officers around the village to remember the position of the boundary, as a way of passing on knowledge and averting future disputes about land ownership.

In the Basque villages of the Pyrenees, ancient carnival rites have a similar purpose. The men of Ituren and Zubieta, for example, wearing dunces' caps and sheepskins with huge sheeps' bells tied on their backs, process from house to house ringing the bells to protect the inhabitants and their flocks from evil spirits.

A great many folklore traditions surround the Green Man, who embodies the vegetative energy of nature. He is the ancient legendary guardian of woodlands, forests and trees, who keeps out of his territory any threatening ogres or other evil spirits. Images of the Green Man, with his head emerging from foliage, have been found all over the world, but he is most closely associated with northern Europe. In England he is personified as "Jack-in-the-Green", a leaf-draped character associated with traditional May Day revels, such as the chimney sweeps' festival still held in Rochester, Kent. His prancing about was held to ward off evil from every house he passed, and from the township in general.

In Scotland and northern England, the old Norse custom of "first-footing" is still observed. A dark-haired man must be the first person to step across the threshold of a house immediately after midnight on the last day of the year. This is thought to bring luck to the household during the year

△ Wood from the birch tree was traditionally used in cleansing rituals, to expel evil spirits and to drive out the spirits of the old year.

▽ The green, or "wild", men of Europe signified the uncontrollable energy of nature, and their dances were often part of feasts and festivals.

▽ Garlic is well known to have a cleansing effect on the body, but in the old days it was also believed to drive out inner demons.

through the gap between them in order to cleanse them of the influence of any evil spirits. (As a bonus, the process also got rid of cattle ticks.) The villagers would then throw a party and jump over the bonfires themselves to benefit from the magical cleansing process and bring good luck. The tradition of "leaping the Beltane fires" has never entirely died out, and is still enacted by Wiccans and other pagans.

Throughout the world, the warmth and atmosphere of a friendly fire has always been recognized as a "magical aura" of safety and protection from the powers of darkness. This may be why chimney sweeps and unglamorous lumps of coal have inherited their reputation as bringers of good luck.

A need to feel that some kind of spiritual energy safeguards the places we enter has always been present in the background of our society. Even though most people are unaware of the origins of the traditions they observe or participate in, the old customs thrive because they are still relevant to our spiritual life in the modern age.

▽ **Many pagan festivals were associated with light, as the bringer of life, and candles and other flames are still used in modern ritual.**

△ **The warmth of an open fire in winter conjures light, life and comfort from the cold. It is also a link with the fire festivals of the past.**

ahead, in other words, to clear its space of "negative energies". Very often, the first-footer brings with him a lump of coal, intended as a magical token to ensure that there will always be the warmth of a friendly fire in the home. The first-footer may also bring some bread and some salt, symbolizing a plentiful supply of food. He must not carry any weapons or sharp tools, and no one in the house must speak until the coal has been placed by the fire and the first-footer has poured a glass of whisky and toasted the head of the household.

clearing personal space

Another New Year folk tradition is wassailing, the giving of a salutation for good health and wellbeing with a cup of spiced ale, to clear away any evil spirits residing within a person's body. The term "wassail" comes from the Anglo-Saxon *wæs hæl*, meaning "be whole" or "be well". There is a story of this traditional personal space clearing toast being offered to Vortigern, last Roman king of Britain, in the sixth century.

The night of 30 April to 1 May constitutes the pagan festival of Beltane. This is a fire festival whose name is Gaelic for "blaze-kindling". It used to be the custom for the pagan priesthood to light two fires, and for the villagers' cattle to be driven

Wisdom for the modern age

The principles of keeping spaces clear remain the same today as they have always been. Where once the services of the witch doctor or tribal shaman were employed, it is now the feng shui consultant, the dowser, the earth healer or the psychic who is most often consulted. Some of the most modern and sophisticated companies employ the services of space clearing professionals to alleviate or avoid problems in the workplace.

The feng shui practitioner might, for example, advise on an auspicious placement of the furniture, or place a *pa kua* mirror in a strategic position to deflect negativity.

The services of the modern dowser may reveal underground water-courses, electrical interference or areas of geopathic stress, and the dowser may suggest ways to divert the obtrusive energy around the building.

The psychic may point to restless energy fields or other psychic interference affecting the environment, and offer protective solutions. Experiments in the USA and other parts of the world to clear environmental pollution using earth acupuncture and assistance from elemental spirits have proved to be very successful. It may be tempting to scoff at unseen forces,

but if such methods work, why not use them? Today, earth healers worldwide acknowledge and work with energy lines, just as Australian aborigines and other tribal cultures have done for thousands of years.

When considering why a space needs clearing, it is relevant to take into account unseen factors that can be the root cause of any problems the occupants are experiencing, such as geopathic stress or sick building syndrome, especially if the symptoms persist. The detection and correction of both conditions is best achieved by a professional dowser or architectural expert.

symptoms of geopathic stress

Geopathic stress is caused by disruption of the natural energy lines of the earth's grid system. These lines can be disturbed by any human activity, such as erecting buildings, damming rivers, or lowering water tables. Areas affected by geopathic stress can induce fatigue, depression, immune disorders,

◁ Traditional ways of using the land, such as these rice terraces carved from the hillsides, work in harmony with natural forces.

▽ When a modern metropolis is built without regard for the natural environment, it becomes a breeding ground for pollution and stress.

▷ Hectic lives in busy cities leave little time for
the calm and quiet repose that is needed for
health and wellbeing.

headaches, irritability, behavioural problems
and insomnia. An environment affected by
geopathic stress will affect all its occupants
but not necessarily all in the same way. A
general malaise hangs over the area, and its
presence is often uncomfortably endured.
These days dowsers are regularly called in
to divert geopathic stress by using copper
rods. Copper is a good conductor of energy,
and by placing rods vertically in the earth
the dowser can re-route the disturbed
energy around an affected property.

sick building syndrome

This is another form of stress experienced
in modern society. Its specific causes remain
unconfirmed, but contributory factors seem
to include external pollutants such as car
fumes entering a poorly ventilated area,
chemicals from indoor appliances and
furniture, such as the fireproofing on
upholstery and carpets, chemicals from
office equipment such as photocopiers, and
modern cleaning agents, as well as biological
contamination from bacteria and moulds.
Generally, lack of clean air, poor ventilation
and the aggravating qualities of several
chemical compounds when put together
can lead to symptoms such as headaches,
dry coughs, itchy skin, dizziness, poor
concentration and fatigue.

The architecture of previous ages
considered its surroundings and took a pride
in its shape and form; our ancestors lived in
homes made completely of natural
materials. Modern building materials are
treated with a cocktail of chemicals. Homes
and workplaces are filled with fire-retardant
chemicals, wall-insulation chemicals and
cleaning fumes, and we also have to contend
with external factors from the surrounding
environment, such as emissions from
factories, garages and agricultural farmland.
Treatment for sick building syndrome is
simple – it involves providing adequate,
clean ventilation and removing the irritant
factors as far as possible.

the modern world

In the past, our primary concerns would
have been for the success of our crops, the
welfare of our herds and our personal health
and security. Today, in the developed world,
our basic needs are largely catered for by
the structures of society, so that our concerns
now mainly focus upon success and
achievement, prosperity and happiness. We
live in a fast-paced consumer society, where
more and more gadgets are provided for our
use and entertainment, but it becomes
increasingly difficult to find peace and quiet.

A century ago, most people were living
far closer to nature. Even for those who
lived in cities, travel was at a slower pace,
often that of the horse or the bicycle, and
everyone's day-to-day existence involved
much more physical exercise and fresh air.
Though life was undoubtedly more
strenuous in many ways, many of the stresses
we have to contend with in today's world
were unknown.

As we fill our homes and workplaces
with more and more modern technology,
it is important that we do not become
enslaved by it. We need to remain aware of
the many different ways in which it can
adversely affect the environment in which
we live or work.

▽ Modern technology means that we can now
travel the world with ease, but it also means
increased noise and loss of green places.

Harmonious Living

It is difficult to reach a state of inner peace if our
material surroundings are in turmoil, filled with clutter
and riotous colour. In our inner being there is often
another kind of clutter – mental and spiritual. If we can
learn to encourage harmony in our daily lives, we will
have taken a big inner step away from the oppressive
weight of riotous environments, which scream for
attention and produce spiritual negativity.

The location of space

Where is space? The initial answer might be: "Space is all around us – everywhere." This, though, is not really true. The space that surrounds us is normally full of bits and pieces. Actually we tend to dislike space, although we may never have stopped to think about it. If there is a big space on a wall, we are likely to hang a picture there. If there is a large empty floor space, we put a rug on it. If there is an empty shelf available, we stand ornaments or books on it. An empty patch of garden can have a shrub planted in it. Most human beings are compulsive fillers of space.

The state of mind that produces this reflex action to "put something there" has been brought about by the steady increase in materialistic consumerism. We have become indoctrinated into the belief that success – and therefore "good" – equals possessions; that the greatest success equals the greatest number of possessions; and that failure – and therefore "bad" – equals lack of possessions. This is a thought-pattern that has spread throughout the developed world.

▽ **The sensitive placement of objects in a room can create areas or oases of calm in which to relax and unwind.**

finding space

Eastern thought has supplied the opposite philosophy: success lies not in possessions or material wealth but in freedom from their grip. This is an idea diametrically opposed to the driving force of a capitalist consumer society. The philosophy of Zen Buddhism

△ **Uncluttered rooms decorated with simple themes of shape and colour can offer the senses both space and clarity.**

is reductionism, which has a weak echo in Western society in the saying (more usually applied to fashion) "Less is more".

As an example of the difference between these two philosophical outlooks, compare a well-stocked flower garden with a Zen garden. Your own familiar garden may be filled with plants, a lawn, paths, seats, ornaments and a patio. A Zen garden, on the other hand, might consist of nothing more than a layer of gravel or beach shingle, with a single large boulder standing in the middle. Rather than filling the area with many objects and colours, the Zen idea is to draw attention to a defined space by virtue of the simple surfaces and textures contained within it. The beautiful flower garden encourages us to focus upon its contents: in contrast, in a Zen garden we are encouraged to become aware of the location of space.

LOOKING AT SPACE

This mental exercise helps to train the mind to become aware of space rather than the objects that fill it.

When you look in any direction, try to make yourself aware of the spaces between objects, rather than the objects themselves, as though what you were seeing was a picture on paper and you were able to use scissors to cut out the objects themselves, leaving only the spaces between them. This exercise can expand the perceptions and help you to escape from preoccupations with the material world.

△ **The simplicity of the Zen garden leads the mind to concentrate on the space that is defined by it, rather than an accumulation of objects.**

This is not just a design concept. Coming to terms with it involves a fundamental alteration, even a reversal, of an entrenched point of view. By developing our awareness of the importance of space, we can actually nurture and improve the space in our own homes, rather than trying to fill it with displays of possessions and material trophies. By so doing, we can actually become aware of the location of space, and begin to appreciate the space that really surrounds us and in which we live.

Gaining such an awareness of the location of space is an important step in learning how to evaluate its character, and

◁ **A garden may be well cared-for and full of beautiful flowers, yet too cluttered and busy to inspire us with a sense of tranquillity.**

in sensing the ebbing and flowing tensions of the subtle webs of energy that course through it. If we can extend our awareness, our subtle psychic "feelers", into the spatial areas we inhabit and move within, we will be much better equipped to deal decisively and positively with any negative or oppressive vibrations (energies) we may find attempting to encroach upon us and undermine our emotional balance.

An awareness of space can help us to bring ourselves out of the habit of valuing possessions too highly. Preoccupation with the ownership of objects sets us at the centre of a cluttered world which limits us spiritually. To leave those limitations behind, we need to learn to value the release of such ties and anchors. In general, we too easily come to value objects for their own sake and not for what they represent. Once we can achieve freedom from the domination of material possessions, we can begin to set our spirit soaring.

The influence of colour

In any environment, colour can have a significant effect on the overall atmosphere. Hot colours will raise the energy levels of people in a room, and cool colours will calm and soothe. Confusion with colours can lead to confusion within human energy patterns. When you spend time in such a space, it can lead you to ask "Do I relax here or do I move about?" Therefore, when you are considering the atmosphere you wish to create in an interior, the first step is to decide whether you want the area to be a stimulating or a relaxing space.

Colours at the red/yellow end of the visible spectrum are stimulating, and colours at the blue/green end are soothing and relaxing. It becomes clear that to consider putting shades of red and yellow into a hyperactive child's bedroom would not have a calming effect upon his or her psyche. Conversely, if you have a lazy child who hates to get up in the mornings, a bright and vibrant colour scheme could be a very good choice. The same applies to any living

▽ **A vibrantly coloured room may inspire you with the energy and confidence to face the day.**

△ **Water features bring the sounds of nature into a room and have a soothing effect**.

or working space. Before you choose a colour for a room you should consider the characters of the people using it and the purpose or focus of the room. For example, a room where a lot of intellectual work needs to be done – such as a study or office – would benefit from having a yellow colour scheme. The bathroom, where you would wish to relax and unwind, could be decorated with colours from the blue/green end of the spectrum.

COLOUR EFFECTS
Within the broad division of the spectrum, each colour evokes specific responses.

STIMULATING COLOURS
Red: evokes confidence, power, strength and purpose.
Orange: invites brightness and joy, creativity and a positive attitude.
Sunshine yellow: encourages mental activity, stimulates thought, invigorates the nervous system.
Pink: as a blend of red and white, it holds the passions of red in check, encourages friendship, harmony in relationships and warm feelings.

SOOTHING COLOURS
All shades of blue: cooling and calming to the spirit and to over-emotional people, but can be unfeeling and cold if over-used.
Violet and mauve: warmer than blue because they contain a certain amount of red, these colours blend activity with rest and work well in living and dining areas.
Green: as the colour of nature, green is the harmonizer of the heart, helping us to be ourselves and to feel at peace with our surroundings.
Pastel colours: gentle on the eye and perfect for balancing any bright and colourful decorative objects.

colour and Ayurveda

Ayurveda is the ancient Indian science of life. It acknowledges three basic personality types, or *doshas*: fiery, airy, and watery. Everyone is a mixture of the three types, but in most people one quality is dominant. If the dominant dosha becomes too strong it can lead to problems, so it needs to be brought back into balance.

In Ayurvedic terms a fiery personality (*pitta*) is a blend of water and fire. This active, creative and sometimes dominant personality benefits from the blue/green end of the spectrum. Someone of this type finds it hard to relax. Therefore indoor fountains, plant displays, natural furniture and an appropriate blue/green colour on the walls will help to calm and balance the fire. With too much stimulation, this personality will be unable to unwind and relax. A fiery personality who occupies a red room is likely to become a bad-tempered workaholic.

The airy personality (*vata*) benefits most from surroundings decorated in warm and earthy colours such as terracotta, sand yellow, creams and warm browns. These colours help to earth this particular personality type, which has a tendency to drift off and perhaps not achieve everything it sets out to do. Full of ideas, the airy personality often has several projects on the go at the same time, never quite getting the time to finish them off. The airy personality benefits from an environment that features rocks and stone, natural earthy fabrics such as canvas and cotton, and objects that evoke safety and warmth, such as rugs and cushions, with gentle, subdued lighting. This personality would find it hard to live with the brighter yellows.

The watery personality (*kapha*) is a blend of water and earth. These people are emotional by nature, very sensitive but with a tendency to be inactive or insecure. Ideal colours for the watery personality type include pink, mauve, red, yellow or orange. Moving water helps to encourage their activity and dynamism in expression. They would not be suited to cold blues.

colour and the elements

Each of the four traditional elements – Air, Fire, Water and Earth – has a colour associated with it that is balanced by a complementary colour. Air is represented by yellow, which is balanced by violet. Fire is represented by red, which is balanced by green. Water is represented by blue and balanced by orange, and Earth is represented by shades of green, balanced by shades of red. From this it becomes clear that a room can contain a complementary clash of colours that will still have the same ideological focus. For example, a fiery room can include orange and blue and still be a room that conjures activity and creativity.

When we want to use colour to good effect, a little research can go a long, long way to creating the desired balance at home or at work, so that our surroundings don't clash with who we are.

▽ Take time to consider what results you are trying to achieve in your rooms and spaces.

A balanced interior

Human beings are governed and motivated in all things by their own psychology – the inner workings of the mind, and particularly the unconscious mind. Since each person's mind is unique and has been formed by different events, thoughts, experiences and genetic sequences, no two people have identical feelings, tastes or preferences. Therefore the ideal surroundings for one person may be considered jarring, tasteless, or lacking in harmony by another.

It is impossible to say that there is a single correct standard for everyone to adopt in order to ensure that a room, or their whole home, will be perfectly balanced for all those who live in it or visit it. There are, however, some general ideas and suggestions that individuals can adapt and adjust with intelligence and perception to suit their own unique needs.

These obvious but simple measures can affect us deeply at an unconscious level. When we spend time in rooms that have personal meaning, awareness of space and ease of access, we experience uplifted spirits, contentment, relaxation and the enhancement of inner tranquillity and peace. If we plan our interiors with sensitivity and care, we can create the states of mind we desire by the way we orient and theme our home or workspace.

placement and movement

Some guidelines for the planning process are fairly obvious and universal. For example, it is important not to have a lot of clutter or items of furniture placed too near the access points of a room. When you are planning the layout of any room, you need to concentrate on the room's function and how people are going to use the space. In the case of a bedroom or an office, this may be a fairly simple task, but your living rooms may need to fulfil a range of functions, with members of the family pursuing different activities in the same space.

You can enjoy finding the best-looking placements for decorations and furniture, but do not lose sight of the use to be made of them and the access that will be needed.

△ The careful placement of a few sensitively arranged items can provide a stunning focal point in a room.

◁ Choose furniture that fits harmoniously into its surroundings; a symmetrical arrangement can create a satisfying visual balance.

For example, a bookcase may look lovely beside the door, but it will not be such a good position if someone entering the room in a hurry throws the door open against a person who is looking for a book. Allow for the opening of cupboard doors and drawers, and don't place other pieces of furniture so close to them that they are difficult to use.

You should also visualize all the "roads" in a room. Every room has routes within it that are frequently used. At its simplest, this may be the actual doorway into the room, as well as perhaps the route between a sofa and the television, or between the dining table and the kitchen. Plan around these routes, keeping them clear of anything that may impede direct progress.

▷ The routes people take when moving around your home should be kept clear and unobstructed by furniture. Easy access into and around the kitchen is especially important.

decorative themes

It can be effective to follow a particular theme in a room, or even within certain areas of a room. This is part of the art of successful interior design. Homes and offices are divided into specific areas precisely for this reason – offering a basic theme for each room, such as eating, relaxing or sleeping.

How rooms look should reflect their purpose. In general terms, the bedrooms should be calming and peaceful, the kitchen bright, warm and practical, the sitting room comfortable and relaxing. The use of colour is an obvious way to create a warm, welcoming atmosphere in a room, but other

themes can be used to give a sense of unity to your decoration. A room might have an ethnic feel, for example, or be furnished with pieces from a particular period.

△ When placing decorative objects around the home, remain aware of thoroughfares so that you do not create obstructions and precious items remain safe.

comfort and proportion

Furniture should be in proportion to the size of the room so that it doesn't seem overcrowded. Even the most comfortable sofa will begin to look uninviting if it is at odds with the rest of the room. You also need to strike a comfortable midpoint between starkness and fussiness. In most cases, you will be furnishing rooms with items you already possess, but it is worth looking at all your furniture objectively to decide what you really want to keep and what would be better replaced.

Lighting can have a profound influence on the atmosphere of a space, creating excitement and drama or a sense of relaxation. Installing adaptable background and accent lighting means you can change the mood at the flick of a switch.

Avoid unnecessary and irritating clutter, and balance the contents of your rooms. By doing so the rooms' appearance is pleasing to the eye but also, equally importantly, to the soul, and you will be able to create harmonious interior spaces that generate feelings of spiritual comfort and inner wellbeing, whatever your personal style.

◁ To induce peaceful sleep, a bedroom needs to feel calm and balanced, uncluttered but also not too stark and minimalist.

Spatial harmony

The physical contents of an area are important contributors to our sense of peace and comfort, but the physical dimension works best when it forms the foundation for achieving the same conditions on a spiritual level. This is sometimes called the "spatial" level because it provides space for the energies that contribute to our wellbeing. A simple space clearing ritual can be used to promote spiritual tranquillity, and effectively to de-tox the spiritual atmosphere of the room. This can lead us to feel supported and nourished by our living or working space, rather than overwhelmed by its clutter, whether this is on a spiritual or physical level.

a ritual for harmony

This ritual is designed to bring home the fact that there is far more to the cosmic whole than is normally experienced. It enables you, spiritually, to step outside yourself into a greater moment, gaining a wider perspective of the universe and your place within it. From the centre of yourself, the warmth and comfort of this broadened vision of life will spread out into the environment of the area you are in, calming negative vibrations and bringing in their place a feeling of great peace and tranquillity, clearing the space around you of all disruptive energies.

Just after the sun has set, or during the early evening, lay out a simple altar with two white candles, a cup or bowl of water, a small heap of salt in a saucer or bowl, a small green houseplant, and some lotus incense in a holder.

Light the candles and incense. If possible, play some quiet, relaxing music in the background. Kneel calmly facing the altar. Relax your body, mind and emotions, allowing the mystical atmosphere you are creating to envelope your senses.

Lower your head with your eyes closed while you take a few slow, deep breaths. Repeat the following:

I see flame. Flame is energy. Energy is vibration. There was fire and energy at the beginning of all things. This fire and energy were caused by me. Thus do I confirm my identity with creation.

Take a pinch of the salt and gently sprinkle it into the cup of water, then sprinkle a few drops of water from your fingertips over the altar. Next, pick up the plant carefully in both hands and contemplate it. Become aware of its natural beauty, colours and shape, and say:

This plant is energy. It is the latest generation in an unbroken chain from the beginning of all life. Its ancestors caused it to be here and now. These flames I see were not, but I caused them to be here and now. Yet were flames ordained also at

△ **Before beginning the ritual for harmony, light the candles and some lotus incense, and spend some time in meditation.**

the beginning. Thus was this living plant ordained, and thus was I, too, ordained to be here with them now at the joining together of our lines through eternity. So with all energy. So with all life.

Replace the plant carefully on the altar, considering how profound the plant's life is. Then repeat the following:

I see the sun and I do not question it. I see the stars and I do not question them. I see the seasons and I do not question them. Sunset and sunrise, I question them not, but behold they are beautiful even if no eye sees them.

ATMOSPHERES OF A SPACE

When we spend time in an area, we react to its atmosphere on a number of different levels, both consciously and unconsciously. Broadly speaking, this can be divided into four categories.

Physical atmosphere: the material level, which is tangible and solid. It includes the structure of the space, the furniture in it and all the solid, visible items.

Emotional atmosphere: the feeling level. It influences mood or sentiment, creating feelings of peace, inspiration or creativity through the use of colour, texture and shape. It can be described as the comfort factor.

Mental atmosphere: the formulative level of ideas, thought patterns and judgement. The use of colour, shape, sound and light can raise or lower mental activity. A simple example would be the use of bright or subdued lighting.

Spiritual atmosphere: the spatial level. It influences our state of being and gives meaning and depth to the other atmospheres of an environment, providing the space for particular energies to exist. The spiritual atmosphere around us provides a meaningful connection between the seen and unseen worlds.

Pause for a few moments to contemplate what you have said, then finish the ritual with the following words:

I have now seen myself, and I do not question it. I see myself in the light of a greater truth. I am a reflection in the eye of the universe. I am part of the Infinite throughout time from the first moment that ever was. [Here extend your arms towards the candles.] *May this light never be extinguished in my heart, but be with me through all times and all seasons. So shall it be.*

△ **Add a little salt to the bowl of water, then dip your fingertips into the water and sprinkle a few drops over the altar.**

This ends the ritual. Stay for a few moments in quiet contemplation, aware of your thoughts, feelings and the calming spiritual vibrations produced by the ritual.

△ **As you hold the plant in your hands, appreciate its unique beauty and sense its natural energy.**

▽ **Do not hurry through this ritual but spend some time during it to sit back and think about the words you are repeating, and sense the spiritual atmosphere you are creating.**

Inner space

As well as clearing the space around us, we need to learn ways to keep our inner environment clean and clear. In simple terms, we can view ourselves as having four layers: physical, emotional, mental and spiritual. In order to maintain a harmonious inner space, ideally we need to consider all four levels.

the inner you

Physically, your inner space will be influenced by your lifestyle and what you choose to eat and drink. You may like to consider changing things in your daily life that do not really serve you – or are actually harmful to you – such as too many late nights, poor eating habits, or any addictive patterns involved with as your alcohol or drug consumption.

On a physical level, it is helpful to be more disciplined about transcending your "bad" habits. A weak physical level can significantly affect your emotional, mental and spiritual health. On an emotional level, you should consider the effect your moods and emotions have on your environment.

Again, self-discipline and working to understand your emotional make-up will help to alleviate heated arguments, stress levels and heavy atmospheres. At this level, you need to consider "relationship" – how you relate to the world and from what emotional perspective you see things. When you look closely at your emotional responses

△ **Inner space is as important as the space around us. Regular relaxing yoga routines are very helpful to the inner state.**

to life, you may realize that they are outdated, linked to wounds from the past that have yet to heal.

On a mental level, it is normally a cluttered mind that suffers mental stress, anxiety, insomnia or depression. Albert Einstein said: "A clever mind is one that is trained to forget the trivial." It is advisable to consider physical exercise, which is known to reduce stress levels, or to begin practising a spiritual discipline such as yoga, t'ai chi or meditation. The benefits of meditation have been well documented: it allows us to relate to who we truly are without falling into the common traps of everyday life.

It is what we are within, rather than what we do, that is the important factor. It is the soul or spirit of the individual that colours life and identifies his or her relationship with the greater whole.

◁ **Drinking lots of spring water rather than coffee or tea will increase energy levels and reduce fatigue.**

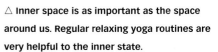

▷ Choose a chair for your meditation that allows you to sit comfortably but with your back straight. Place your feet flat on the floor and let your hands rest in your lap.

▽ Set an alarm clock or timer for the duration of your meditation so that you do not have to think about the time passing.

meditation for inner cleanliness

A period of meditation allows you the time and space to keep your inner world clean and clear, while at the same time creating space for spiritual harmony to filter down through the other layers. By spending time in quiet contemplation, you are creating an opportunity to simply be and so allow yourself the pause to catch up, or perhaps to unwind, without external stimulus or diversion. This enables you to centre and calm stressful states and thus bring about inner peace.

By meditating each day, you can subtly infuse your surroundings with balanced and peaceful vibrations, rather than the stress and anxiety of daily life. With regular meditation, you will feel revitalized physically, your mind will feel refreshed and your emotions calm. From here it is easier to step into each day with confidence and faith. Tasks become simpler to complete. It is as if meditation stretches time, and where before you may have felt the need to rush,

it is now possible to move at a pace free from stress and pressure.

Here is a simple daily meditation to keep you and your home, office or hotel room free from stress.

Set an alarm clock to ring after 10 minutes and place it beneath a cushion. Sit comfortably on a straight-backed chair with your feet flat on the floor, or sit cross-legged on the floor supported with pillows or cushions beneath you.

Imagine that your spine is being gently stretched upwards towards the heavens and at the same time downwards to the earth, and that the central point of balance is in your abdomen. Breathe fully, slowly and deeply, concentrating only upon your breathing. Breathe in "Peace", and allow the breath to infuse your whole being. Breathe out "Free from fear". At first your thoughts may race, your concentration may wander,

▷ As you slowly open your eyes, imagine the sunrise coming out of your eyes and shining light on to a new day.

and you may feel restless. Simply continue to breathe and bring your mind back to the words on the rising and falling breaths. Gradually you will feel a calming influence as you maintain your focus on your breathing. Sit in contemplation until the alarm clock rings. On an outbreath, gently open your eyes and get up slowly.

The Tools of Space Clearing

Tools are important to human beings — for whom the twin foundations of knowledge and the use of tools have been the basis of success as a species — and, like all skills, space clearing has its special implements. Whether you choose to follow a particular magical tradition such as Wicca, or take a more general approach, there are many things that can help to enhance your rituals and spiritual actions.

Scents and aromas

In the world of sensation, scents and fragrances play a very important part in controlling our feelings and responses. Smell stimulates a response by association, sometimes triggering clear and detailed memories of past experiences that we had long forgotten.

Foul or acrid fumes repel us, whereas sweet or fragrant aromas tend to draw us closer to their source. This is the basis for the choice of the different scents and incenses used during particular space clearing rituals. Just as they attract or repel us, some scents attract negative vibrations and others drive them away.

In the human world, our natural reaction to unpleasant smells is to try to get away from them, but in the spirit world, negative vibrations are attracted by dirt, dust, debris, carrion and uncleanliness, because they have the opportunity to "feed" off the presence of energy that is being held there. This is the reason why cleanliness is considered so important as a way to keep spaces clear of old or stale vibrations.

▽ The sweet scent of the jasmine plant can help to keep the atmosphere positively charged once a space has been cleared.

repelling negativity

In situations where a strongly negative atmosphere is experienced and serious space clearing is needed, the ideal aromas to drive away negativity are hot, spicy, vibrant and dynamic. These fiery scents include asafoetida, fumitory, pepper, garlic and chilli. Asafoetida, in particular, smells so foul when it is being burnt that the natural human response is a particularly averse one. This has a psychic effect on the person performing the space clearing of pushing all negativity away with a force of repulsion as strong as the smell itself.

The same principle applies to the use of fumitory – a herb used to expel negative vibrations of a lesser nature. The dried herb is sprinkled on to hot charcoal and fumigates the room with a smell that we would not consider particularly pleasant. However, it serves the purpose of clearing the room of psychic debris before it is filled with any positive input or charge. Both asafoetida and fumitory can be used to clean a space in situations where you need to

△ Scented flowers used as decoration in the home send subtle messages to the brain as well as stimulating the senses.

▽ Hot, spicy aromas such as garlic, pepper and chilli are associated with the fire element and are all strongly protective.

You can perform a simple test using a lighted candle to see if the psychic atmosphere of an area is clear. All you need for this is a candle and holder, matches and an absence of draughts.

Fit the candle securely into its holder and stand it on a table that is out of any draughts. Light the candle and sit quietly and calmly by the table, but far enough away so that your breath does not disturb the flame. In a well-balanced room, the candle flame should burn gently with a small golden yellow flame, flickering only now and then with the natural movement of air through the room. If the candle flame sputters, burns blue, behaves erratically, jumps rapidly or sparks, you have confirmation that the psychic atmosphere is charged and would benefit from a space clearing.

"start again", perhaps when you are taking over a new office or moving into a new home. They can also be useful when gentler routines have not seemed to work for any length of time.

Once a psychically clean room has been established in this way, it is advisable to maintain the standard by making the space less attractive to negative energies – keeping clutter to a minimum, having a regular cleaning routine, and ensuring that life energy in the environment is positively charged by introducing healthy plants, dust-free carpets, fresh air, light and comfort. In this way, the space will serve you, rather than those things you are trying to avoid.

aromatic influences

Here is a quick guide to scents and aromas that will repel negativity, attract harmony and protection, or balance an environment. All the fragrances can be obtained in the form of aromatherapy oils, incense sticks, gums and resins or loose herbs. Use whichever form you prefer.

Aromatherapy oils should be added to water in an aromatherapy burner, gums and resins should be burned on hot charcoal in a charcoal burner, and loose herbs can also

△ **Sprinkle some dried fumitory on burning charcoal to repel negative vibrations from a room, ready for a fresh beginning.**

be sprinkled over hot charcoal. The dried leaves of some herbs can simply be lit and left to smoulder in a suitable container, but you will need to experiment with the different herbs to discover which leaves ignite well on their own, and which benefit from the extra heat of charcoal.

Once a clearing has been established, a choice of balancing or harmonizing fragrances can be used to help maintain the clarity of the space and ensure a pleasant atmosphere for the occupants of the room. This acts to keep the space positively charged until it is felt that another clearing may be necessary.

These scents attract harmony and protection in any environment where they are burnt: frankincense, myrrh, lotus, rose and geranium.

These scents repel negative vibrations and can be used when a room needs clearing: cypress, juniper, fumitory, and sage.

These scents encourage and enhance feelings of peace and calm: bayberry, gardenia, magnolia, and rose.

Essences and remedies

Since the pioneering work of Dr Edward Bach in the 1930s, there has been a strong and steady increase in the use of vibrational remedies for a variety of physical, mental and emotional complaints. Bach developed a method of harnessing the natural energies of flowers by floating the blooms in pure water and leaving them for a certain time in sunlight, which draws the healing essence from the flower into the water.

From the humble beginnings of the 28 original Bach flower remedies, there are now thousands of essences from all around the world, covering a wide range of sources, from ocean to crystal, animal to tree. Each essence has its own particular qualities that are channelled into pure water and then preserved in alcohol. Vibrational essences act on the "subtle anatomy", or the body's life force, in a very similar way to homeopathic remedies. At this level, the essences work to influence and heal imbalances in energy patterns.

remedies to cleanse the body

Just as rooms and environments can be affected by undue negativity, so can the physical body. At times when stress seems overwhelming, emotions are running high, or perhaps deep fatigue from too many demands is hindering clarity and peace, any of the following remedies will be helpful in cleansing negativity.

△ Spritzing an area with water to which you have added a few drops of essential oils or flower essences can be a quick and easy way to lighten and clear an atmosphere.

White yarrow: works to strengthen the aura and acts as a shield against negative environmental influences.

Angelica: an all-round auric strengthener and protector, bringing the ability to cope with challenges or difficulties that could otherwise affect performance.

Crab apple: cleanses the body and soul of unnecessary or outdated vibrations.

Olive: an energy reviver that is helpful at times when you feel overworked, overwhelmed or just tired.

Vanilla: acts like a psychic shield, allowing you to maintain control of your environmental atmospheres without being affected by them.

Lotus: a spiritual harmonizer.

When you are making up a remedy mix, the order of application offers a map for the consciousness – an energy path for the psyche to follow. Adding the last essence encourages the energy to aim for spiritual harmony and peace.

A SPACE CLEARING ROOM SPRITZER

The following recipe can be made up and stored in a spray bottle. Spritz it around a room to clear negativity, emotional memories, mental stresses or psychic unrest.

The mixture is quick and simple to make and offers a convenient, quick-fix solution for clearing an atmosphere when time is short, such as cleansing between clients when you are at work, for example.

3 drops pine oil (purifies and refines energy)
3 drops rose geranium oil (atmospheric harmonizer)
3 drops cypress oil (closes astral doors)
5 drops lavender oil (mental cleanser and harmonizer)
7 drops myrrh oil (for consecration and protection)
7 drops crab apple flower essence (general cleanser)
1 tsp vodka
distilled water

Clean out a spritzer bottle with warm, salted water, rinse and allow to dry. Measure the aromatherapy oils and the flower essence into the bottle. Add the vodka, which preserves the mixture and allows the oils to blend more cohesively with the water. Top up the bottle with distilled water. Seal and shake gently to blend. Spray around yourself and your working or living area whenever you feel that the spirits need lifting or clearing.

▷ Honeysuckle flower essence is helpful when you are dwelling too much on past experiences and feel unable to move forward.

a cleansing mix

A mixture of the cleansing remedies can be taken when you feel you need an energetic protector and pick-me-up. Like all vibrational remedies, this mixture works by flooding out negative feelings. If you have been repressing your emotions, some unexpected feelings may be stirred up, but the remedy is safe and has no side effects.

Either place 7 drops of the mixture directly on your tongue, or mix 7 drops in spring water and sip it throughout the day. (If you are dropping it straight on to your tongue, don't allow the dropper actually to touch the tongue, to avoid the possibility of bacteria entering the remedy bottle.) While taking the mixture, avoid drinks containing caffeine, because it interferes with the remedy's healing path in the body.

you will need

spring water
vodka
7 drops crab apple flower essence
7 drops olive flower essence
7 drops white yarrow flower essence
7 drops angelica flower essence
7 drops vanilla flower essence
1 drop lotus flower essence

Rinse out an essence bottle with spring water. Fill the bottle one third full with vodka and then add the six flower essences in the order listed. Top up the mixture with spring water and shake gently to infuse the essences. Label the bottle "Cleansing Mix" and add the date it was made.

This essence can be kept for three months and should be stored in a cool, dark environment when not in use. If it becomes cloudy during this time, discard it and make up a fresh mix.

▷ To ensure inner balance, you can sip a cleansing mix of flower essences whenever you feel that stresses are rising in you.

Smoke and fire

Fire is intimately linked with light, and candlelight is often used during peace vigils and meditations to symbolize the spirit of remembrance and peace. Apart from its historical link as a symbol of light and hope, fire has also long been an instrument of purification. The ancient Celtic fire festivals, such as the winter festival of Yule, involved fires or beacons, not only to represent the light of life, but also to assist the community in driving away unwanted influences. A new log was kindled from the previous year's log, which had been extinguished, preserved and re-lit to ensure continuity and blessing from one year to the next.

In modern times, fire is used mainly as a source of warmth and not so much for its powers of cleansing and purifying, although there are several ways in which fire can be used in space clearing.

▽ **The lighting of red candles in a room invokes the positive energy of Fire, the element of purification and transformation.**

candles

The simplest way to represent the Fire element in the home or office is with candles or lanterns, and one of the simplest fire rituals is to make an affirmation as you light a candle. This could be something like "May there be peace in this place", or "By the power of Fire, this room is filled with brightness and strength", or perhaps you might like to say "With this flame to protect me, no harm may enter here." The affirmation can be about anything or anyone you would like to call on to fill your environment. Your intent will be carried symbolically by the burning candle for as long as it remains alight.

When you are working with a black candle, light it and let it burn for up to one hour (but do not leave it unattended during this time) before extinguishing it and removing it from the room to be buried or discarded respectfully in the earth. You should then replace the black candle with a white one, allowing that to burn for

△ **The symbolic act of burning away negativity serves to mirror that occurring in our lives.**

REMOVING NEGATIVITY

A candle can be used to remove negativity by utilizing the flame to burn it away. This can be done by writing down those things you wish to release from the environment (such as the energy left in the room after a heated argument) and letting the written message be consumed by the candle flame. Once the paper has been lit, drop it into a fireproof container and let it burn to ashes completely. You can then scatter the ashes outside in the wind, as you visualize the negativity being blown away.

▷ Sprinkle some sacred herbs on to an open fire to conjure a mystical atmosphere.

another hour. As you light the white candle, affirm your call for peaceful vibrations to prevail in the place.

open fires

If you have an open fire, or a garden where a fire can be lit, you may like to build a stronger relationship with the purifying abilities of the Fire element by having that intention when you light the fire. Instead of simply laying a fire for warmth, add a handful of purifying herbs, with offerings to the Fire spirits such as a handful of peppercorns or a few sprinklings of tobacco. Add your intention that, as the fire burns, it will provide protection, and call for the spirits to be ever watchful to drive away negative influences from your home or land. The smoke from the burning herbs will infuse the environment with a protective haze. The open fire is no longer a place of winter practicality, but becomes a magical cauldron in which to gaze and observe the spirits as they dance away the dark.

▽ Laying flowers at the base of a candle can act as a focus for what you wish to call on or change.

colours, flowers and herbs

When you are working with Fire affirmations, certain candle colours will complement your particular requirements, and the following list offers a basic guide to colour correspondences.

To enhance an affirmation further, you can also surround the base of your candle with flowers or herbs chosen to complement and strengthen the focus of your ritual.

Red is for power, strength and protection, and is the colour of Fire; surround a red candle with carnations.

Black absorbs negativity and draws away psychic intrusion; surround a black candle with rue or sage leaves.

Green promotes harmony and emotional balance; surround the base of the candle with roses.

Light blue is for healing vibrations and peace; surround a blue candle with white jasmine flowers.

Pink represents love, romance, happiness and felicity; surround the base of a pink candle with pansies.

Yellow promotes change, new beginnings, wisdom and understanding; surround a yellow candle with lavender.

Orange is for healthy atmospheres, positivity and creativity; surround an orange candle with cloves.

White is for purity, balance and all general ritual work; surround the candle base with white lilies or camellias.

Music and sound

Sound is a form of vibration, which is at the root of our existence. Albert Einstein asserted that living things are not solid matter but a dance of atoms in space, and when we look closely at our physical nature, this is indeed the case. All matter vibrates, emitting waves of energy, and within a certain range of frequencies we respond to these vibrations as sound.

Sound can be used for protection, clearing or harmonizing, depending on the level and tone of the sounds used. Loud, shocking noises, such as fireworks or drums, for example, have long been used by many different cultures to drive out evil spirits. Conversely the gentle, almost inaudible, sound of a mother's heartbeat is capable of soothing a baby to sleep.

Our response to sound is largely determined by the associations we make with a particular noise. Sounds of nature can be either stirring or soothing, as can music.

▽ A gentle, repetitive sound such as a chime can be used to induce a feeling of peace in an environment that needs calming.

For thousands of years the power of sound has been encapsulated in the use of voiced mantras and chants by many traditions throughout the world. Repetition of the "Aum" mantra, for example, can be used to harmonize an environment. It is a simple, safe and effective method. A variety of sacred mantras and chants can be sung or played, either to clear a space or to fill it with a particular vibration after a space clearing has been done.

△ Rhythmic sounds, especially in the form of drumming, are used in shamanic ritual to summon the assistance of the spirit world.

noise pollution

If you consider for a moment the myriad modern day sounds humans emit, which ride over and above the hum of earth's organic life, it is not surprising that noise pollution is now a well-established problem. Traffic, machinery, appliances, loud music

▷ Tibetan singing bowls can produce a variety of sound vibrations that touch the body with resonance.

and voices can all contribute to noise pollution. Many of us will have experienced a craving for peace and quiet as a result.

As we tune into the more subtle sounds of the earth, and simplify our lives, we have to acknowledge this orchestra of noise more seriously as a major contributor to stress and distress at home and work. We all need to consider how much we ourselves contribute to noise pollution, and take steps to naturalize and neutralize our part in it. By consciously filling our environment with more harmonious sounds and music, we can bring a depth and meaning to our world way beyond mere entertainment value. If you are looking for ways to naturalize the sounds around you, it is well worth exploring what is now produced by the New Age music industry. The sounds of nature and her creatures, such as whale song, waterfalls, or waves on the shore, are often found in the background of what is known as "ambient" music.

the powers of sound

Sound, music and the voice can all be used very effectively for space clearing. Fast or loud music and sounds will increase energy in an environment, whereas quiet, slow, rhythmic sounds will induce a sense of peace and tranquillity.

A drum, when played loudly and with authority, will help to expel negative energies, and when played rhythmically it will harmonize and raise the Earth element. Wind instruments, the didgeridoo, cymbals, tingshaws (Tibetan bells) and gongs can help to alleviate stress, mental chatter and frenzied atmospheres. Sacred instruments such as the bamboo flute, sitar or aeolian harp can also balance Air atmospheres. Crystal singing bowls can be utilized to balance the Water element, along with water features such as fountains, fish tanks and watery music. These are ideal for harmonizing emotions and for removing emotional conflict from living and working areas.

A MANTRA TO LORD SHIVA
The following mantra to the Hindu deity Shiva is a powerful way to clear an environment of any unnecessary vibrations, especially those that are blocking you personally, or stifling spiritual peace or understanding. Always burn a candle when performing this chant.

1 Sit in front of the candle and any representations you may have of Lord Shiva, such as a statue. Chant "Om namah Shivaya" (pronounced "Om narmar Shiv-eye-yah") rhythmically for at least 10 minutes.

2 If you have a set of rosary beads, you can perform the chant the traditional 108 times, moving one bead round with each repetition. For particularly difficult problems you can chant this mantra over a period of 40 days. The mantra can also be used as part of a regular spiritual practice, which will strengthen its influence upon you and your surroundings.

Crystals and pendulums

Because we are all subtly influenced by our environment and will be affected by it at a subconscious level, we may need help to reveal to our conscious minds what we are sensing subconsciously.

Crystals, as part of the earth's structure, emit energy waves at natural frequencies in harmony with our own biological make-up, and for this reason they can help to balance and harmonize our inner and outer environments. In fact, some parts of the human body are actually crystalline structures, including our teeth.

In dowsing, a pendulum acts in relation to our energetic impulses, revealing positive or negative responses to questioning, and we can use this technique to reveal the cause of a sense of disharmony.

▽ **The amethyst is part of the quartz family of crystals and is safe and reliable for daily use in counteracting electromagnetic emissions.**

using crystals

As children of the earth we need to acknowledge that we function best when we are in harmony with nature, and all kinds of crystals can play a significant part in maintaining that harmony.

Crystal clusters are excellent at keeping communal spaces clear. Their many points direct and charge energy positively, and placing a crystal cluster in a negatively charged room will clear it quite quickly. To clear negativity, use a smoky quartz cluster, to alleviate stress, use an amethyst cluster, and for harmonizing and emotional cleansing, a clear quartz cluster. If the problem is excess energy, crystals that will ground it effectively include smoky quartz, obsidian, hematite, chrysocolla, yellow fluorite, onyx and turquoise.

Modern electrical appliances give out electromagnetic energy at frequencies way beyond nature's own. To give an example,

△ **Many crystals, including turquoise, quartz and obsidian, have beneficial protective and harmonizing qualities.**

the earth's electromagnetic field functions between 1 and 30Hz. Human brainwaves range from 5–30Hz. Electrical appliances are much higher than natural frequencies, and range from 35–100Hz. We may be subjected to these high frequencies for a considerable length of time if we have to work with electrical equipment such as computers; placing crystals around them will help to counteract any harmful effects.

Rainbow crystals (those that have rainbow colours within them) placed on a sunny windowsill can work to bring the colours of joy to a depressed room. They also work well where moods need lightening. Rainbow colours are most commonly found in clear quartz crystals. Twin crystals are attached to each other but have two separate terminations at one end. They can be used to heal relationships and underlying relationship difficulties.

You can wear or carry any of the crystals suggested here by scaling down the size to smaller stones or single points.

◁ You can dowse using a pendulum to find out which areas of your home or office may be out of balance.

indicate "yes" and "no"), to give it some kind of momentum to work with. To avoid concerns that you are influencing the outcome, after asking a question, empty your mind of everything except the words "I wonder what the answer will be?" and wait for the pendulum to respond.

To use a pendulum as an assessment tool for space clearing, draw a scaled-down floor plan of your chosen building, writing which room is which on your sketch. Hold a pendulum in your right hand. Place your left index finger on one area of the sketch and ask the pendulum "Is this room energetically balanced?" When you receive an answer, make a note of it. If the answer is "yes", move on to the next room. If it is "no", go on to ask a series of simple questions to discover what may be causing the problem, such as "Is this room emotionally charged?" or "Is it affected by electrical emissions?" and so on, until you find what is affecting the area.

dowsing

A simple dowsing technique can help you to discover if there are any areas of your home or workplace that are energetically unbalanced. Once any imbalances have been uncovered, you can correct them using whichever space clearing exercise seems most appropriate.

Before you begin, you need to discover which pendulum swing indicates a "yes" and which indicates a "no". The simplest way to find out is to ask a question such as "Is my name [*state your real name*]?" and wait to see what movement the pendulum makes. You will then know which swing means a "yes". To discover a "no" swing, ask the pendulum "Is my name [*state a false name*]?" and wait to see the movement.

Once you have established your "yes" and "no" swings, you can start asking questions. If at any time the pendulum behaves in a different way to your yes/no swings, it usually indicates that you need to re-phrase your question. A common error is to ask a question with more than one possible answer, such as "Is this room balanced or not?" It is important to ask questions of the pendulum that require a straight "yes" or "no" answer. If you reduce the question to "Is this room balanced?" the pendulum will be able to give a definitive answer.

Another common problem when working with a pendulum is complete lack of movement. To facilitate a response, dowsers may swing the pendulum to and fro (avoiding the particular movements that

HOLDING A PENDULUM
Hold the chain between the thumb, index and middle fingers, leaving about 15cm/6in above the pendulum free. Hold the chain with the fingers pointing downwards so the pendulum can swing freely.

Magical implements

Just about anything can be used as a magical implement, and throughout the history of magic, just about everything has been. However, over time certain tools have become paramount and in general they are associated with the four elements – Air, Fire, Water and Earth – together with a fifth, the Quintessence or Spirit, which unites the other four.

The magical symbol of the pentagram, the five-pointed interlocking star, represents this concept, bringing together the five elements that are necessary to sustain life: each of the four lower points of the figure represents one of the physical elements, while the topmost point represents Spirit. The pentagram is often traced during rituals and symbolizes protection and wholeness.

magic and the elements

Each of the physical elements has its own magical tool. The sword is associated with Air, the wand with Fire, the cup or chalice with Water and the pentacle with Earth. The athame (pronounced "ath-ay-me") is a general-purpose tool, which is used as a psychic pointer.

There has been some controversy amongst occultists regarding the correct tools to use to represent the elements of Air and Fire. Many magicians use the wand for Fire and the sword (or dagger) for Air, as

▽ **The traditional altar tools of the Wiccan practitioner are the chalice or cup, athame (knife), wand (stick) and pentacle (salver).**

△ **Shamans decorate their magical items with power objects such as feathers and claws.**

▷ **The tools you use in magical ritual can be as simple as an ordinary black-handled kitchen knife and a glass bowl. The important thing is to use what feels right to you.**

this is how they are depicted in packs of Tarot cards originating from the 19th-century occult Order of the Golden Dawn. Others believe that this was a blind intended to confuse the uninitiated and, instead, prefer to use the wand for Air and the sword or knife for Fire. But in magic, the only thing to avoid is worrying about it. The basic rule is to find the way that feels right for you and stick to it.

In the ancient past, magicians tended to be educated scholars and practised ceremonial "high magic". As they were high-born they were permitted to carry swords and therefore used them as implements for their magic. Witches, on the other hand, originated from the village wise-person. They were very often followers of the old pre-Christian fertility religion called Wicca and were usually advocates of "low magic". Witches did not have access to the ceremonial regalia of high magic and instead developed their tools from ordinary household objects such as bowls, platters and kitchen knives. They were usually well-versed in herbal lore.

The magical implement that is appropriate to any particular ritual depends on the nature of the ritual, or "working". Emotional matters are governed by the Water element, competitive matters by Fire, mental matters by Air and worldly matters such as finance and success by Earth. This is a very generalized picture, however. Another use of the Earth element, for instance, is in calming energies and dispelling hostile psychic vibrations, as well as for self-defence against occult attack. The idea behind this – as with electricity – is to run excess and unwanted energies to earth. Thus, the Earth element is regularly used in space clearing.

assembling the tools

A sword is probably the most difficult and expensive item to obtain, but like all the other implements can be purchased from occult suppliers. You can easily make the other magical implements yourself, using a little imagination.

The pentacle originated as a platter or salver. It can be made of any material, but is usually a round flat piece of metal or wood: a wooden breadboard or coaster is very suitable, and you can paint a pentagram on it yourself. An ordinary black-handled kitchen knife can be used as an athame, and any glass bowl or stemmed glass from your kitchen can serve as a chalice. Much folklore is associated with the magic wand: according to tradition, it had to be cut in one slash on the last stroke of midnight. This is not really necessary, but it is a way of showing respect and gratitude for anything that you take from nature, and this is important.

▽ **The Fire element can be quickly represented by a lit candle, and the act of lighting it takes on a symbolic meaning of its own.**

THE HAND AS A MAGICAL IMPLEMENT

At times when it is not advisable or possible to use a blade in a ritual, you can substitute the fingers of your hand as a pointer, imagining that they are like the blade. The hand can be held in a symbolic position, in which the first finger represents Isis, the female, and the middle finger represents Osiris, the male. The thumb is positioned between these two fingers, and the posture thus invokes the protection of the god and goddess over their child, Horus.

Space Clearing Rituals

A ritual is an act repeated in a formalized manner to give it greater meaning and focus our concentration upon it, and ritualistic behaviour of various kinds helps to give structure and pattern to our lives. The application of rituals for space clearing greatly enhances our energy and determination, helping us to bring abstract knowledge into physical play to accomplish stronger results.

Preparing for ritual

One of the ways ritual magic works is through what is known as psychodrama, in which a physical enactment – involving sight, sound and the other senses – produces a corresponding change of consciousness, especially in the subconscious mind. This is the primal area of the mind – the basic and ancient root of the human consciousness. As the psychologist Carl Jung showed, it recognizes and communicates in symbols only, not in logical linguistics. Within it are stored not only our personal memories but also our racial memories, reaching back through thousands of years, which come up to the surface layers of our mind in the form of instinct. Some experts believe that we retain not just racial but species memories – that our deeper minds may contain the memories of our pre-human ancestors.

The subconscious reacts to enacted behaviour just as it reacts to real situations occurring spontaneously, so it can help if you treat a ritual like a theatrical production, learning your part as though it were in a play. Instead of standing self-consciously mumbling the words under your breath, this approach can encourage you to be bold with your movements and loud and confident in your declaration of the words.

purifying and cleansing the area

Any proper magical ritual, including space clearing, needs to be "written on a clean slate". If there are psychic impurities or negative energies present when the ritual is carried out, they can intrude and interfere, contaminating the result and sometimes changing it completely. As a modern analogy, we might think of such impure energy as a kind of "occult computer virus". A purifying and cleansing routine acts like an anti-virus programme. There are two areas that can benefit: the environment in which you intend to perform a space clearing, and yourself.

Every culture has its own purifying and cleansing methods, from the Christian "bell, book and candle" to the pagan "rites of passage", and there are a great many to choose from. The simplest method is burning a suitable incense and carrying it round the area, calming your mind and projecting that calmness out into the room with the smoke wafting from the incense.

A slightly more intricate version, practised by occultists, is called the Rose Cross ritual. The lighted incense is carried around the room in a pattern, travelling from corner to corner, in a cross shape, then circling the middle of the cross. The shape resembles a cross with a rose in its centre, which is the symbol of the Rosicrucian Brotherhood, an occult order dating from before 1614.

▽ **It is important to approach an area you are preparing for space clearing in a dignified and respectful manner.**

▷ Keep a bowl of sand ready for when you want to extinguish the smudge stick.

smudging

The most popular purifying and cleansing technique is probably smudging, a shamanic method which has enjoyed a widespread revival in recent years. This method has several advantages. Its shamanic origin means it lends itself to just about any magical path without causing contention, so it can be used as a prologue to any kind of space clearing ritual. It is very simple but extremely effective and because it needs a little more input from you, it encourages magical thought and activity while you are putting together the basic tools for the ceremony: a smudge stick and a smudge fan.

The smudge stick is simply a bundle of dried herbs, usually including sage. The fan should be made of feathers, a single feather can also be used. The purpose of the fan is to waft the smoke all over the area, over the walls, floor and ceiling and round the doors, windows and any other openings into the room, such as the fireplace. The nature of the herbs and the intention of the person who gathered and tied them, together with the action of the fan, drives away any negative energies lingering in an area.

▽ As you fan the smoke, strengthen the action by visualizing the herbs' cleansing qualities.

MAKING A SMUDGE STICK

It is very rewarding to grow and dry your own herbs, thus ensuring that their magical qualities are tended during all stages of growth, and that you honour the spirits of the herbs when cutting them. The three suggested here (three is a magical number) are all for purification. The best variety of sage to use is American white sage or mountain sage (*Salvia apiana*). All the herbs must be completely dry.

YOU WILL NEED

dried sage stalks
dried lavender flower stalks
dried thyme stalks
natural twine

Gather all the dried herb stalks together and arrange them in an intertwined bundle. Bind the stalks loosely with twine and trim the ends to neaten the bundle. Light one end, extinguish the flame, and let the smoke rise to fill the area.

Preparing yourself

For any ritual cleansing work, preparing yourself is a very important prerequisite. There is a saying that "cleanliness is next to godliness", and it is an esoteric belief that harmful negative energies – or evil influences – will fasten on to any dirt on the body of an individual commencing a ritual. (This applies equally to the clothing you are wearing, so fresh, clean clothes are also recommended.) Apart from this consideration, relaxing in a hot bath, especially one made fragrant with herbs, before a space clearing ritual serves to put the conscious and unconscious parts of the mind in closer touch with one another.

While you are bathing, imagine that you are cleansing away all impurities from your body and soul and, as the water runs out of the bath, visualize all those impurities draining away from you. You may like to anoint yourself with rose geranium essential oil diluted in some sweet almond oil.

△ Bathing ensures that all impurities are removed from the physical body prior to a space clearing ritual.

Alternatively, scent some almond oil with one or two leaves harvested from a *Pelargonium graveolens* plant you have bought to help with your magical and ritual preparations, thus ensuring a regular supply of the natural herb. Always harvest leaves with respect and care for your plant.

Another preparation often used, in religious activity as well as in magic, is fasting. This is a valid technique, as it helps to separate the mind from its material bonds by encouraging a semi-trancelike state. However, it is not an essential preparation for space clearing. You may like to consider a purifying diet instead, but check with your GP first as to whether this is advisable. If you feel that this is appropriate, you should begin the diet five days before you plan to carry out your ritual.

◁ You can anoint your body with rosewater or an oil blend containing rose geranium essential oil before performing a cleansing ritual.

▷ Preparation of your body and mind before you begin any ritual carries the same importance as the ritual itself.

mental and psychic preparation

It is important to be in the right frame of mind when undertaking any ritual work, so mental and psychic preparation is also recommended. For space clearing purposes, the correct frame of mind is relaxed, confident, at peace with yourself, calm, positive and assured.

After you have bathed, or made other physical preparations, a period of meditation immediately preceding the start of a ritual will help to achieve calm and composure. Space clearing is a spiritual process that can be quite draining, and its success will depend on your mental preparation and state of mind. Meditation can be accompanied by some quiet, spiritually inspiring music and burning a suitable incense, which should not be too thick or heavily scented: a light fragrance is best for the preparation before a ritual, leaving the heavier aromas for the ritual itself, in cases where they are considered to be necessary.

A banishing ritual can be performed after the meditation period. This will prepare the working area for the main ritual to come, and it will also put your mind into a receptive state for ritual work.

There are a great many things that can disturb the harmony of nearby energies: for example, a serious argument that took place the previous day between the couple living next door could have left "heaving" psychic vibrations, like a sea with a rough swell where there ought to be smooth water. Such vibrations can weaken the result of a space clearing ritual, or even make it completely ineffective.

A banishing ritual is like pouring oil on troubled waters, to smooth psychic shockwaves. Such troubled vibrations can spread out over a surprisingly large distance, and they need to be eliminated before space clearing can be properly undertaken, so adequate preparation is an important part of the ritual itself.

HERBAL BATH MIX

All the ingredients for this mix are easily available to buy, or they can be grown in a herb garden or window-box. They are all associated with purification and cleansing. Use fresh herbs if possible.

YOU WILL NEED

2 tsp organic oats
small square of cotton muslin
7 basil leaves
3 bay leaves
3 sprigs oregano
1 sprig tarragon
pinch of rock or sea salt
thread to secure

Pile the herbs in the centre of the muslin square, then add the oats. Top with the rock or sea salt, pick up the corners of the muslin and tie with thread. Hang the sachet from the bath tap so that the water is infused with the essence of the mixture.

Magical circles

Magic evolved through the ages into two broad types, referred to as "low magic" and "high magic". These terms are very generalized and the two often merge seamlessly together. Low magic was practised by the simple and poor: peasants who had no access to education, riches or reading and writing. This is the kind of magic that originated with the tribal shaman, or the wise woman mixing her herbs in a steaming cauldron. High magic grew out of it and became the province of the rich, the nobility and the educated.

As an example of the essential difference between high and low magic, a kitchen knife was often used as a "psychic pointer" in low magic, and this evolved into the athame, the ritual pointing knife used by witches. In contrast, the upper classes were permitted to carry swords, which were usually forbidden to the peasantry, and therefore in high magic a ritual sword is frequently used as a pointer instead of the athame. The magical implements used today no longer have any association of this kind with class structure. Today's witches use swords freely, and ritual magicians use herbs and athames.

◁ A handful of sacred herbs can be put into a heatproof container and burnt to raise bright vibrations in a room.

△ A visual magic circle can be created by forming a ring on the floor with night lights or small candles.

casting a circle

In both high and low magic, a magic circle is considered indispensable. The idea, greatly simplified, is that this creates what might be called a protective "energy field" around the place of working, through which no hostile or negative astral forces can penetrate. (Although it is seen with the eyes as a circle on the ground, the mind should perceive it as a sphere.) Casting a magic circle is an important part of witchcraft, or Wicca, which follows the traditions of the "low" magic of the ordinary people.

In casting a magic circle, great importance is attached to astral beings called the Guardians of the Watchtowers. The "watchtowers" are the four compass points and the four elements of Air, Fire, Water and Earth to which they are linked (Air corresponds with east, Fire with south, Water with west and Earth with north). The Guardians of the Watchtowers protect those who invoke their aid and ensure the security of the circle. In low magic, especially in Wicca, complex rituals and magical regalia are not normally used.

a simple space clearing

This can be used anywhere as a space clearing procedure, and is a short and simple ritual. But in spite of its simplicity, it is a powerful piece of low magic. As with any magical or mystical activity, you should prepare yourself beforehand. Make sure you

▽ Drawing a magic circle around yourself using an athame, or ceremonial knife, follows a tradition that is many centuries old.

choose a time when you will not be interrupted. A short period of meditation is recommended to calm the mind and spirit, and to eliminate all disruptive thoughts from daily life intruding on the ritual.

The first part of the spell involves casting a magic circle. For this, if you do not have an athame you can use an ordinary kitchen knife as a pointer, preferably one with either a black or a natural wood handle, or you can use your hand.

performing the ritual

Having meditated, stand facing north. Slowly raise the knife or your hand to point in that direction, then turn to the right to face east, imagining that you are drawing a line of pure light in the air as you move. Then turn again to face south, then west, then north again until the circle is complete. As you do this, repeat the following circle-opening invocation, saying each line as you face the appropriate point of the compass:

I call the Guardians of the North, protect this
place from earthly wrath.
I call the Guardians of the East to calm the airs
and bring me peace.
I call the Guardians of the South, protect me from
the fire's red mouth.
I call the Guardians of the West to lay the stormy
seas to rest.

When you have completed the circle, remain facing north, relax and say:

Let blessings be upon this place,
and let my Circle clear this space
of spirits wicked, cruel or fell,
so that I in peace may dwell.

Imagine the circle you have cast is spreading out through the universe like the ripples in a pool, bringing tranquillity and peace to its centre, which is you and your space.

▽ Ripples in water, moving outwards, will eventually be still and calm, like the space you have just cleared.

A zodiac ritual

This space clearing ritual draws on your astrological sign to personalize it and give it power. Use the chart of sun signs to select the correct corresponding tools and materials, and insert the name of your sign where appropriate in the wording.

All astral or psychic energies are intimately connected with zodiacal influences, but while virtually everyone has heard of the zodiac, fewer actually know its definition. While the earth makes its annual orbit of the sun, from earth we perceive this movement as if the sun is travelling along an imaginary line across the sky, called the ecliptic. The zodiac is the name given by astrologers to the band of 12 constellations that appear along the ecliptic through the year. During each 30-day period of the year, the sun appears to rise against the background of one of these groups of stars, and that constellation is said to be the sun sign of anyone born in that period.

The zodiac space clearing ritual has 12 variations which all use the same ritual framework, and there are two ways to choose the appropriate zodiac sign to include in it. You can either choose your own birth sign (or that of anyone you may be helping) or select whichever sign covers the date on which you are to perform the

△ **This variation of the zodiac ritual uses turquoise, benzoin and the chalice to fit with the sign Scorpio.**

ritual (you can check this in the horoscope section of a newspaper if you are unfamiliar with all the zodiac dates).

preparation

Set up the altar so that you will face east when standing in front of it. You will need an altar cloth, an incense burner, a small heap of salt in a container, and the four magical implements: wand, pentacle, sword/athame and cup/chalice (all four should be present, even if only one is to be used in the ritual). Place the tool corresponding to the chosen zodiac sign near the front of the altar. The cup or chalice should contain a small amount of water, whether or not you will be using it.

the ritual

Light the incense and the candles. Pick up the cup or chalice and sprinkle a pinch of salt in the water, saying: "Thus do I cleanse and purify thee, oh spirit of Water, that thou mayest aid me." If you are not using the cup further, replace it on the altar.

Take up the appropriate magical tool and hold it out towards the east, at arm's length. State in a commanding voice:

By the ancient magic of [zodiac sign] *I call now upon the spirits of time and space to assist me in cleansing this place of all impurities. By this* [name of tool], *the symbol of the authority over*

SUN SIGNS AND CORRESPONDING TOOLS

SIGN	INCENSE	MAGICAL TOOL	CANDLE COLOUR
Aries	Dragon's blood, lily	Wand	Scarlet
Taurus	Storax, mallow	Pentacle	Red, orange
Gemini	Orchid, wormwood	Sword/athame	Orange
Cancer	Lotus	Cup/chalice	Amber
Leo	Sunflower, olibanum	Wand	Yellow
Virgo	Lily, sandalwood	Pentacle	Yellow-green
Libra	Aloe, galbanum	Sword/athame	Emerald green
Scorpio	Benzoin	Cup/chalice	Turquoise
Sagittarius	Lignum aloes	Wand	Blue
Capricorn	Hemp, musk	Pentacle	Indigo/black
Aquarius	Galbanum	Sword/athame	Violet
Pisces	Opium, ambergris	Cup/chalice	Crimson

again, repeating the action for the fourth and last time.

Replace the magical tool on the altar and cross your wrists over your breast, fists clenched, right wrist outermost (in what is called the "Osiris risen" position). In a very firm and commanding voice, say this:

Let no creature of any sphere now malign this place. Let all malignity depart hence, and all good enter herein. Let no disturbing influence or visitation descend upon this protected place.

Take up the cup once more, whether it was the main magical tool or not. In a dignified manner, carry it round the perimeter of the area you are clearing. As you go, sprinkle occasional drops of water with your fingertips. This forms a magical circle of protection around the area that hostile astral forces cannot penetrate.

End the ritual by returning to the altar, turning your back to it and announcing to the world: "Go ye in peace!"

▽ **When sprinkling your water in an area imagine it is holy water charged with light and blessings.**

△ **Be clear and authoritative when speaking the words of a zodiac ritual, believe in what you say.**

the occult powers of [zodiac sign], *I command that all that is hostile, of negative intent or malicious of form or mind, depart hence. Depart, I say, and return not, for the forces of* [zodiac sign] *stand now guard upon this place of enchantment. Thus is my will! Thus is my command! Thus is my power!*

Turn to the right so that you are facing south, thrust the magical tool forward in that direction and bark out loudly the word "AVAUNT!" (meaning "depart"). Turn to the right again to face west, again thrust the magical tool forward and say again, "AVAUNT!" Turn to the north and repeat the action, and finally return to face east

A shamanic ritual

NATIVE AMERICAN SACRED HERBS

For thousands of years, the indigenous people of North America have maintained a very close relationship with the plant kingdom. They use many herbs for healing, protection and blessings, but their four most sacred herbs for purification and protection are sweetgrass, sage, cedar and tobacco.

Sweetgrass is traditionally used for self-blessing, for keeping evil spirits away from the home and to purify tools and equipment, because its sweet smell calls up the good spirits. It is plaited into a braid, then the end is lit and the smoke wafted over magical tools or around the room.

Sage is a powerful cleanser and purifier, and native Americans have been known to sit on sage leaves in sweat lodges, thus physically linking into its purifying abilities. The leaves can also be used for smudging, either loose or in smudge sticks. The most effective types are white or mountain sage and desert sage.

Cedar is an evergreen tree also known as the Tree of Life; it is a very powerful psychic and spiritual cleanser. Smudging with cedar is advised when conditions are particularly difficult or obstructive, as its powers deal with the more "problematic" energies. It can be obtained loose and dried, to be sprinkled on hot charcoal when required.

Tobacco is used for offerings to the Great Spirit and to the elemental and natural powers of creation. Tobacco is also cast into the sweat lodge fire as an offering to the fire spirits, and is sometimes given to elders and medicine men as a mark of respect.

The word "shaman" comes from the Tungusic dialect of the Ural–Altaic tribes of Siberia, but it is now used to describe individuals of many traditions throughout the world that commune with the natural and supernatural world.

The shaman employs sacred herbs, drums and chants to summon the assistance of the spirit world, in order to cleanse a person, situation or environment of any perceived negative or stale influences.

the ritual

The shamanic ritual outlined here calls upon the powers of the drum, of sacred herbs, and of the *inyan* (the stone people of the native Americans) to cleanse and purify an area.

YOU WILL NEED

loose dried sage
smudge bowl or shell
black or dark feather
large stone chosen for
  its individuality
tobacco
drum

▽ **Begin the ritual by smudging yourself and the large stone with smoke from the smouldering sage. Use a feather to fan the smoke.**

▷ **Beat the drum while moving in a spiral around the room, towards the centre.**

Place the sage in the smudge bowl and light it. Use the feather to fan the smoke around yourself and over the large stone.

Take a pinch of tobacco and stand in the centre of the area you are clearing. Facing north, say "Great Spirit, I honour you, and humbly seek your presence within this grandfather rock." Place the pinch of tobacco at the central point of the room. Pick up the large stone and, holding it to your heart, ask it to help you to clear the environment by absorbing any stray energies. Set the stone in the centre of the room on top of the tobacco, saying, "Mitake oyasin" ("For we are all related").

Take another pinch of tobacco and, still facing north, hold out your hand in that direction. Call with feeling and respect, "Buffalo." Place the tobacco on the floor to the north. Take another pinch of tobacco, face the east and call: "Hawk." Place the tobacco on the floor to the east. Repeat the gesture for the south, saying, "Coyote," and for the west, saying, "Bear."

Turn to face north again and now say, "Guardians of the four winds, I – your brother/sister – do call your presence here."

▽ **Hold the grandfather rock to your heart and ask it to help you in your task.**

Stand the smudge bowl on the stone so that the smoke coils up through the room.

Take up the drum and, beginning at the edge of the area, walk clockwise in a spiral until you reach the centre, drumming the atmosphere towards the stone. Drum over the stone into the herbs, visualizing the stray energies coiling away in the smoke. Thank the Great Spirit, grandfather rock, and the four guardians for their help. Repeat "Mitake oyasin" and remove the smudge bowl from the stone. Take the stone outside to rest on the earth in order to discharge any remaining energy into the ground.

▷ **As the smoke coils through the room, sit for a moment and visualize the cleansing process.**

A ritual in the Zen style

Zen is a philosophy of Chinese origin, adopted by the Japanese in the 12th century, that has its own unique identity within the wider practice of Buddhism. The name is derived from the Chinese word *ch'an* which, in turn, originates from the Sanskrit *dhyana*, meaning "meditation". The essential concept of Zen is that a true state of perfection – nirvana – is attained only when all is reduced (or expanded) to nothing. It cannot be reached while the surface of life ripples with emotion, desire, concern, ambition, curiosity or selfishness.

A number of "koans" (exercises in paradox) originate from Zen teachings and give an indication of what needs to be accomplished by the mind of the acolyte who seeks nirvana. Perhaps the most famous of these questions is "What is the sound of one hand clapping?" If everything is reduced (or elevated) to its ultimate state of non-being, perfection has been reached. Zen rituals, therefore, tend toward simplicity, quiet, stillness and deep inner reflection to

▽ A room decorated and furnished in accordance with the philosophy of Zen will always reflect spaciousness and composure.

△ Zen epitomizes simplicity, and rituals in the Zen style are likewise always simple.

create an atmosphere of intense and almost solid peace; they are ideal for dispelling any form of psychic disharmony or negative energy in space clearing.

Because this ritual comes from the eastern rather than the western tradition, it is not necessary to precede it with a banishing ritual, though this can be done if you feel it is appropriate.

PRONUNCIATION

"Aum" (or "Om") is spoken after taking as deep a breath as possible. It begins with the sound "Ahh", moving into "Om" (like the first syllable of "omelette") and continuing the "mm" for as long as the out-breath lasts. This word is held to symbolize all the sounds in the universe.

▷ **A clear mind is the perfected state of Zen. Meditation is an ideal practice to help you move towards such a state.**

preparation

Arrange for as much silence and stillness as the surroundings permit. If possible, use a gong to mark the beginning and end of the ritual: otherwise, find something else that will produce a similar clear, simple sound, such as a stone to bang gently on a small block of wood. You will also need a low table or altar covered with a plain black cloth and a few sticks of sandalwood incense in a suitable container.

Set up the altar as close as possible to the exact centre of the area you wish to include in the space clearing, so that you can sit or kneel before it facing east.

the ritual

Light the incense. Kneel on a cushion or sit on a straight-backed chair before the altar, or adopt the lotus position if you prefer. When you are settled, perform the fourfold breath to still your thoughts: to do this,

▽ **A simple sound, such as the striking of a gong or chime, is used to mark the beginning and ending of a Zen ritual.**

breathe in to an unhurried count of four, hold your breath for a count of four, breathe out for a count of four and hold your breath again for a count of four, then take the next breath and repeat the sequence. Continue to practise the fourfold breath for a few minutes, until you feel a state of great calm begin to unfold.

When you feel sufficiently calm and at ease with your surroundings, gently sound the gong once. As the sound fades, begin to chant the single word "Aum" as slowly as possible. Keep your head bowed towards the altar. Repeat the chant 10–12 times, taking care throughout to avoid any feeling of "hurrying things along".

Once you have reached the end the chanting, take two or three more fourfold breaths, then slowly bow towards the east, with your hands held at your chest in an attitude of prayer. In this position, repeat a single long "Aum". Your mind should now be clear enough to concentrate your thoughts. Close your eyes and make your mental image as sharp as you can, aiming for a reality equivalent to having your eyes open. This may take a little practice before you undertake the ritual itself. Visualize a circular ripple of light in the centre of your abdomen, slowly spreading out horizontally, like the ripples from a stone tossed into a pool filmed in slow motion. As this circle of light reaches the horizon, it continues out into the universe and to infinity. Continue to observe this visualization for several minutes.

To end the ritual, stand up, place your hands in the prayer position at your chest as before and bow deeply from the waist. Sound the gong once more to close.

An angelic space clearing

The concept of angelic beings is familiar in the Judaeo-Christian tradition, in which these high and pure spiritual entities act as messengers, protectors and guides to humans. Some angels, such as Gabriel, are mentioned in the Bible, but in fact they predate the Biblical period, originating in earlier cultures such as those of Sumer, Babylon and Ur (in modern Iraq). Angelic invocation formed the basis of many ancient occult practices, and individual angels were traditionally associated with various entities, such as the seven ancient planets, specific days of the week, certain colours, incenses, symbols and powers. There are stories of angels being seen on battlefields or by individuals in danger, whose lives were saved by the angelic beings.

If you are attracted to this kind of spiritual conception, you may well draw the strongest benefit from performing an angelic

THE ATTRIBUTES OF ANGELS

Traditional correspondences exist for each angelic presence, and this list will help you to call upon the assistance of the most appropriate angel for your needs. In your ritual, utilize the appropriate symbols for the angel you choose.

ANGEL/CHARACTER	HELPFUL FOR	DAY	COLOUR	SYMBOL	INCENSE
Michael Angel of the sun, guardian and protector	Summon to encourage success, or with issues involving the maintenance of stamina or physical health	Sunday	orange/gold	six-pointed star	olibanum
Gabriel Angel of the moon, protector of women and children	Summon for fertility, healing, psychic abilities and all issues concerning harmony in the home	Monday	pale blue	nine-pointed star	myrrh, jasmine
Samael Angel of Mars, protector and guardian, guide to men	Summon to protect against violence, to dispel negative opposition and to obtain justice in your life	Tuesday	red	five-pointed star	tobacco, dragon's blood
Raphael Angel of Mercury	Summon to protect during times of change, upheaval or travel and for issues of mental stress.	Wednesday	yellow	eight-pointed star	galbanum, storax
Sachiel Angel of Jupiter	Summon when you are seeking justice, or protection of your financial situation or status	Thursday	purple	square	cedar
Anael Angel of Venus	Summon when conflict involves relatives or friends, where emotional harmony or love may be lacking	Friday	green	seven-pointed (or mystic) star	rose, red sandalwood
Cassiel Angel of Saturn	Summon in cases involving the protection of property, land or possessions, to clear obstacles such as chronic health conditions, or in situations where you feel blocked by another's actions	Saturday	indigo or black	straight line	myrrh

△ Each angel has an association with a particular colour and fragrance: use the appropriate candles and incense on the altar.

▽ Light the incense and leave it to smoulder while you spend about 15 minutes each day in contemplation of your chosen angelic power.

▽ To end the ritual, extinguish the candles with respect and give thanks to the energies that will respond to your call.

space clearing. When an angelic presence is invited into the place you wish to be cleared, it will leave a lingering protective power and the strong influence of its own characteristics, which will make the place feel calm, tranquil and thoroughly cleared of all hostile or negative influences.

an angelic altar

When you have decided which angel is most appropriate for your needs, you can set up an altar to your chosen protector. This is done very simply by assembling two candles in the colour that corresponds to your angel, and the correct incense, perhaps with an image or symbol to focus your thoughts. Place a candle on each side of the incense container and write in appropriately coloured ink the name of the angel you wish to call upon, drawing the symbol of that angel above the name.

Light the candles and the incense and sit before the altar for about 15 minutes each day, asking for assistance and/or intervention on your behalf in dealing with the situation or energy you are trying to clear. Repeat your request three times and then sit quietly in contemplation of your angel and the help you will receive. Extinguish the candles with respect and give thanks to the energies that will respond to your call.

A druid space clearing

We know very little about the Druids of old, because they were members of a culture that kept no written records. The knowledge we have comes almost entirely from a few books written by the Romans, who were responsible for exterminating the Druids ruthlessly. The typical Druid seems to have been an athletic warrior who possessed remarkable knowledge. From childhood, he would have committed to memory the wisdom, culture and history of the Celts, all of which was transmitted orally.

The Druids were the priesthood of the Gaulish tribes, also known as the Celts, who populated west and central Europe in the pre-Roman era. Later invaders, such as the Anglo Saxons (who reached Britain from Germany after the Romans had abandoned the islands), pushed the Celts into the most remote areas of Europe, including Scotland, Cornwall, Wales, Brittany and the Basque region of northern Spain.

The Druids regarded oak trees and mistletoe as sacred: when we "kiss under the mistletoe" at Christmas, we are actually enacting part of an ancient pagan fertility rite. They also practised human sacrifice (often by burning their victims in groups inside wooden cages shaped like giant human figures), which was the Romans' declared reason for stamping them out. However, it is more likely that the Druids were destroyed because they were the intellectual leaders of Celtic society, and were capable of organizing resistance against Roman rule.

The modern order of Druids was invented in the 18th century, probably as a rival to Freemasonry, and has no direct

GOD OF THE EARTH
"Father Dis" was worshipped by the Druids as the god of the earth. The Romans equated Dis with their god Pluto and the Greek god Hades, the rulers of the underworld.

△ Druidic rituals were often performed in groves of oaks, the most venerated of trees and sacred in ancient times to the sky-gods.

▽ Today we are more often surrounded by buildings than the wonders of nature, but we can still express our respect for the natural world.

△ **Having set twigs and boughs around the space to be cleared, arrange the candles and incense around the room and light them.**

produce an aura of calm about yourself. When you feel calm, approach the east of the area. Stand and draw a deep breath. Without shouting, use the breath to declaim authoritatively: "There is peace!" Now approach the south, take another deep breath and again use it to declaim: "There is peace!" Repeat in exactly the same way to the west, and finally to the north.

Returning to face the east, adopt the occult salute of Dis, by crossing the forearms at the level of the forehead, with clenched fists. In this position, take another deep breath and state levelly and quietly: "I have peace! Let peace prevail!" Lower the arms and visualize the atmosphere of peace spreading like a white mist throughout the area. Gather up the twigs and burn them ceremonially outside or on an open fire indoors. If fire poses a problem, you can bury the twigs, preferably beneath an oak tree. In this case, let the oak tree know what you are burying and why.

connection with the Celtic priesthood. Some writers have suggested that Druidism and Wicca share a common origin in the remote past, and there seem to be some grounds for this. Wicca is known to be a combination of the native lunar-based agricultural tradition with the sun-worship brought by the migrating Beaker people of the Bronze Age, around 1500 BC. Thus Wicca observes four lunar festivals (known as the major Sabbats) and four solar festivals (the lesser Sabbats). It is possible that Druidism in Roman Gaul was descended from the sun-worshipping aspect of the Beaker folk, before their beliefs merged with the native religion.

This space clearing ritual is based on the romantic Druid idyll constructed in the modern period, rather than on the accounts

of Roman historians, who accorded only a few lines to ancient Druidic practices, which were evidently not pleasant.

preparation

You will need to gather several twigs of oak leaves from the ground (they should not be picked from the tree). In winter you can use bare oak twigs. A few sprigs of mistletoe can be added if available, but be aware that the white berries are poisonous. Select an "Earth" incense such as sage, pine or patchouli, and candles in Earth colours: black, brown, olive-green, mustard-yellow or white. No altar is used in this ritual.

the ritual

Set the twigs and leaves around the space to be cleared. Arrange the incense and candles carefully here and there around the area and light them.

Stand for several moments, breathing in slowly and deeply, with your eyes closed, to

▽ **Stand quietly in the centre of the area, breathing deeply, to calm yourself before beginning the ritual.**

Hedgewitch rituals

The term "hedgewitch" describes a magical practitioner who works alone and very much according to individual style and belief. In days of old, the hedgewitch would have been called upon regularly to assist in house blessings and clearings, in the protection of property and personal possessions, and also to act as an oracle to discover the reasons behind any problems and hindrances. Traditionally, he or she would have lived on the edge of the community, surrounded by hedgerows and perhaps also concealed behind the garden hedge around the house.

Living in harmony with nature, hedgewitches use their knowledge of herbs,

▽ **Hedgewitches have a very close link to the spirit world, and to elementals like the fairies.**

flowers, roots and leaves to make up concoctions for such purposes as healing, protection or fertility. A hedgewitch is able to keep one foot in the material world and the other in the world of spirit, and this is what the hedge represents: the veil between the worlds. The hedgewitch might use any of the following for space clearing.

spirits of place

Everything in the world is made up of energy and this includes the energy that makes up the blueprint for the home and place of work. For the purposes of communicating with them, the various energies around us can be called spirits of place. By communing regularly with the spirits of place, the hedgewitch can discover what is causing particular problems to arise.

fairies and elementals

A hedgewitch believes strongly in the elemental energies that inhabit gardens, plants and other natural objects. These entities are a vital part of the energetic life force system, and together are known as elementals because they are related to the four elements, and each shares the characteristics of the element to which it is related. They are called sylphs (those that are related to the Air element), salamanders (those that are related to Fire), undines (related to Water) and gnomes (related to Earth). Fairies and dryads are nature spirits and the hedgewitch will work with both elementals and nature spirits when seeking causes of inbalance.

Creating an elemental area will provide these helpful spirits with a space to be close to you and will be somewhere you can connect with them at times when you need their assistance. At first you may not believe in them, but once you have made an elemental space and asked for their assistance, you will find that something will happen that will definitely shift your belief towards their existence.

△ **Obsidian, onyx, flint and other dark stones are frequently used by hedgewitches for their rituals and charms.**

dark crystals and stones

Any dark stone can be programmed to draw in negative vibrations from its local environment. Placing dark stones in a problem area can help to cleanse it before it is filled with symbols and objects of warmth and light.

Flint is commonly found throughout most of the world and this stone is a powerful protector against psychic or negative intrusions.

sharp objects

To give protection against negative influences, place needles, pins, thorns, prickles, or any other sharp objects in a jar, then fill it with a mixture of protective herbs. The jar should then be sealed and left in the area that seems to be causing problems. It can also be placed under the bed for protection at night. Putting rusty iron nails around your property, facing away

△ Hedgewitches will often grow and harvest their own herbs, for use both in rituals and charms and for healing.

from the walls, is another traditional means of protection, and will guard against any kind of opposition.

a horseshoe

An iron horseshoe should be displayed with its horns facing to the left in the shape of a crescent moon. Iron is the metal of Mars – the planet of power, strength and courage. A horseshoe placed in this way displays the properties of Mars and moon goddesses.

spells, charms and amulets

Charms such as runic symbols, or those made specifically for an individual, can be used for protection, as well as natural amulets

▽ Hedgewitches display a horseshoe on its side, with its horns facing left like the crescent moon, to invoke the power of moon goddesses.

like oak leaves, onion and nettle. A protection spell is one of the skills sought from a hedgewitch.

herbs and spices

The hedgewitch frequently uses herbs and spices in her work and those commonly used in space clearing include the following:

Angelica: an all-round protective plant.
Asafoetida: removes all negativity, but smells acrid, so is used only in severe cases.
Cactus: all spiny plants and tree branches offer protection. Prickly plants or stems in the home or workplace will deflect negativity from the surrounding area.
Fumitory: to expel negative thought forms.
Garlic: the strong smell and taste of garlic deters negativity. Cloves of peeled garlic can be strung over door frames, or placed in strategic positions and replaced once a week with fresh cloves.
Rowan: all parts of the rowan tree have magical protective properties. String the leaves and berries into a garland and place them around whatever you wish to gain protection for, keeping it out of reach of small children or babies.
Yarrow: a powerful psychic protector.
Salt: central to many of the hedgewitch's practices, salt is one of the sacred items for all magical practitioners. It is a crystal and its cleansing powers mean that it is held in great respect.

▽ Garlic has powerful cleansing properties on both the physical and energetic levels.

A HEDGEWITCH SALT CLEANSING

This ritual can be performed once a week to keep your home or workplace clear and clean. Sweep up any old salt and take it outside your property boundary before repeating the ritual.

Begin at the doorway and move clockwise around the room. Take a pinch of undyed natural sea or rock salt and sprinkle it in the first corner saying as you do so, "Clean and clear this corner [or window, or fireplace] be, from all that is not good for me." Repeat in all four corners, around the door frames, windows, and fireplace, in the same way.

▽ Salt is absorptive and has been used for centuries as a cleanser.

Space Clearing for Life

Wherever we are, we become aware of an atmosphere that we perceive through our deepest senses. The atmosphere of each place is subtly different from any other and can profoundly influence our mood. If you dislike the appearance of a room, you can change it, and the same is true of its atmosphere. Space clearing can make a room feel the way you want it to.

To dispel a negative atmosphere

The "atmosphere" of a place can be experienced by those in it as good or bad, but what exactly is it? In occult terms, an atmosphere is a "thought-form" of a certain type. Just as living creatures may have tiny parasites living on them, the psyche has its own form of parasites that attach themselves to it, and these are referred to by occultists as thought-forms.

Thought-forms can be extremely valuable when a magician deliberately creates them, and they form a major part of magic. Unfortunately, the unco-ordinated and primal regions of the mind (the regions responsible, amongst other things, for our dreams) are just as capable of generating a subconscious thought-form as the controlled regions are of deliberately producing a conscious one.

On the subliminal unconscious level, the mind is very susceptible to the psychic vibrations inherent in a place, or produced by people who have been there before, or even by people living nearby and not actually in the place itself. Such vibrations are received by the subconscious mind, rather like a radio set receiving broadcast messages, and a thought-form is created that reflects the nature of the broadcast – it may be happy, sad, gloomy, cheerful, spooky, holy, welcoming, resentful and so on. In our upper, conscious mind we are not aware of how this information – this feeling – arrived inside us, but we recognize it and describe it as the "atmosphere" of a place.

Any kind of good, positive atmosphere is welcome and wholesome, but we sometimes need to cure a negative, unwholesome one. This can be achieved in two ways. We can generate a sufficient quantity of positive psychic vibrations and literally blast them into the affected area, like a kind-of "psychic fly-spray", to change the nature of the vibrations emitted (like changing the broadcast signal). This is the process called exorcism, and it requires tremendous psychic strength and control: it is not recommended unless you are an expert. Also, in nearly every case it is unnecessary, like using a sledgehammer to crack a walnut.

The second way is generally much more useful, helpful and simpler: to continue the broadcast analogy, we can re-tune the receiver so that it picks up a better signal – and the "receiver", of course, is ourselves. In other words, we endeavour to change our own state of mind so that the unwelcome vibrations are no longer received. This process helps us to become stronger, more psychically capable, and less vulnerable to negative influences.

Rituals that produce changes inside ourselves – changes of consciousness – need to be approached with care and sensitivity, and they work best when they are kept short and simple, unless you are a fully trained and proficient occultist.

◁ As you light your central candle, visualize the flame protecting you and your space.

▷ The fourfold breath is used to calm and centre yourself before the ritual.

the ritual

You will need a selection of white candles and tea lights, including one large white candle, and a rattle such as the one described right. Distribute the candles about the floor of the room and light them. Use as many or as few as you feel is appropriate.

Sit on a cushion in the centre of the room. Light the large white candle and place it on the floor directly in front of you. Spend several minutes performing the fourfold breath (breathe in for a count of four, hold for four, breathe out for four, hold for four before taking the next breath). Then pick up your rattle in your right hand and repeat the following in a deep and warning tone:

Pay attention (shake rattle)
Snake is here (shake rattle)
It is true
Snake is coming (shake rattle)
So beware adversary – snake is ready to strike. (shake rattle loudly)

Then repeat the following chant:

Life is love; love is life; let there be an end to strife.
Let the good replace all bad; let love release all spirits sad.

Let my will reveal the power, starting at this present hour,
To enhance the energy, so that I possess the key,
To allow all ills to go, and to let the goodness flow,
Into this place where I now kneel, let love begin all things to heal.

Repeat the chant several times. Visualize all negativity departing from you at great speed, as you chase it away and re-claim what is rightfully yours.

▽ All kinds of noise will chase away negativity, but the noise of your rattle has the added potency of the power of the rattlesnake.

MAKING A RATTLE

Rattles can conjure the ominous sounds of the rattlesnake as it warns of its presence by shaking its tail. The rattle when used in ceremony can either summon the energy of snake to protect, or can warn intrusive energies that they should step back and withdraw. You will need an empty aluminium drinks can, some paper, and a handful of dried long grain rice. Remove the ring pull completely, empty the contents, wash and thoroughly dry the aluminium can. Place the can on the paper and draw round the circular base to form a circle the same size. Cut out the circle. Pour the rice grains in through the ring-pull hole. Place the paper circle over the top of the can to cover the ring pull hole and glue in place. Decorate your can as you feel drawn to do. When it is completed, pass your rattle through the smoke of burning sage, calling for the powers of the rattlesnake to enter your shamanic rattle and for snake to help you.

Dedicate your rattle to Sosho (the snake) and to the spirit of life before using it.

To change an atmosphere

Sometimes the atmosphere of a space needs to be changed if its function is to be altered. For example, if a former bedroom, which has acquired a relaxed atmosphere over the years, is changed into a sitting room, psychically sensitive people may feel drowsy when they spend time in the room. If the planning department of a company moves out of an office and the accounts department moves in, employers may wonder why the accounting staff now seem to be spending so much time in earnest discussion. The atmospheres in these spaces are not particularly negative – they are just misplaced echoes of former thought-forms, each with a residual power of subliminal

persuasion, that need to be overwritten by a more appropriate one.

Transmuting one positive atmosphere into another can be done with a ritual in which you begin by focusing on the old atmosphere, and then swing your focus to the new atmosphere, whatever it may be. This could also be described as stamping a new psychic impression upon a place.

CANDLE COLOURS

Use this list to help you choose candles in the most appropriate colour, which will represent the new function of the room and enhance the atmosphere you are seeking to create.

Red: active areas, energy, dynamism.
Orange: creative areas, socializing, a supportive ambience.
Yellow: thought, the mind, offices and places of study and learning.
Green: areas of relaxation, harmony, balance, calm.
Blue: peace, calm, relaxation.
Violet: warmth and relaxation. A combination of blue and pink, it is ideal for areas where both liveliness and rest are required, such as a dining room.
Pink: inspiration, happiness, positivity.
Purple: depth, reflection, authority, contemplation, for areas requiring stillness, depth and meaning, such as a meditation room.
Silver: magic, dreams, the feminine, for changing a very masculine room into a more feminine one.

Gold: prosperity, abundance, the masculine, for changing a feminine room into a more masculine one.
Brown: grounding, practicality, commitment, for an atmosphere that requires stability and reliable energy. Ideal when changing a mentally oriented space to a more practical one, such as a kitchen or utility room.

YOU WILL NEED

4 small tumbled rose quartz crystals
altar
white candle
2–3 candles in a colour that reflects the new usage of the space
small token of the original use of the space
black cloth large enough to cover or contain the token
rose geranium essential oil and burner
small token of the new atmosphere

the ritual

Set up an altar in the middle of the room using appropriate colours to reflect the change you are making. Put the white candle in the centre of the altar with the three coloured candles arranged in a triangle around it. Put everything you are going to use in the ritual on the altar for a few moments, then take the rose quartz crystals and put them in each corner of the room.

Take the object you have chosen to represent the old atmosphere, and place it in the western quarter of the room. Take the object that is representing the new atmosphere of the room and place it in the eastern quarter. Light all the candles. Start the ritual at the east side of the altar, facing west. Take a few deep, calming breaths and say the following:

◁ As you clap your hands, visualize the sounds driving away the old atmosphere of work, business and stressful activity.

△ After removing the old object, bring in the new one and place it in a central position in the room as a focus point for the new energies.

CLAPPING HANDS

Like any loud and sudden noise, clapping the hands serves to alert and charge the atmosphere. It has the effect of startling a room's energies into an awakened and expectant state.

Go! Depart! Begone ye hence! Avaunt I say, this is my will!
Be ended, finished, changed, transposed,
Leave no disturbing echoes still!

Clap your hands loudly, then take the cloth over to the object in the west and cover it. Return to the altar, but this time stand at the west side facing east, in the opposite direction to the earlier part of the ritual. Say the following:

Now welcome be, now welcome stay, now welcome is for evermore!
Be started, newborn, fresh, unfurled,
And bring thy presence to the fore!

Go to the object in the east that represents the new atmosphere and bring it reverentially to the altar to place it there. Sit beside the altar and leave the item there for several minutes while you meditate on it. As you do so, absorb the new atmosphere that is emerging in the room and reflect it back at the object.

When you feel this is complete and the atmosphere has been altered, close the ritual by extinguishing the candles. Dismantle the altar and remove the object that represented the old atmosphere from the room. Leave the object that represents the new atmosphere in a prominent position on a windowsill or shelf.

To make a place feel special

When we expect visitors and spend time preparing for their stay, our aim is to make our home feel especially welcoming. If we are holding a dinner party, we take great care both to prepare good food and to provide a jovial atmosphere. It is important to us to provide for our guests' physical comfort, and we are also concerned about doing the equivalent on a psychic level.

There are two key words that relate to making a place feel special, both materially and magically, and these are "pride" and "respect". Without one, we will not feel the other. When both these elements are brought into play, our place – whatever and wherever it may be – will begin to fill with that special atmosphere of sparkle and excitement.

YOU WILL NEED

altar and orange altar cloth
2 orange or gold candles
frankincense incense and charcoal
    burner or essential oil and burner
wand
additional orange candles for dark
    areas
rosewater in small bowl

the ritual

Position the altar so that you will face east when standing before it. Arrange the cloth and the two candles in holders upon it, together with the incense or essential oil burner and the wand. Place the additional candles randomly around the room in the shadowy areas that light does not normally illuminate, and where the candle glow will enhance the richness of the room's appearance. The aim is to achieve a depth of perspective in the room, so try to arrange the candles in a non-linear way. Try to avoid having any two candles at a similar distance from the altar.

Light all the candles, then stand in front of the altar and bow your head. Take several deep and calming breaths. Use the wand to

"draw" a solar hexagram in the air in front of you above the altar. The hexagram, a six-pointed star (identical to the "Star of David") is associated with the zodiac, the planets and the sun. At its centre, "draw" the symbol of the sun: a small circle with a dot in the middle. As you do this, visualize the outline appearing as a line of brilliant golden light. Then in a commanding voice, say:

Let none undo the spell I cast,
For it is well and three times good;
This place is special now at last,
Be it now full understood!

△ **Candles randomly arranged in this ritual brighten every corner.**

▽ **The solar hexagram is a six-rayed star with a representation of the sun in the centre.**

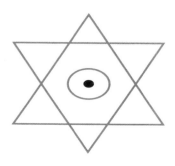

▷ When drawing the hexagram visualize its lines as brilliant golden light.

CREATING AN ENTRANCE

In magical terms, the doorway or entrance to a space is symbolic of a new beginning or a journey of discovery and change. It is therefore an ideal setting to affirm the new atmosphere you are calling in, by using decorations to make the place feel special as you enter.

Bead curtains add a sense of mystery and magic.

Foliage, such as rosemary, ivy and laurel, garlanded around a door frame invites protection, fun and harmony into the room.

Flowers and herbs invite connections with the natural world and convey a sense of ease and relaxation.

Fairy lights strung around the doorway create a sense of light and warmth, and invite the fairies into your space.

Images and charms hung over the door attract specific qualities: angels invite blessings, protective deities offer strength and coins invite prosperous exchanges.

Now pick up the bowl of rosewater and, as you walk clockwise around the edge of the room, dip your fingers in the water and then brush your hand over the walls and floor areas. As you do so, say, "Blessed be this boundary". Where there are areas of the room that might be damaged by the rosewater, pass your hand over the walls a little distance away. It is helpful to visualize that the blessing water is creating a sphere of happiness and peace, as you mark out the boundary of the room.

To close the ritual, extinguish all the candles, starting with the furthest away from the altar and ending with the nearest. Give thanks and discard any remaining rosewater into the earth.

▷ As you distribute rosewater around the room concentrate on what you are doing and visualize a sphere of happiness being created.

To give a sense of belonging

To generate a sense of belonging in a space, we need to start off by feeling special there, and then begin to form a bond with it. A space clearing ritual performed with this intent first needs to produce a subtle change of consciousness. Then, at a second level, it needs to establish an aura of association connecting us with the place.

As you develop your awareness of the energy in a room you will be able to sense any imbalance that creates a disturbing or unsatisfactory atmosphere. Such imbalance can be defined in terms of the four elements, and you can consider ways in which you could bring each element into the space, by introducing them in ways that are relevant to you personally. First it is necessary to find which element is required, and each imbalance will tend to manifest within you in a distinct way as you spend time in the room.

▽ **A bedroom may have everything it needs to be serene and peaceful, but you might still feel that its atmosphere is lacking something.**

sensing the need

Calm and centre yourself before entering the room, then go in and sit down in the centre of the floor, or on the most important piece of furniture, such as a bed in a bedroom, or the sofa in a sitting room. Make your body into a complete circuit by putting both feet flat on the floor or surface, with one hand resting on each knee. After about three minutes, turn your hands palm upwards on your knees and begin to sense the area, also taking into account how you normally feel when you are in the room for any length of time. An imbalance between the elements may be indicated by any of the following feelings:

Crowded – compulsive, mentally intense: too much Air.

Forgetful – unable to remember or recall information, absent-minded: too little Air.

Explosive – having difficulty in keeping one's temper, or a compulsion to outdo everyone: too much Fire.

Disempowered – overly meek and submissive: too little Fire.

QUICK FIXES
Elemental imbalances can be quickly corrected by introducing any of the following items into a space:

Air: music, wind chimes, images of air creatures such as birds, lavender fragrance.
Fire: candlelight, gold or orange materials, fire creatures such as the phoenix, lion or dragonfly, frankincense or copal fragrance.
Water: a fountain, water garden, fish-tank or bowl of water, images of water creatures or plants, jasmine fragrance.
Earth: plants, herbs, crystals, images of earth-dwellers such as prairie dogs or badgers, cypress fragrance.

▽ **A bowl of water with some jasmine flowers will help to balance a room.**

▷ To be able to sense the need of a room, you will want to be calm, relaxed and receptive.

ELEMENTAL BULBS

Once the needs of your environment have been established, you can balance or summon the relevant element into your room by installing a painted and patterned light bulb.

Air: violet circles on a yellow background.

Fire: red flames on a green background.

Water: blue bands on an orange background.

Earth: citrine and russet brown diamonds.

Overwhelmed – being or feeling too emotional: too much Water.

Insensitive – being unfeeling, callous, hurtful or cold: too little Water.

Dull – reluctant to change anything: too much Earth.

Restless – desiring to change things continuously for no reason: too little Earth.

elemental lighting

Install the appropriate elemental light bulb in the room, preferably in the central light fitting, and light some incense of the appropriate fragrance. Breathe deeply, calming the mind. Absorb the atmosphere and the character produced by the colours from the light falling upon the walls of the room. Then repeat one of the following statements, according to the element:

From Air I arise, in Air I live, in Air my kin, to Air I shall return.

From Fire I leap, in Fire I triumph, in Fire my kindred, to Fire I shall return.

From Water I spring, in Water I form, in Water my kingdom, to Water I shall return.

From Earth I come, in Earth I dwell, on Earth my people, to Earth I shall return.

Meditate upon bonding spiritually with your chosen element. Visualize, as appropriate, clouds for Air, gentle flames for Fire, rivulets for Water or roots for Earth stemming from you and twining about the entire area. This will give you a strong feeling of connecting with and belonging intimately to the place, as you become more and more comfortable with the atmosphere you are creating around you with your

ritual. Once you feel that the balance and connection you are seeking in the area have been achieved, remove the bulb and return the lighting in the room to normal.

▽ Let your hands "feel" and sense the area you are intending to balance and clear.

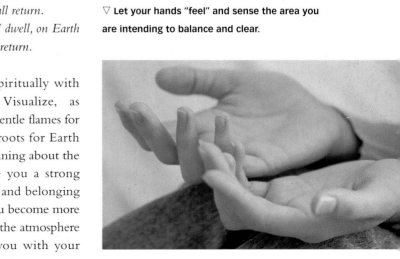

Space clearing for a new beginning

In order to facilitate a new beginning for ourselves, we must first create the space to enable it to materialize in our lives. For this reason, the acknowledgement of endings is highly significant. Our lives follow cycles that are continually changing, evolving and shifting from moment to moment, and nothing in the physical realm remains permanently the same.

In modern society, we have come to fear or abhor most endings, seeing them as associated with failure or as the loss of something we value or want to keep. However, change is not only inevitable but good, and when we are able to let go of things that do not really serve us, or of an experience that has run its course, our lives can open up in very positive ways.

So to attract a new beginning, we must first close the door on that which is ending. This could be a work contract, a relationship, a house move or perhaps grown-up children leaving home; whatever the situation, it is important to create an ending that honours the change, while remaining positive about it. The ceremony can be as simple or elaborate as you wish. The simplest way to honour an ending is to voice the fact in your life and world, and give thanks for what you have experienced as you indicate your intention to let it go and move on to a new beginning.

moving

If you are moving house, cleaning and clearing out naturally become paramount in the process of moving on. After the physical clearing and cleansing has been finished, an ideal way to acknowledge the act spiritually is to sweep the house symbolically with a bundle of birch twigs or a birch broom, imagining each area being purified as you do so. In ancient times, brushwood from the birch tree was used to sweep out the spirits of the old year, preparing the way for the beginning of the new one. Let the house know of your

SYMBOLS OF NEW BEGINNINGS

These are many ways in which you can call for a new beginning, once you have recognized and acknowledged an ending in your life.

• A pair of lodestones placed as a pair in a central area of a room will call for the attraction of a lover.
• If you see shooting stars and comets together in the sky, wishing upon them calls the Sky Father's protection and blessing for any wishes you make.
• The cowrie shell is sacred to the Goddess and empowers wishes for love, friendship and family. Decorate a small pouch with cowrie shells and drop your written wish inside.
• A bowl of seeds (such as sesame, sunflower or pumpkin) with a wish tucked into them, placed on an altar or on the kitchen windowsill, will encourage the growth of whatever you have called for.
• A birch broom propped up beside a doorway will encourage the old to depart and the new to arrive, and will also provide protection for the home.

• Written symbols, such as Beth from the Druidic tree alphabet, or the Greek letter Alpha, will encourage new beginnings. Write them in places of significance, such as over a written wish or trace them in the air in a space where new beginnings are being called for.
• Write a wish on a piece of paper, fold or roll it and place the paper within the cone of a white lily flower, this bloom is sacred to Ostara, the goddess of birth and new life.
• When you are seeking new work or prosperity opportunities, turn silver coins in your pocket on the first night of a new moon to invite growth in your finances.

▷ In Celtic lore, the birch is associated with January, the month dedicated to Janus, the Roman god of new beginnings. Therefore, sweeping with birch twigs symbolizes your call for a new beginning.

△ Sprinkle blessed, or sun charged, water around a room for a new beginning into it. As you do so, focus your mind on what you are doing.

▽ Rosemary is traditionally associated with remembrance and is helpful for rituals that deal with releasing grievances or loss.

intentions in performing this act, and thank it for having been your home. You can also use the birch broom to sweep the new house you are moving into, as a first step to claiming it as your new home. Here it will have the effect of sweeping away the atmosphere created by the previous occupants, creating space for your own spiritual energy.

To prepare your new home for the beginning of your life there, bless it by walking around all the rooms and sprinkling them as you go with drops of water that you have charged with the energy of the sun. This will add vitality and vigour to your new environment.

relationships

At the beginning of a relationship, we want to spend all available time with our new partner. If a parting becomes inevitable, so does our attention to the relationship, which can sometimes end with total silence, resentment and disregard or, conversely, with trauma, abuse and blame. If possible, try to remember the love you once shared, honour each other's differences and accept that your time together has had some value in your lives. If you can achieve this, you will be closing the relationship cycle with love, which will set up the vibration for love to meet your new beginning. It is a question in all cases of starting as you mean to go on.

Space clearing your office

If you have a private office where you can ensure that no one will disturb you, any of the rituals described in this book can be performed in it: you can simply perform one that you find relevant to your needs. However, most people do not have such privacy at work, which can make it awkward to conduct any kind of overt ritual, so an alternative system of conducting a space clearing needs to be employed.

At its purest and most powerful level, magic needs no special equipment or physical actions, including speech; the entire ritual, including all scents, colours and tools, can be imagined through creative visualization. In order to achieve the full-blown magical results of an occult master by this technique, it is necessary to develop and train the mind and willpower so that anything created in the imagination becomes indistinguishable from absolute reality in all respects. However, only a shadow of this ability is required in order to accomplish a practical and effective office space clearing.

preparation

Try to choose a time for the space clearing when you are unlikely to be disturbed. Even though outwardly you will not be doing anything that would raise any eyebrows among your colleagues, you will be better able to concentrate if you are alone.

Before the day you have planned to perform the ritual, obtain a small notepad to form a scrapbook that lends itself to the concept of a silent, mental space clearing. You will also need to collect a number of appropriate images to represent your working environment. These could be taken from magazines and catalogues. Your tools for this ritual will be nothing more complicated than scissors, glue and paper.

the ritual

Cut out the pictures you have collected and use them to assemble a collage, or compound image of the office, by arranging and sticking them together. Remember that it does not need to look like your own office, nor does it need to be artistic or to

△ **As offices are usually crowded and busy places, space clearing at work oftens needs to be a private, mental exercise.**

scale, or to have perfect perspective. You are simply aiming for a surreal general impression of an office environment, not an accurate reconstruction.

Everyone is familiar with the ancient voodoo practice of sticking pins into a doll that represents someone you don't like. This follows the principle of sympathetic magic: the idea is that the doll and the target become inextricably linked, so that whatever happens to one will transfer itself to the other by association. Though this practice is definitely immoral, sympathetic magic can be employed in a similar way to space clear the office.

Just as the doll is only a rough image of a real person, your office collage need only be an approximation of your actual office.

◁ **Create a scrapbook of images that represent your working environment, and use this as a focus for your thoughts.**

▷ **If a co-worker is causing problems, take a cactus to work and place it between you and the offending party to create a symbolic barrier.**

PROTECTION STRATEGIES

Here are some other simple ways to keep your office psychically protected and clear:

• Display some plants and flowers that have protective qualities, such as fern, yarrow and geranium. Put them in waiting rooms and reception areas to reduce any invasive effects upon your space of the energy of visitors.

• Place smoky quartz crystals in the four corners of your office. Cleanse them once a month by soaking them for eight hours in salted spring water. Rinse them thoroughly and before replacing them hold them in your hands while affirming their abilities to continue absorbing stray energies from your office for the month to come.

You can make one collage, or as many versions as you like, until you find an image that you resonate well with. All you now need to do is look at the image you have assembled and, as you concentrate on it, visualize that you are projecting a space clearing energy into the office. This exercise should be repeated several times for maximum effect.

guarding against negativity

There are other things you can do to space clear your office and repel negativity, such as keeping the area clean and free of clutter, just as you would your home. To protect yourself from negativity coming from another worker in your office, take in a cactus and put it between yourself and the offending party.

If when you are at work you feel a sudden vulnerability, try using your mind to project an image of a guardian figure at your office door. This should be someone you feel safe and happy with, who will keep stray energies (or human nuisances) from entering the office. But it is important never to visualize such a guardian as actually taking the offensive against other people, no matter how much they may annoy you. It is a guardian only, not a hostile spirit.

Space clearing on the move

Like space clearing in an office, space clearing "on the move" can be awkward if people who are unsympathetic to spiritual rituals are likely to be present or to arrive on the scene unexpectedly. You may find yourself in a variety of temporary situations where some psychic negativity may make its presence felt and need to be dealt with for your comfort and peace of mind. These could include hotel rooms, holiday accommodation, cars and caravans, as well as public transport: in short, anywhere that you enter for a limited period but cannot conveniently leave if you encounter a negative energy field. While you would probably not become aware of anything negative during a short journey on a bus or in a taxi, a longer journey by air, sea or rail might benefit from space clearing.

A handy ritual based on certain elements of Wicca can fulfil the need for a space

clearing whenever you are on the move. It is unobtrusive and very simple, and can easily be performed in a hotel room or even in a crowded train compartment or a car

△ **Your hotel room might be charming to look at but could have a lingering atmosphere from previous guests that you want to dispel.**

(providing you are not the driver) because everything is carried out in the mind, rather than physically.

The ritual can be done purely as a mental exercise, but an important magical technique that can help greatly when you are doing a mind-working is to visualize yourself actually performing it as a full ritual. This usually takes only a little practice. Try to imagine a "ghost image" of yourself stepping out of your real body, like a double exposure in a film. Visualize your image standing up and saying and doing the things that the physical you is only thinking. The use of this magical double, or doppelganger, is actually an occult method dating back many centuries. In ancient times people believed that a powerful magus was able to send out such a doppelganger that could actually be seen by others who took it for the real person. Such a self-projection was sometimes called a "fetch".

▽ **Ships' cabins can seem cramped and impersonal. Use your space clearing skills to claim the space as your own.**

▷ Try using frankincense or lotus joss sticks, which you can easily include in your luggage, to bless your temporary home.

the ritual

This is a quick and easy method of conducting a space clearing in crowded or cramped conditions. Throughout the ritual, repeat this chant continually in the background of your thoughts:

Echo echo Azarak! Echo echo Zomelak!
Echo echo Babalon! Echo echo Zebulon!

While doing this, imagine a ball of bright blue glowing fire (like the blue part of a hot flame) starting at the centre of your chest and expanding at about the speed at which a party balloon is inflated, until it has filled the whole area with its glow. (If you are visualizing a doppelganger, the glow should emanate from its chest.) This blue ball is begun again and again, repeating its expansion in waves or pulses. As you proceed, the "balloon" of light expands faster each time, until you can do it in time with the chant, so that eventually each three-word phrase covers an expanding blue pulse. Continue this for a few minutes, then stop and relax.

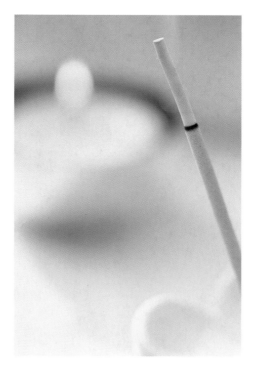

a portable space clearing kit

If you are regularly on the move, it may be a good idea to assemble a portable space clearing kit, to help bring you peace of mind wherever you may be. Include the tools you feel happiest working with, but a good list of items to include would be:

small sage smudge stick
frankincense incense sticks
matches
packets of dried herbs such as
  rosemary, marjoram and dill seeds
salt

△ Salt spread on a mirror or other reflective surface can help to absorb negativity sensed in a room and reflect it away into the light.

The smudge stick and frankincense sticks can be used to "clear the air", and the dried herbs can be sprinkled lightly around the edges of a room to act as a circle of protection if you are occupying a place that makes you feel disturbed or restless. A small handful of salt in each corner can be utilized when the room itself feels in need of cleansing or balancing.

◁ You can make up your own portable space clearing kit quite easily, to ensure happy and successful trips.

▽ Remember that charcoal gets very hot, so take a heatproof container in your kit, and check there are no smoke alarms in your room.

Everyday rituals

The purpose of doing regular daily rituals is not so much to provide a space clearing for a specific room, but to enhance and empower yourself, so that you will have a stronger and more stable foundation. This will help you radiate an aura of authority wherever you go. This practice can also be described as "self charging".

an early morning ritual

The following ritual is a simplified adaptation of an ancient magical technique called "invoking by pentagram", by which various energies can be summoned for a multitude of purposes. In this case, you are summoning a fresh charge of personal psychic energy to strengthen your being, calm all atmospheres you may enter and encourage you to appreciate the joy of a new day.

Light your chosen incense or essential oil. Stand facing a window, towards the east (during warm weather this ritual can also be performed outside facing the sun). Take some slow, deep breaths.

When you are calm, make the sign of the pentagram on your body. To do this, touch the fingertips of your right hand to your

▽ As you touch your forehead to begin the pentagram, say clearly and firmly, "I am Spirit!".

forehead and say, "I am Spirit!" Touch the fingertips to your left hip, saying: "I am Earth!" Touch your right shoulder, saying: "I am Water!" Then touch your left shoulder, saying: "I am Air!" Touch your right hip, saying: "I am Fire!" Finally, touch your forehead again to complete the figure of the pentagram, saying: "Thus I seal my affirmation." Inhale the fragrance of the incense or oil for a few moments before beginning the new day.

△ Choose an incense depending on the qualities you feel you may need to call on during the day.

WAKE-UP HERBS
For protection and purification: frankincense, juniper
For physical energy and success: cinnamon, carnation, cloves
De-stressers: bergamot, cedar.

a bedtime ritual

To end the day, you can use this specially modified version of a much more elaborate ritual known as the Middle Pillar Exercise. This ritual has its origins in the teachings of the cabbala, an immensely powerful Hebrew magical system that may be more than 3,500 years old.

Before you begin the ritual, calm and centre yourself. Stand facing west – the direction of the setting sun – and for a few moments relate to the sun setting on the horizon, whether it is actually still daylight or already dark.

Imagine a beam of brilliant white light shining down on you from an infinite height. As it touches your head, it transforms your entire body into light-filled glass, like a clear bottle of human shape. As the light courses down through your body, it changes hue, moving through all the colours of the rainbow. As these colours flow down, imagine any dark areas of your body being cleansed by the rainbow light pushing the blackness down and out through the soles of your feet. As it flows out of your feet,

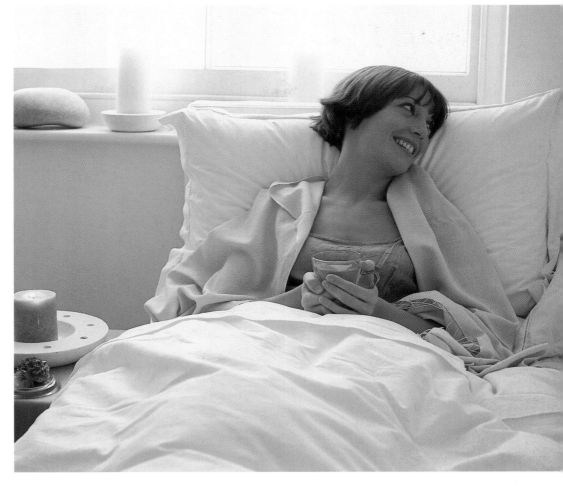

▽ Placing an amethyst under your pillow will help you to achieve a deep and untroubled sleep.

imagine that it is forming a pool or puddle of black mire, and that this pool is then draining away into nothingness, leaving you clean and filled with brilliant, opalescent, rainbow hues.

To add to the effectiveness of the ritual and enhance your ability to sleep, place an amethyst or clear quartz crystal under your pillow before you settle down to sleep.

△ After you have finished your bedtime ritual relax with a cup of dreaming herb tea and allow the tensions of the day to disperse.

A DREAMING TEA MIX

Mix the following herbs to make up a dreaming tea, which can help you to recall your dreams and have a restful night's sleep. (It is not advisable to drink this tea if you are pregnant.)

1 heaped tsp jasmine flowers
1 heaped tsp chamomile flowers
2 sprigs fresh marjoram
a large cup or mug of boiled
*   spring water*

Place all the herbs in a jug and pour over the boiled spring water. Leave to infuse for 5 minutes, then strain into a cup and sweeten with honey if desired. Sip this relaxing tea about half an hour before you go to sleep.

Space clearing people and objects

As we go about our daily lives, we can pick up energy from our journeys, from those we meet and interact with, from our own feelings, thoughts and emotions and from the environment. The level of demand on our energy will determine how often a clearing may be necessary to counteract the effects of negative energy. For someone who is working with people in a caring capacity, such as a therapist, for example, whose clients may be ill, depressed, or temporarily unbalanced in some way, it will sometimes be necessary to clear at least three times a day, if possible, or after seeing each client. For someone whose existence is more solitary, the need for clearing diminishes proportionately.

The same applies to objects: if they are in regular use a daily cleansing routine could be advisable, but if they are used in less specific ways about once a month would be sufficient. For example, if you are working with a protective crystal during an ongoing dispute with a neighbour, this would be considered "regular" usage and a daily cleansing of the crystal would be appropriate. If you work from home or in a small office and simply wish to use crystals to help keep your working environment

▽ Objects such as crystals and ritual implements may need daily or monthly cleansing, depending upon how often they are used.

spiritually clean and clear when no particular issue or problem is evident, then cleansing them once a month will probably be sufficient.

There are a variety of ways in which people and possessions can be cleared of negative vibrations. Some of these have been described on previous pages, such as the use of smoke and fire or herbs and aromas. Outlined here are some specific methods that you can use to cleanse yourself or objects around you: simply choose the technique that best suits your circumstances or requirements.

clapping

Creating loud sounds has been a traditional way of space clearing for centuries. You can use this method when there is very little time available and you wish to clear an object such as a crystal, a piece of jewellery or a seating area. Stand in a commanding position, breathe deeply and centre yourself, then clap your hands firmly a few times around and over the object, imagining as you do so that the energies are being commanded to leave and chased away. You may like to make a positive affirmation after clapping, such as, "Be clear, be bright and filled with light."

absorbing

This clearing is ideal when you have been working hard and feel drained or ungrounded, or for an object that has been put to hard use. It can also be useful when life needs to be slowed down a little. Sprinkle some salt on the floor or in a container and stand on it with bare feet, or place the object on top in the centre, for five minutes. During this time visualize all impurities being absorbed into the salt. When the time is up, brush the salt carefully from the soles of your feet (or from the object) sweep it up and discard it in running water. Rinse the salt from your hands and feet and/or the object.

△ When cleansing an object by clapping over it, you should be authoritative and commanding with your gestures.

▽ Laying your bare feet upon rock salt is a good way to ensure that negative vibrations are drawn away from you. Rinse your feet well afterwards.

△ Laying crystals on your body and relaxing for a few minutes will replenish your energy levels.

crystal cleansing

You can use crystals to clear both objects and people, and this method is most suitable when there is more time available for cleansing. Space clearing yourself will take approximately half an hour, while for objects the ideal time would be overnight or for approximately eight hours. When you are using crystals for cleansing purposes, it is important that they themselves are clean and clear before you use them.

Lie down in a comfortable position and place a smoky quartz crystal beneath your feet with the pointed end facing towards you. Place a clear quartz crystal above your head with the pointed end facing towards you. Place a rose quartz crystal on your chest. Lie quietly for as long as you feel the crystals are having an effect upon you, which should take about 25 minutes. Remove the crystals in reverse order and bury them in the earth for about eight hours before unearthing them and rinsing

them clean. If you do not have a garden, the crystals can be buried in a pot of earth on a windowsill.

To cleanse an object, place it in a dark coloured cloth with a smoky quartz crystal or other black or dark stone such as obsidian. Wrap them up together completely and leave undisturbed overnight. Next morning, remove the object and bury the working crystal in the earth as before.

smudging

Purification using the smoke of smouldering herbs such as sage, thyme and rosemary, is a traditional space clearing method employed by Native Americans. The fragrant smoke has a cleansing effect on the environment, but it is also very useful when you need to clear negativity from a person or object.

You can buy smudge sticks for this purpose, or grow your own herbs and tie the stalks into firm bundles. Simply light the stick, extinguish the flame, and waft the smoke around the object or person to be cleansed. Loose, dried herbs can be burnt and the smoke used in the same way.

▽ For cleansing with smoke, use a feather and a smudge stick to waft the sweet-smelling herbal smoke around you or an object.

Altars and Shrines

An altar is a meeting point, where the divine reaches down to touch the everyday world and where we can concentrate our intentions and desires for spiritual growth. When you visualize an altar, you may imagine a monumental table in a lofty, echoing building, covered with a sumptuous cloth and with ritual objects formally arranged on it. Or perhaps you see an ancient monolith, open to the sky, potent with the memory of mysterious sacrifices and pagan rites. Altars like these are awesome and remote, approached only by priests forbidden to ordinary worshippers. A different kind of altar – a simple shrine where you need no intermediary to help you reach the world of spirit – is the subject of this section. When you create a personal altar you place yourself at the very centre of your own sacred space, bringing the divine right into your life.

The domestic altar is a constant reminder of the search for spiritual fulfilment, anchored in the context of daily life. It can be a focus for prayer, a shrine to honour those you love, a place where you choose to meditate, or somewhere to spend a few minutes in quiet contemplation. The act of creating sacred space is a way of inviting spirit into your home and your life. An altar will grow, change and develop as you do: take it with you on your spiritual journey.

Altars Through Life

A sacred space brings positive energy into your home and life. Your altar and the precious objects you place on it, whether specially made for the purpose, or something that has significance in your life, will help to focus that energy.

A personal altar

It is in times of solitude and quiet reflection that we find the space we need to centre and renew ourselves, and to gain patience and wisdom to deal with all that life throws at us. We need time to see beyond the mundane and the everyday, to find a way of viewing life as a connected whole, and to feel integrated with that whole: to achieve a sense of spirit.

Creating a personal altar is a way of inviting spirit into your home. The sacred space it occupies is available to you all the time, whenever you need an interval of repose to nourish your soul and restore your sense of the sacred. As you use your altar for prayer or meditation you energize it, and its influence widens, flowing out through and around you, to sanctify your home and everyone in it. An altar can be a physical expression of your deepest attachments and longings; by giving them form you bring them into your daily life and empower yourself to achieve what you desire.

△ We instinctively bestow significance and importance on items of remembrance, and make out of them tiny, temporary shrines.

instinctive altars

Most of us display an instinctive need to enshrine what is precious to us. If you look around your home you can probably already find an altar you have created unconsciously – perhaps several. The lovely sea shells you collected during last summer's holiday, the family photographs upon the mantelpiece, the candles and flowers in the centre of the table: we all make such arrangements with love and care, and they inspire us with feelings of harmony and beauty.

Young children naturally make altars of their favourite toys. They will often arrange their most special things so that they can look at them as they go to sleep and find them still there when they wake in the morning. If a child is sick or upset, arranging some pretty things on her bedside table will help to cheer her up. Children have a wonderful ability to invest all kinds of objects with magic. A child will turn a handful of toffee wrappers into jewel-

△ A simple altar for a child that is a collection of their favourite things, will encourage them to build a magical relationship with their spirit.

coloured windows, transforming his familiar surroundings. Fragments of translucent, sea-worn glass, with their delicate colours and subtle texture, are valued as rare marine gemstones. Leaf skeletons or unusual feathers picked up in the park are mysterious treasures – the fresh vision of children can teach us to see such things as they really are: small miracles of natural form.

As children grow up they need to establish their separate identity and personal space. The teenager's room is a shrine to growing individualism (which may mean that it's a mess). Friendships might be celebrated by a whole wall full of photographs, reinforcing the good feeling of being a member of a supportive group. Another wall might be devoted to posters of pop stars, but there may still be a shelf somewhere

◁ Setting aside an area of a room purely for reflection, prayer or meditation will help to bring a spiritual element into your life.

with just a few flowers and a single candle, and you can add items as they become significant. It will evolve as you use it and your relationship with it grows closer and stronger, until all its various elements mirror the many facets of your personality.

practical considerations

Any flat surface can become an altar when it is hallowed by intent. It needs to be somewhere quiet, where no one will bump into it as they pass and where you will be able to stand, sit or kneel before it comfortably. But if it suits you, the surface could be a shelf, a windowsill with a tranquil view beyond, the top of a chest, even the top of the refrigerator.

Traditionally, altars have been made from natural materials, often wood. If you choose to make a shrine on an old piece of furniture, it will hold the resonance of its past use, while a new piece could be the foundation of an altar for new beginnings. Prepare the space the altar will occupy by removing clutter from the surrounding area and cleaning everything until it sparkles.

△ A bowl of floating candles, lit to create a welcoming atmosphere for visitors, is one of the simplest altars.

dedicated to some much-loved toys, whose missing eyes and worn fur show how much emotion was invested in them – a little altar to the childhood that is being left behind.

creating an altar with intent

The altar is a work of intuition and imagination. As you play around with ideas for it, handling and thinking about the objects you are placing on it, you will be feeding into it your own energy and creativity, making it more deeply personal. You will know instinctively when it is right. Allow your creativity to flow freely, straight from your spirit. The intention behind what you place on an altar, and what it represents, is more important than its physical reality.

Your altar can be for you alone, or to share with others. A family altar can work for cohesiveness, like the traditional ancestral altars of the East. A couple could share in the creation of an altar to promote a deeper commitment to one another.

Let your altar grow freely, moving things around, or setting up a new altar whenever you wish. It can begin very simply, perhaps

Altars through the home

Most people have one room that feels special, where the sense of positive energy is most complete. It could be the living room, the kitchen, or a welcoming entrance hall. Traditionally, the hearth is regarded as the centre of the home and is really a prototype altar. But if you want an altar to be very personal to you, you may prefer to have it in a more private place.

Feng shui can help you position your altar effectively, using the directional chart called the *pa gua* to find areas that represent the various aspects of your life. An altar in the wisdom and experience area could benefit your spiritual life, while an altar dedicated to love would be most effective in the relationships area. The *pa gua* can also be imposed on a room to determine the best placement for an altar, or on the altar itself to help you arrange objects on it.

All the different activities that we pursue create distinct types of energy in each room. This is why it can be very difficult to get to sleep in a room that has been full of lively conversation, for instance, or to concentrate on a piece of analytical work in the kitchen. Every altar will be influenced by the energy of its surroundings. You can use this power to create a life-enhancing altar

△ A bedroom altar reminds us as we wake that the spirit of the sacred is always with us.

in any room by drawing on the intrinsic energy of the space, and there is no reason why you shouldn't have several small altars around the house, wherever you feel they are needed.

the bedroom

Most of us want our bedroom to be a sanctuary where we can be wholly ourselves. It is where we take our secrets and prayers, joy and grief. A bedroom altar acts as a focus for these, and for daily rituals to help you greet the day and prepare for night.

◁ This simple bedroom altar to Gaia, the goddess of dreams, includes lillies to invoke calm.

For peaceful rest, place sleep crystals on your altar: amethysts, a piece of jade or obsidian. The scent of lavender or jasmine will help you sleep. Honour the earth deity and goddess of dreams, Gaia, with barley grains or laurel, or include an image of Nephthys, who sheltered the sleeping pharaohs beneath her protective wings.

At bedtime, set a bowl of water scented with jasmine oil near your bed and place your sleep crystals in it. On willow leaves – to help your wishes come true – write what you wish to come to you in sleep.

▷ Our working environment, like any other, benefits from a spiritual atmosphere. An office

THE FOUR DIRECTIONS

Ancient traditions honour the four directions of the compass, and attribute specific qualities to each one. The custom is preserved in the architecture of Christian churches and Buddhist temples, where the altar always stands in the east. By placing an altar in a particular direction, you can harness its particular qualities.

EAST: new beginning and rebirth.
SOUTH: motivation, creativity and growth.
WEST: healing and transformation.
NORTH: looking within.
There is, however, a Buddhist saying, 'Where faces the yogi, there is the east of the yogi': in other words, 'the east within' – your own state of mind – is more important than geographical direction.

the study or office

An altar in the workplace will generate positive energy to help you concentrate. Wisdom and inspiration are personified by Thoth, the scribe of the Egyptian gods who wrote down the wisdom of the universe.

Yellow candles assist communication and learning. Helpful crystals include emerald, to give insight, azurite, for clarity, and hematite, to aid reasoning and memory.

the hallway

The Roman god Janus is a traditional protective deity, and could stand on a shrine by the door, or it could house a guardian animal such as a dog, lion or tiger. Sacred objects at the entrance help to sanctify the whole of your home, and you will carry blessings with you as you leave.

the kitchen

At the hub of the house, the kitchen is a potent place. The energy of the earth – in the form of food – is transformed by the magical process of cooking, which demands creativity and concentration. An altar for

◁ A kitchen altar can incorporate any kind of food, although traditionally it would have included grains, honey and spices.

hospitality could be dedicated to Hestia, goddess of the hearth and home, or to Demeter, goddess of abundance and unconditional love. Leave offerings of rice, grains, fruit or honey for the nature spirits and light the altar candles each time you prepare a meal. A shrine behind the sink would engage your attention as you work there. You could hang herbs and flowers, chilli and garlic around the window like a garland, or decorate the sill with evergreens.

the living room

To promote harmony between your family and friends, set up an altar to the four elements on the mantelpiece. This could combine salt for earth, a red candle for fire, sea shells for water and feathers for air.

Green is the colour of harmonious relationships. To create a prayer bowl, place a clear quartz cluster in a green bowl filled with spring water and invite members of the family to write down their prayers for others and tuck them under the bowl.

Collecting natural offerings

We are part of the natural world, even if urban living makes us feel removed from it. We rely on nature for food and sustenance, and have a responsibility as its caretakers. Placing natural objects on an altar helps to reinforce its connection with earth energies, and underlines our commitment to preserving the natural world.

Nearly everyone has at some time brought home a beautiful stone or sea shell as a souvenir of a precious day, or because it came from a place that made us feel happy, somewhere we felt a sense of spiritual peace. The resonance of that experience clings to the object for ever. In school, the tradition of maintaining a nature table encourages children to share their unusual and beautiful natural finds with others. This kind of display also involves a kind of reverence for the wonders of the earth, and can become a visual calendar, recording the cycle of the seasons.

Reverence for nature of course precludes stealing from it: if you are moved by a beautiful natural environment, the last thing you want to do is disturb it. Rather than cutting flowers or trees, you may prefer to take only things that have fallen. Leave an offering to signify your appreciation of the gift. This could be a traditional offering, such as

tobacco – which is considered a sacred herb by native Americans – or salt, sacred to the Celts. Or express your gratitude in a simple action, such as clearing away litter.

flowers and trees

Plants are great healers, both physically and spiritually. If you respond particularly strongly to a flower or tree, keep it or an image of it on your altar. Trees are powerful emblems of nature, and each has its special attributes and symbolism.

According to legend, the birth of Gautama Buddha was greeted with birdsong and showers of sweet tea and fragrant flowers, and this is why fresh flowers are placed on Buddhist altars. Flowers are a universal symbol of youth and gentleness, and an appreciation of their beauty has helped civilizations to flourish artistically since

△ **Driftwood carried by the oceans conveys the blessings of the Goddess and can be placed on an altar dedicated to emotional healing.**

▽ **Flowers are filled with grace and beauty, and can remind us of our own innate qualities of innocence and purity.**

▽ **Fossils represent the ancestors and past life memory. Placing a fossil on an altar will aid memory and help us find our roots.**

▷ Pebbles and stones represent the earth element. Their presence on an altar can help to stabilize stress-filled atmospheres.

TREE ASSOCIATIONS

APPLE: youth, beauty, innocence.

ASH: the world tree, purification and cleansing.

BAY: guardian of the house, protection against illness.

BEECH: stability, flow of energy, protector of knowledge.

DOGWOOD: charm and finesse.

HAWTHORN: marriage, fertility, protection of children.

HAZEL: wisdom and fertility, used to divine water.

OAK: wisdom, strength and endurance.

ROWAN: protection against evil.

WILLOW: love and regeneration, lunar and feminine rhythms.

YEW: immortality, transformation and inner wisdom.

ancient times. Their brief lives encapsulate the cycle of birth, life and return to the earth to nurture the next generation. A single flower is an expression of natural but fleeting perfection. Gazing into it, you can find peace and serenity that you can take into yourself.

herbs

The use of herbs – for healing, spiritual cleansing and magic – has a long history. Many are tried and tested remedies, and almost every plant is useful in some way.

Herbs are used as talismans in magic: St John's wort, for example, is hung over windows and doors on Midsummer's Day to cleanse and protect the house. They can be placed on an altar to represent particular qualities. Basil, for example, is said to protect from pain, and sage is a purifying herb.

fruits, nuts and grains

At harvest time, it is traditional to bring offerings of nuts, fruit and grain to the altar to give thanks for the abundance of nature. The fruits brought for blessing contain within them the seeds of next year's crop, so this ritual of thanksgiving also includes a prayer for fertility in the future.

stones and sea shells

A stone belongs to the earth and brings grounding energy to the altar. It conveys the character of the place where it originated: the moving river bed, the windswept seashore or the eternal mountains. Rocks and stones also carry the resonance of millions of years of history, and fossils remind us even more vividly of the antiquity of earth's life story, of which we are a part.

Emblems of the sea, shells are associated with its fluid, feminine energy. They signify water, the element of the emotions. They also have traditional links with regeneration, baptism and prosperity.

feathers

Representing the element of air, feathers symbolize the connection between earth and heaven, and therefore between humanity and the creator. Their complex structures and natural beauty make them valuable objects for contemplation during meditation.

▽ Feathers represent birds, who are honoured as a link between earth and heaven.

Objects of beauty

While you are assembling your altar, it will help you to decide on the form it is to take if you constantly keep in mind your purpose and intention: that you are honouring the spiritual centre of your life and providing a focus for it. All the elements you bring to the altar, such as candles, incense, pictures and objects that are important to you, are tools to help you to this end. Make your altar beautiful, so that each time you see it, it lifts your heart.

sacred images

Deities from any religion may have a personal symbolism for you, whether or not you are an adherent of any faith. A statue of the Buddha in meditation could help with your own meditation and prayer, for example, while a picture or statue of St Francis of Assisi may have special meaning if you have a deep affinity with animals.

In the Christian church, the symbolic power of imagery is seen in the icon, a visual expression of faith. The Byzantine artists of the early Church developed a characteristic style for the painting of these holy pictures, using a language of symbols to transmit the tenets of Christianity to worshippers who could not read the scriptures for themselves. Because God had appeared on earth in human form, it was felt that the image of the human Christ could be por-

▽ **Statues of female or male figures will honour the archetype you wish to represent.**

△ **Creating an altar with objects of personal meaning can reinforce spiritual connections.**

trayed to help the faithful understand the nature and intention of God.

Icons can be anything from small paintings on wood panels or paper, to large frescoes. Their nature is defined not by their size but by their sacred subject matter and the traditional style and symbolism used to depict its essence. They are recognized universally as objects of great beauty and power. In the West, they tend to be regarded as symbols of faith, comparable with a cruci-

fix or a stained glass window. In the mystical tradition of the Orthodox church, however, they are precious objects of prayer, veneration and contemplation.

If you wish to bring the blessings of the Goddess into your life, dedicate your altar to her by enshrining her image. This might be a reproduction of a fertility figure, or a

▷ Angels are believed to provide protection and guidance. An angelic altar brings loving support

ANIMAL SYMBOLISM

Images of animals can be used on the altar to symbolize an aspect of your character or to help you focus on a quality you desire.

BEAR: receptive female energy, earth wisdom, introspection.
BISON: wisdom of the elders.
CAT: independence, intuition.
DEER: security and protection.
DOG or WOLF: loyalty, family.
DOLPHIN: understanding.
EAGLE: divine and earthly power.
FROG: cleansing, emotional healing.
HARE: quickness of thought.
HERON: self-reliance.
HORSE: freedom, power.
LION: strength.
LIZARD: illusions, letting go.
OWL: magic, wisdom.
RABBIT: fertility.
ROBIN: new beginnings.
TURTLE: endurance, experience, knowledge.

△ The points of a crystal help to direct energy. They can also help to channel healing thoughts.

counsellors and guardians

If you call on a guardian angel for spiritual support, you can place a picture or figurine of a beautiful angel on your altar to focus your prayer. Photographs of loved ones who have died will remind you that they are still part of your life; pictures that show them full of happiness and vitality help you to remember your whole relationship with them, not just the fact that you have lost them. Seek their wisdom and advice as you remember them.

In the shamanic tradition, everyone has a spirit ally in the form of an animal. Your guardian animal could be one that you particularly identify with, or you may want to call upon an animal spirit whose energy can help you in a time of need. Placing an image on your altar will deepen your connection with your animal ally. Your prayers might be inspired by a picture of a soaring bird: birds are traditionally seen as spiritual messengers, flying between earth and heaven.

gemstones and crystals

Crystals – points of sparkling light created in the darkness of the earth – are potent emblems of spiritual illumination, purity and durability. The ancient Greeks considered all quartz crystals to be fragments that had fallen from the perfect crystal of truth that resided on Mount Olympus. As well as being objects of great beauty, crystals and

gemstones are storehouses of powerful energies, and magical powers of healing and protection have been ascribed to them. Each crystal is believed to have a distinct spiritual nature and to exert a specific influence on the human spirit; each has its own associations and symbolism. Place crystals to which you feel drawn on your altar to endow it with their special power.

△ A crystal's structure can serve to align and harmonize the physical and mental worlds.

statue or painting of one of the many aspects of the Goddess worshipped by ancient cultures, such as Isis the compassionate mother of the Egyptians, Athene the Greek goddess of wisdom and craft, or Diana, the moon deity who lights up the darkness within. By invoking the Goddess and seeking her ancient wisdom you will find an aspect of her in yourself. Bringing her into the heart of the home in this way upholds a tradition that has been practised throughout history.

Objects of symbolic value

Everyone has a collection of treasures that represent memories of close relationships and happy times, and such things have a place on a home altar. They probably already have their own special places, either on display like little shrines where we see them each day, or nestling secretly and safely where we can always find them when we feel the need to touch them and remember. A private arrangement of this kind can be a good place to start exploring a relationship with a personal altar.

A lock of hair, a baby's first shoes, or a trinket from a wedding cake are traditional mementos that many people keep all their lives. Other items are precious because they were gifts: they carry the memory of the giver, as well as the positive energy associated with the act of giving. Placing objects of symbolic value on an altar sets them in a new context that makes us see them afresh. It acknowledges the importance of all that they represent.

seasonal symbols

Altars can change with the seasons, celebrating the coming of spring with fresh flowers and seeds, or ushering in the Christmas festivities with garlands of evergreens. Special seasonal items could be arranged on an altar in honour of the traditional festivals of the Celtic eightfold year. For city dwellers, especially, seasonal altars reaffirm a connection with nature.

△ Tiny items of personal significance can be kept safe on your altar in a pretty bag.

abstract symbols

Symbols predate writing as a means of conveying ideas. Ancient symbols were carved, painted, stitched and worked in metal for magical purposes, to ward off evil or to invoke gods. Some signs, identified as archetypes, appear to be universally understood. A symbol gains its significance from the emotional and spiritual weight it carries. Like music and art, symbolism is a language of the emotions.

Some of the most compelling symbols are the simplest, such as the circle that represents the cycle of life, death and rebirth. The spiral, too, stands for the cycle of existence, but its outward motion also symbolizes growth and the energy of the vortex. In Celtic symbolism, the triple spiral stands for the three stages of life personified by the Triple Goddess: maiden, mother and crone.

The cross is the emblem of Christianity, and also represents the four cardinal directions. In pre-Columbian America the cross was a fertility symbol related to the four rain-bearing winds. The *ankh*, a cross surmounted by a loop, was an ancient Egyptian symbol of immortality.

The pentacle, or five-pointed star, is an ancient symbol of harmony and mystic power. When used magically it is inscribed on a disc. It is a female symbol related to the earth element.

Ancient graphic symbols such as these can bring their energy and associations to your altar. By painting or carving them yourself, you will enhance your connection with them: it is worth learning new craft skills to achieve this.

▽ Altars can provide a focus for poignant memories and remind us of the good in our lives.

RUNES AND THEIR MEANINGS

ᚠ FEOH: spiritual richness.

ᚢ UR: strength in a time of change.

ᚦ THORN: contemplation before action.

ᚩ ANSUR: messages and new opportunities.

ᚱ RAD: the wheel of life, a journey or quest.

ᚲ KEN: enlightenment and inspiration.

ᚷ GEOFU: a spiritual gift, love and partnership.

ᚹ WYNN: success and achievement.

ᚺ HAGALL: strength to face a challenge.

ᚾ NIED: need.

ᛁ IS: standstill, preparation before moving on.

ᛡ JARA: harvest, reward for past effort.

ᛇ EOH: transformation.

ᛈ PEORTH: choice, taking charge.

ᛉ ELHAZ: protection within.

ᛋ SIGEL: good fortune.

ᛏ TYR: dedication, perseverance.

ᛒ BEORC: new beginnings.

ᛖ EHWAZ: progress.

ᛗ MANN: destiny.

ᛚ LAGU: attunement to creation.

ᛜ ING: the inner spark.

ᛞ DAEG: the light.

ᛟ OTHEL: focus and freedom.

runes

The runes are a sacred writing system of northern Europe, which, according to legend, appeared to the god Odin during a shamanic initiation rite. They were his gift of knowledge to humanity, and they are empowered with ancient wisdom. Runes can be used as guides for meditation and divination, as protective talismans and in wishing ceremonies.

portable altars

Some people like to know that their personal altar is completely private to them. If you feel this way, you could arrange a beautiful small shrine inside a cupboard or box. A small wooden box makes a lovely altar, because you can lay out all your sacred things on the flat lid. It is also portable, so you can take it with you when travelling – especially useful if you are making a difficult trip and need spiritual support. Alternatively, when you leave home you could carry with you a crystal that you have programmed at your home altar (see *Rites and Ritual* at the end of this chapter).

△ **A portable altar kit can be an excellent idea if you are often on the move, and wish to carry the essence of your home with you.**

△ **Runes are used for spiritual guidance, and can also add a symbolic message to an altar.**

Candles and incense

Candles embody the positive symbolism of light as spiritual illumination, and the fragile candle flame is a powerful emblem of the individual soul, especially in a time of darkness and distress. Other lights, such as oil lamps and lanterns, can have a similar reassuring significance, and a perpetual flame on an altar stands for the constant presence of the divine.

Watching a lighted candle can be an aid to meditation and, like the candle flame, the fragrance of incense helps to focus the senses and calm chattering thoughts. Incense smoke has a symbolic status on the altar as an offering and is also used in ritual purification. It is an integral element of worship in many traditions.

altar candles

The lighting of candles is a simple ceremonial act that initiates and hallows ritual. It acts as an announcement of the intention to worship. In the Catholic church, a prescribed number of candles must be lit before

each mass, the number varying depending on the solemnity of the service. It is common practice to light a candle and leave it to burn out before the shrine of a saint as an act of devotion, symbolizing both prayer and sacrifice. Candles are also used to mark rites of passage, from baptism to funerals. Placed around a coffin, their light is believed to protect the dead from evil during the vulnerable time of transition.

The Christian use of altar candles was adopted from older traditions, and candles have been significant in religion and magic since the earliest times. The ancient Egyptians, who practised dream incubation, would sit in a cave staring at a candle flame until they saw a deity in it. When they went to sleep the deity would answer their question.

The feast of Candlemas at the beginning of February was grafted on to the pagan fire festival Imbolc. A traditional feature was the blessing of all the candles that were to be used in the church for the rest of the year.

△ **Candle-gazing can increase concentration, and can be helpful when focus is required**.

Candlemas is a time of purification and dedication, and is a good time to clean and rededicate an altar.

△ **Resins produce impressive clouds of fragrant smoke, infusing the environment with scent.**

△ **White candles represent purity and simplicity and can be used for any ceremony or ritual.**

COLOUR ASSOCIATIONS FOR CANDLES

WHITE: spiritual enlightenment, healing, peace and purity; can be substituted for any other colour for ritual use.

YELLOW: intelligence, communication, concentration, movement.

ORANGE: attraction, stimulation, strength, luck.

GOLD: understanding, confidence, prosperity, cosmic influences; honours solar deities.

PINK: harmony, nurturing, family, affection.

RED: energy, life, courage, passion.

VIOLET or PURPLE: spirituality, inner harmony, wisdom.

INDIGO: cleansing, meditation.

BLUE: wisdom, inspiration, truth, healing; honours lunar deities.

GREEN: love, nature, renewal, abundance.

BROWN: home, wealth, stability, older family members.

SILVER or GREY: secrets, compromise.

BLACK: conclusions; banishes guilt, regret and negativity.

magic and ritual

Traditional candle magic often involves writing the name of something you wish for on a piece of paper and then burning the paper in the candle flame, so that the wish is carried away in the smoke. In another candle charm, a symbol of the wish is engraved in the wax. As the candle burns down, the melted wax dripping down its

side may form an image to indicate how your wish might come true.

For ritual use, candles can be empowered by 'dressing' or anointing them with oil, to cleanse them of energies and influences from the past. The oil is wiped from the middle of the candle to the ends if the ritual aims to send energy out, or from the ends to the middle if the intention is to achieve or attract something.

In pagan tradition, the candle flame represents the element of fire, associated with life, creative energy and passion. Blowing candles out is said to be an affront to fire, and will have the effect of blowing away your intent or desire. It is best to let the candle burn down completely, although this is not always possible. Tibetan Buddhists consider that in blowing out a candle they are blowing away the breath of life, so pinch out the flame instead. For the same reason, incense sticks should be waved rather than blown before the altar.

incense

The burning of incense on the altar is a gentle form of offering, with its associations of purity and sweetness. It clears the sacred space of invasive thoughts and images, giving a feeling of peace and serenity. It allows your spirit to soar above the mundane.

Combustible incense, in the form of joss-sticks and cones, is readily available.

◁ Incense comes in many forms, from cones to loose herbs and resins. All the different scents have particular associations and symbolism.

Alternatively, mixtures of fragrant resins, herbs and spices can be bought or prepared at home for burning on a charcoal block. For this you will need an incense burner, preferably with a stand or feet to protect the altar. Line the burner with a layer of sand to stabilize it and insulate it further. Concentrate on your intent as you light the incense, so that it is charged with your positive thoughts and the scented smoke drifts upwards carrying your prayers with it.

There may be times when you prefer to scent your altar with more delicate fragrances than incense. You can use essential oils in an aromatherapy burner, natural pot pourri mixtures or scented flowers.

INCENSE ASSOCIATIONS

COPAL: for honouring the gods, cleansing, and to bless love.

FRANGIPANI: for the blessing of friendship and love.

FRANKINCENSE: for cleansing and blessing, banishing bad influences and enhancing insight.

HONEYSUCKLE: for healing and psychic power.

JASMINE: for increasing sensitivity and to bless meditation.

LOTUS: for clearing the mind.

MUSK: for courage and vitality.

MYRRH: for purifying and cleansing of negative thoughts.

PATCHOULI: for grounding, fertility, protection and prosperity.

PINE: for strength and reversal of negative energies.

ROSE: for emotional healing and the expression of feelings.

SANDALWOOD: for protection, healing, and granting of wishes.

VANILLA: for rejuvenation, love and mental concentration.

WHITE SAGE: for purifying and cleansing sacred space.

Rites and ritual

Setting up an altar at home is one step on your spiritual path, but the journey continues. Although your journey is an inward one, a sacred place serves as a reminder of the way. Each time you use it in personal ceremonies and rituals you strengthen the positive energy it holds for you.

If you share the altar with your partner or family, the occasions on which you come together for worship and ritual help to reinforce the bonds between you. Or you may think of your altar as a private and personal space, somewhere you can go when you are angry or upset to be quiet and restore your calm and inner strength. Use it to nourish your soul and help you unwind at the end of a tiring day. At difficult times of transition, use it as a support, and at times of peace, go to the altar to give thanks.

preparation

To prepare for your ceremonies, you should purify your sacred space by cleaning the room and clearing away clutter, and cleanse yourself so that you feel refreshed and energized. See that the altar is clean and free of dust, the flowers are fresh and candles new.

▽ Calming the mind with meditation helps to cope with stress, and builds inner strength.

△ Sage gets its name from *saga*, meaning 'wise woman', and burning it summons protection.

Burn some incense or white sage to clear away any negative energy from the area.

If you include crystals on your altar, cleanse them to clear past vibrations so that they become personal to you. You can do this in various ways: smoke is a gentle cleanser, or they can be placed in sunlight or moonlight, or washed in rain or spring water.

It is a good idea to devise a formal beginning for your time before the altar: light a candle or some incense to quieten your thoughts and prepare you to concentrate all your energy on the subject of your meditation or prayer. Focusing on deep, relaxed breathing helps to still your mind.

▽ Singing bowls can produce a variety of sound vibrations that touch the body with resonance.

◁ An offering of salt made to an earth goddess such as Gaia helps to build a close relationship with the earth.

▽ Mark the beginning or end of a ritual by ringing a bell or some chimes.

daily ritual

Greeting the morning with a small ritual is a positive way to start a new day, and doing this before an altar sanctifies the act. If you practise yoga, for instance, you can perform your salutations to the sun in your sacred space. The ritual will strengthen your spiritual bond with creation while the movements invigorate your body.

Remember that you can change the format of your worship freely, as your needs and ideas change: you are not just an observer, as in a formal religious ritual. You might wish to read a text that inspires you, or recite a poem that helps you express your emotions. Singing, striking a singing bowl, playing a musical instrument or listening to music could form part of your ritual.

prayer and meditation

If you are accustomed to saying daily prayers, or spending a particular period of time in meditation, your altar can become the focus of these regular practices. Prayer and meditation are complementary routes to spiritual development. As a request for help or guidance, or thanksgiving, prayer is active, while meditation is a passive exercise in contemplation, quietening the mind to increase its receptivity and allow the subconscious to surface.

Using an affirmation can help to focus your meditation. Create a thought that feels right to you: it needn't describe your present reality, but the reality you dream of. The affirmation is a way to make your dream real. Repeat the positive thought again and again, silently or aloud, to allow it to sink into your unconscious mind.

programming a crystal

You can use the energy of your affirmation to programme a crystal on your altar (choose one that has properties appropriate to your particular goal, such as rose quartz for love or citrine for abundance). Hold the crystal in both hands and gaze into it as you concentrate on your wish. Breathe deeply and each time you inhale repeat the affirmation and picture what you want. As you exhale, project your desire into the crystal. You can also write your wish on a piece of paper and leave it under the crystal.

If you are travelling, or when you go to work each day, keep the programmed crystal near you by carrying it in a small bag.

offerings

As part of your ceremony, place an offering on your altar as an expression of gratitude for the blessings of your life. Leaving a gift for another person on the altar for a while before you give it will endow it with positive energy and reinforce its value as a token of love. Adopt a way of closing your ceremony that you can repeat each time. Play a piece of music, say a farewell prayer, a thank you, or simply "amen", to give you a feeling of completion.

△ A prayer can be as simple as a few moments of silent communion with the spirit.

Altars of the Elements

The ideas that follow for establishing your personal altar are based on using the Four Elements as a starting point. By doing this you have a framework in which to express symbolism and communicate wishes and desires.

The element of air

Air is the element of life and breath – when we cease to breathe, life ends. Speediest and most ethereal of the elements, it rules the east, the direction of the sunrise. Because it is associated with the new day and with the freshness of the new year, air symbolizes new

▽ The fresh, fast-moving element of air helps us to disperse the clouds of ignorance and doubt.

beginnings, enterprise, infancy and the generative energy of the seed. It is creative, focused, aware.

In the form of wind, air may be a gentle, cooling breeze or it may have the destructive force of a hurricane. Its energy is projective. Because air is the element of the four winds, it governs movement and is associated with travel, freedom and new dis-

△ The air element corresponds with the east, the direction of the rising sun, and with the morning.

coveries. It is also the element of thought and ideas – the fresh, moving force of the open mind, of intellect and the imagination.

▽ Creatures of the air, birds symbolize the connection between earth and heaven.

▷ Use incense and yellow flowers and candles on your altar to symbolize the qualities of air.

Those in whom air is the dominant element are rational and analytical.

In daily life the areas governed by air include workplaces, offices, meeting rooms, schools and libraries, as well as places concerned with travel, such as railway stations and airports. It presides over the eastern quarter of a room or building. In the natural world, air's places are mountain tops, windy plains and clear or cloudy skies.

The power of the mind can include psychic ability, and air governs the arts of divination and visualization. It enhances positive thinking, allowing the mind to expand into wider realms, and to connect personal experience with the universal.

gods of the air

Deities associated with air are Shu, Thoth, Hermes and Mercury. Shu was the Egyptian god of the air who, with his consort Tefnut (the goddess of moisture), created the earth and sky. The Egyptian moon god Thoth was the sacred scribe of Osiris. As the god of wisdom, he was

endowed with secret knowledge. It was said that his book of magic contained spells that would give the user power over all the gods, and that between them his books contained all the wisdom of the world. He eventually became associated with the Greek god Hermes, the messenger of the Olympian gods, who could travel as fast as thought.

Hermes was versatile and changeable, eloquent and inventive, the personification of consciousness. His quick wits and slippery character made him the patron of thieves and merchants as well as travellers. His Roman equivalent was Mercury, whose cult spread widely among the Celtic and Germanic peoples of the Roman Empire. The latter identified him with Wotan or Odin, the god of speech, breath, wind, storm and magic. Mercury gave us the word 'mercurial' to describe a volatile, lively, quicksilver character. Invoke these deities to bless an altar with the energy of air.

THE ATHAME
Wiccans use this ritual knife to draw circles, control elemental spirits and direct energy during ceremonies. It has a dark handle and a double edge. It is seldom used for actual cutting, and would never be used as a weapon. It represents the masculine force on the altar.

AIR CORRESPONDENCES
DIRECTION: east.
SEASON: spring.
TIME: dawn.
MOON PHASE: new.
PLANETS: sun, Mercury, Uranus.
GENDER: masculine.
COLOURS: yellow and violet.
SENSES: hearing and smell.
MAGICAL TOOLS: wand, athame, sword.
INSTRUMENTS: wind instruments.
CREATURES: birds, winged insects.
NATURAL SYMBOLS: feathers, incense smoke, fragrant flowers.
TREES: elder, eucalyptus.
HERBS: comfrey, lavender, mint.
INCENSE: sandalwood, lemon.
MINERALS: mercury, aventurine, topaz.
SIGNS: Gemini, Libra, Aquarius.
ARCHANGEL: Raphael.

An altar for new beginnings

The most challenging times in life are those of transition. At moments when we are breaking with old customs and habits, or taking on new responsibilities, we need a boost to our self-confidence to stop us feeling uncertain, isolated or afraid. The established routines of our everyday lives have to be abandoned, and we may doubt our ability to meet a new challenge. We need to feel supported.

In traditional societies, the moment of setting out on a new chapter in life is invariably marked by some form of ritual that offers this kind of spiritual support, but in modern times many of the old ceremonies have been curtailed or lost. Others that do survive – such as weddings – have become so commercialized that their spiritual value can be hard to hold on to.

A simple ceremony at your altar will help you focus your thoughts and find the resolution to make a bold leap into the new. If you have just fallen in love you could be entering a new relationship that will be central to your whole future. If you are expecting a child the focus of your life is about to change radically. If you are moving house or starting a new job, you will be embarking on a series of new encounters and opportunities to shape your future.

△ The yellow triangle and violet circle both symbolize the air element.

◁ For new beginnings, such as the dawn of spring, yellow and violet flowers are ideal as they are the colours associated with a fresh start.

Sometimes the impetus towards a fresh start has to arise from sadder circumstances, such as divorce, children growing up and leaving home, or moving to a new area, away from people you love. At such times, the transition is one from grief and loss to healing and moving forward. The creative act of setting up an altar can be part of the process of transformation.

Invoke the element of air to inspire you with confidence and hope for a new beginning. Set your altar in the easterly quarter of a room, so that when you stand before it you are facing east, the direction of the sunrise. If possible, arrange it under a window so that it is bathed in the morning sunshine. Place a bell on the altar.

To symbolize new growth and natural energy you could add a vase of flowers: choose violet and yellow flowers, the colours of the air element, to help you focus your intent. Burn incense containing rosemary to clarify your thoughts. White candles represent new beginnings and clear vision.

◁ **The number three is associated with manifestations – ringing your bell three times will help to call new realities into your life.**

AN INCENSE MIXTURE FOR FOCUS

Incense is a tool of the air element, and will help to clarify your thoughts.
2 parts dried rosemary
1 part dried thyme
1 part lemongrass
Few drops rosemary essential oil

Pound all the dry ingredients together using a pestle and mortar, then add the essential oil. Mix the oil in well with your fingertips. Burn a few pinches of incense on the altar, using a charcoal block.

ritual for a new start

The time of the waxing moon is the period between the new and the full moon, when the half moon can be seen in the sky during the first part of the night. This is the

▽ **Burn a pinch or two of incense in the morning to cleanse your mind for the day ahead.**

time of new beginnings, and during this period you can perform a simple ritual to help you approach the next part of your life with confidence. As you meditate before your altar, focus on your hopes and wishes for the future. Write these down on a piece of yellow paper cut into a triangle, and lay the triangle on a larger violet or blue circlet of paper or cloth on the altar.

Place the bell on top of the piece of paper. Each morning of the period of the waxing moon – as near sunrise as possible – come to the altar and ring the bell three times as you visualize your hopes and wishes being realized and achieved.

THE SEASON OF NEW BEGINNINGS

The pagan festival of Ostara is celebrated at the Vernal Equinox, around 21 March in the northern hemisphere and 23 September in the southern hemisphere, when day and night are of equal length and the sun begins its ascendancy: a time of balance and regeneration. Ostara signals the return of spring and is a festival of new life and fertility. This is the time to plant seeds and initiate new plans. An altar to celebrate Ostara could be decorated with spring flowers and herbs: celandine, daffodil, primroses, violets, sage, tansy and thyme. Yellow and green candles represent clear focus, optimism and new growth.

An altar for meditation

Creating a personal altar in a garden is a rewarding way to acknowledge our connection with nature, and provides a tranquil space for quiet thought and meditation. It can be a breathing space, both literally and metaphorically, where the freshness of the breeze, the scent of leaves and flowers and the sound of birds inspire us with a sense of gratitude and awareness.

Meditation is a way of focusing the mind, stilling the endless mental chatter that distracts us from concentrated thought. It is not a way of escaping from the reality of our everyday responsibilities. It increases awareness and enables us to live fully in each moment with contentment and serenity.

According to Zen Buddhism, the practice of gardening is itself an active form of meditation. The size of the garden is not important: the message of Zen is that the large can be experienced in the small, and

▽ **Taking a little time with your designs helps the mind become relaxed and centred.**

△ **The patterns you create in your miniature Zen garden will contain potent messages to and from your subconscious, and will help to integrate your inner and outer worlds.**

the meaning of the whole world can be seen in a grain of sand. The garden is the universe in microcosm. The concept can be adapted to your own garden, where you can fashion a serene space for meditation with stones, gravel and moss, inspired by the temple gardens of Japan.

gardens of contemplation

Respect for nature and a sense of connectedness with natural cycles are basic tenets of Zen Buddhist thought. Zen arrived in Japan from China in the 11th century, and its emphasis on contemplation and tranquillity found a natural counterpart in the Japanese love of simplicity. Buddhist monks applied the concepts of Zen to their daily

▷ Once you are satisfied with the patterns you have made, move on to your meditation.

lives, and designed their living quarters and gardens in accordance with them, producing simple, peaceful spaces for meditation in perfect accord with nature.

Zen gardens are often conceived as miniature re-creations of natural scenes, such as mountains and forests. Composed of simple elements such as moss, leaves, stones and water, they are timeless havens of silent contemplation. Paths meander, and a stream may be crossed by a zig-zagging 'eightfold' bridge, forcing the visitor to move slowly and appreciate each vista.

In a 'dry' garden, a natural scene is recreated without water. The rocks are arranged with artful judgement to appear as if naturally strewn in beds of pale gravel, which is carefully raked. The elements of such a garden are symbolic: the stones represent the great age of the universe, and the swirling patterns in the gravel imitate the river flowing around them. Some stones lie hidden or partly buried in the gravel, so that the eye is led down beneath the surface, just as in meditation Buddhists look within themselves to seek enlightenment.

Symbols also abound in the plants that grow in Japanese gardens, and these ideas can be used to enhance the significance of elements in your own outdoor sacred space. Evergreen pines, for example, stand for longevity, and the fleeting, delicate plum blossom that appears in the cold of early spring is a symbol of courage.

FORM AND EMPTINESS

The serenity of a Zen garden has an almost hypnotic effect, and you can use its combination of form and emptiness as a starting point for a meditation. When you have worked on your Zen garden, and created a pattern that springs from your inner consciousness, sit back and contemplate it. Empty your mind of its clutter and confusion and absorb the simplicity and peace of the natural forms in front of you.

a miniature zen garden

You can create a garden on a miniature scale, following the ideas of Zen, on a wooden platter or tray. The process of creating and working in the garden itself becomes a form of meditation, helping to soothe the mind and reduce stress.

Fill the tray with sand or fine gravel, and arrange some groups of beautiful pebbles in it. The stones you use could be found anywhere: in the street, in the park, on the beach. Once you begin to look at them properly you will be amazed at their beauty and form. Gazing on the stones you choose for your garden – all of them millions of years old – may prompt you to see your life in a new perspective.

You may decide to make your garden entirely with sand and pebbles. This art of gardening is called *bonseki* in Japan, and is the 'dry' equivalent of bonsai. Or you can add fresh flowers or small plants to represent living natural forms. Use a stick or a small rake to create spirals and circles in the sand around the stones and plants. These patterns can be smoothed away and redrawn whenever you come to the garden: they evoke the fluidity of the present moment and the impermanence of human life.

Try to dedicate a few moments a day to contemplation. Even if your time for meditation is short, the garden can become a small oasis of peace and quiet where you can find some spiritual freedom.

An altar for motivation

We are all motivated by many different things: physical and emotional drives, the need to survive, self-satisfaction and pleasure, our values, interests and ambitions, rewards, fears and established habits. Often the different influences that press upon us oppose each other in confusing and defeating ways. It's very easy to spend too much time and energy on activities that seem urgent but aren't really important. Instead we need to concentrate on the issues that may not seem so urgent, but are actually much more important to us, such as clarifying what we want our lives to be, fostering good relationships with others, and preserving our health by exercising, eating properly and getting enough rest.

Motivation comes with feeling capable, self-directed and hopeful, and challenging and positive goals are motivating in themselves. Pinning your hopes on impossible dreams, on the other hand, simply becomes frustrating: deep down you know you will not succeed, so you build in the idea of failure before you begin.

It's important to set goals that are achievable but that stretch your capabilities: this is a fine balance and needs careful thought –

◁ Choose incense ingredients that mirror and magnify your intent or goal.

△ Orange or yellow flowers on your motivation altar will inspire creative thinking.

about what you really want to do, and about yourself. You have to listen to your inner voice, and face honestly how you are feeling about a situation: sometimes an apparent lack of motivation conceals anxiety about beginning a difficult task. Once you acknowledge that you are fearful it is easier to face up to your fear and see the problem objectively. Break a seemingly impossible task down into tiny steps and do the first one – once you've started, the next step ceases to feel so momentous.

Lack of motivation can often stem from simple fatigue. If you're feeling frantic, don't be afraid to take a break. Stand back from

your situation and re-organize it. However busy you are, make time for exercise, proper meals and sleep. Don't wear yourself out meeting other people's expectations if they are unreasonable.

moving forward

Making an altar invites change into your life. It is a positive statement that you intend to focus your inner resources and move forward. With most of the things that we find difficult, the hardest part of all is beginning: the creation of an altar is an act of faith that gets you started and underlines the seriousness of your endeavours. The altar is a

229

◁ **When you are setting your goals, include only those that you can realistically expect to meet.**

INCENSE FOR MOTIVATION

2 parts cinnamon
2 parts frankincense grains
1 part nutmeg
1 part allspice
1 part ginseng
1 part juniper berries
Few drops frankincense essential oil

Pound all the dry ingredients with a pestle and mortar, then add the essential oil. Burn a few grains at a time on a charcoal block.

tangible expression of your intent to set aside time to evaluate your dreams and wishes. As a place where you can contemplate your life, it will help you to set worthwhile goals and to achieve them.

As air is the element of the intellect and the imagination, of dreams and ideas, its influence is important in an altar dedicated to motivation. When you feel sluggish and unable to get going, visualize a fresh breeze blowing away the cobwebs of your mind, bringing clear thought and inspiration. Add a little fire to your altar, too, to inspire you with drive and creativity. Fire is the element of change and helps to break old habits.

Your altar for motivation should sparkle with energy and light. Place it in a sunny window so that when you come to it in the morning the freshness and beauty of the new day greet you and fill you with optimism. If possible, use the windowsill as the altar, and on fine days open the window to let in the morning air.

Choose a beautiful, shimmering piece of fabric, such as a length of organza shot with gold, to use as an altar cloth, and decorate the altar with yellow and orange flowers. Yellow candles will help you to concentrate single-mindedly on your goals. Include an incense burner on which you can sprinkle a few grains each morning. Your altar ritual can include reviewing the achievements of the previous day and writing out your list of goals for the forthcoming day.

A TIMETABLE FOR ACHIEVEMENT

Planning your day effectively helps you to stay in control, which increases motivation. It also helps you to decide on priorities. Get into the habit of making weekly and daily schedules that are based on realistic goals, rather than a wish list that is impossible to achieve. Set clear starting and stopping times for work sessions, with proper breaks. Include plenty of time for rest and recreation, and allow some flexibility for unforeseen demands.

The element of fire

△ The turbulent, uncontrollable energy of lava illustrates fire's governance over the passions.

Fire is both creative and destructive. It can cleanse and purify, but it consumes: it is the only one of the four elements that cannot exist without feeding on something else. It creates warm, welcoming homes and cooks our food, but it is dangerous and can get out of control. It has the power to transform everything it touches.

Fire rules the south, the direction of the sun's fiercest heat (in the northern hemi-sphere), and it is related to motivation, creativity and passion. Its energy is quick-acting, forceful and positive and its power can be frightening. It symbolizes the inner child, the spirit within and the creative spark. Because it is the element of the passions, it gives courage and strength to fight for faith and quality of life. Those in whom it is dominant are passionate and intense. Fire consumes obstacles to faith and trust, and banishes negativity.

Areas governed by fire are kitchens, fire-places and boiler rooms, gyms and athletics fields, and creative spaces such as studios and playrooms. Fire presides over the southern quarter of a room or building. In the nat-ural world, its places are deserts, hot springs and volcanoes.

Fire governs the sense of sight, it also inspires the need to offer and accept the power of touch. It is the element of physi-cal challenge, sensation and sexual energy. It celebrates life.

▽ Fire can be dangerous and destructive, but it may burn away obstacles to new growth.

FIRE METAL

One of the fire metals, iron, is found on earth in its pure form only in meteorites. It is present in our blood, and is essential for physical energy and clear thinking. Wearing it as a talisman is said to increase physical strength. In some cultures, an iron talisman is worn as protec-tion against evil or negative energy: for this reason Sikhs wear an iron or steel bangle called a *kara* on their right wrist at all times.

▷ The lighting of a candle on the altar is a simple act that initiates ceremony as well as honouring the element of fire.

gods and goddesses of fire

Some of the deities associated with fire are Re, Sekhmet, Apollo and Lugh.

Re was worshipped by the ancient Egyptians as their pre-eminent solar deity. As a creator god, he brought order out of chaos – from his tears, the first human beings were formed. He was born each morning and journeyed across the sky in his solar boat, entering the underworld each night to do battle with the cosmic serpent, Apep. 'Son of Re' was one of the titles bestowed on the pharaoh. Re's daughter was the sun goddess Sekhmet, 'the Powerful One', who was usually portrayed with the head of a lioness. Re sent Sekhmet as his 'Eye', the terrible burning power of the sun, to punish the wickedness of humankind, but at the last moment saved his creation from total destruction by diverting Sekhmet's frenzied rage. Sekhmet was the terrifying aspect of Hathor, the goddess of joy and maternal love.

In Greek mythology, the sun was guided across the sky by Apollo, who also represents light, truth and clarity. He was the god of medicine and of music, and was the patron of the nine Muses, the embodiments of the creative imagination. The Celtic sky-god Lugh was a deity of the sun and the weather, and his spear is sometimes seen as a fork of lightning. As the god of skills and arts, he could be honoured by an offering of a creative work. The pagan summer festival of Lughnasadh, celebrated at the beginning of the harvest, is held in his name. Invoke these deities to bless an altar with the energy of fire.

▽ The lion is a universal symbol of strength and courage. Medieval alchemists also used it to represent transformation through fire.

FIRE CORRESPONDENCES

DIRECTION: south.
SEASON: summer.
TIME: midday.
MOON PHASE: first quarter.
PLANETS: Mars, Pluto.
GENDER: masculine.
COLOURS: red and orange.
SENSE: sight.
MAGICAL TOOLS: candles, lanterns, solar icons, wand.
INSTRUMENTS: stringed instruments.
CREATURES: dragon, snake, lion, ram, phoenix.
NATURAL SYMBOLS: flame, lava.
TREES: oak, hawthorn.
HERBS: basil, bay, garlic, hyssop, juniper, rosemary, rue.
INCENSE: frankincense, cinnamon, basil.
MINERALS: brass, gold, iron, fire opal, garnet, hematite, red jasper, sardonyx, flint.
SIGNS: Aries, Leo, Sagittarius.
ARCHANGEL: Michael.

An altar for creativity

Assembling a personal altar is a wonderful act of self-expression, and is in itself a creative act. Dedicating the altar to creativity recognizes and honours your powers of invention and originality. It is a very positive way to affirm your own talent. If you dream of a creative endeavour but have not dared to pursue it for fear that you will fail, bringing your dreams to your altar can help to dispel your inhibitions.

The spirit of creation flows through every one of us. We may describe it as divine inspiration, chi, life force or quintessence, but it is the energy that we put into everything we create – whether that thing is a sculpture, a letter or a meal. No narrow definitions apply here: creativity should not be confined to writing, painting or other 'artistic' pursuits. It is important for everything we do to be approached creatively, giving spiritual value to even the most mundane tasks.

inspiration

To inspire literally means to 'breathe into', and the ancient Greek poets, whose word it is, would invoke one of the nine Muses to inspire them. They saw themselves as channels through which the divine voice could be heard. As a focus of positive energy,

△ The creative altar should be filled with colours of the rainbow, inviting variety, vibrancy and colour into your own world as a result.

▽ Focus your creative altar by adding elements that symbolize your own artistic endeavour in your chosen field.

◁ Displaying items associated with babies may help someone who is eager to conceive.

▽ If you are expecting a baby, give expression to your hopes and dreams for your child at the altar.

the altar is a place to tune into the creative spirit and call on it to inspire us.

In addition to inspiration, the creative process demands hard work, discipline, judgement and the courage to make mistakes and learn from them. At the altar we can find the motivation to acquire the skills we need to express ourselves. In our own sacred space we can leave behind the limits of self-consciousness, so that our open minds attract fresh ideas like magnets, faster than they can be expressed. It is in this state of intuitive awareness – a form of meditation – that creativity flows.

creating the altar

Make your altar a thing of shimmering beauty to awaken your senses and fill you with the joy of creation. Dress it with a rainbow of colour and let its flamboyance give you the confidence to express yourself in other ways as you have here. The objects you choose to put on it can reflect whichever creative opportunities you want to explore, such as brushes and paints for artistic endeavour, or pens and paper if you are searching for the courage to express yourself in writing. Use this special place to try out your dreams, and bring your own creations to beautify your altar.

an altar for fertility

The most profound act of creation is that of new life itself. If you are trying to have a baby, the energy of your creativity altar can be devoted to your desire to conceive. Some of the world's most ancient altars were erected for this purpose, celebrating the fertility of the earth and of women with the element of fire, the spark of life.

If this is the special purpose of your altar, include on it objects that speak of abundance and new growth, such as seeds and flowers, and add some beautiful images of parenthood and babies. You could also include a figure of the great Goddess to ally yourself with her fertile power.

IMBOLC: THE LIGHT OF INSPIRATION

The festival of the return of light is at the beginning of February, and honours the Celtic triple goddess Brigid, a fire deity, celebrating her union with the god of light. It is a time of inspiration and creativity, when rituals are performed to bless new love, fertility, and the planning of new projects. Imbolc is predominantly a female festival, and Brigid blesses women's self-expression and creativity.

At this season, the goddess is honoured in her maiden aspect as the patron of inspiration and poetry. By tradition, if a white cloth is left outside overnight at Imbolc, the goddess will bless it with inspiration.

THE FULL MOON

When the moon is full, its energy is opposed to that of the sun as they are on opposite sides of the earth, and the moon rises as the sun sets. The time of the full moon is therefore a period of high potency. It is the best time for rituals at the altar to encourage fertility, passion and abundance. In ancient times, women would rise before dawn on the day of the full moon and go into the fields. There they would wash themselves in the morning dew, asking the moon to bless them with children.

An altar for positive outcomes

It has long been acknowledged that if you have a clear idea of what you want you are far more likely to achieve it. Thought is a form of energy, and positive thinking contributes energetically to the fulfilment of your desire. Just as an artist has an idea that leads to the creation of a work of art, ideas are the first step to creating your future.

You should begin by thinking clearly about what you want. This is an effective way to make things happen, rather than simply allowing them to happen to you. Ideas, thoughts and wishes are running through our minds all day, but often we hardly give our-selves the chance to hold on to them before they disappear. Voicing such thoughts in a conscious way harnesses their energy to help us work towards their successful fulfilment.

When you are facing a challenging situation it is easy to focus on all the difficulties that might arise and to become preoccupied with the chance of failure. While it's important to have a realistic idea of what you are facing, the negative energy created by worry and fear can be paralysing. You may spend more time identifying all that could go wrong than in constructing a detailed and positive image of the outcome you want. A daily ceremony at your altar helps to focus your energy on what you want to happen.

The life-affirming qualities of an altar dedicated to the element of fire will support you and give you the courage to achieve success. Place on your altar images that symbolize courage and strength, such as a lion, a picture of a great oak tree or an object made of its wood. An image of the Archangel Michael would invoke his aid: he is the angel of fire and prince of the sun, who assists in matters of achievement and ambition.

▽ **Use orange candles and images of strength and power on an altar to ensure success.**

▽ **Invoke the aid of the Archangel Michael on your fire altar by lighting a candle in front of his image. The image of a lion is also a potent one for a fire altar.**

HERBS AND SPICES FOR SUCCESS

BASIL: gives protection, repels negativity and brings wealth. Leaves carried in the pocket bring luck in gambling, scattered on a shop floor they bring business success.

BERGAMOT: attracts success and prosperity. Rubbing the oil on money before it is spent will ensure the return of riches; the leaves in a purse attract money.

CINNAMON: draws money, protection and success.

CLOVE: banishes any hostile or negative forces and helps to gain whatever is sought.

VERVAIN: attracts money, protection; transforms enemies into friends.

△ **When burning a wish it is vital to ensure that the paper is completely burnt to ashes.**

TURQUOISE: THE LUCKY STONE

A popular amulet, turquoise has many protective qualities. It is said to guard its owner against ill-health and poverty, and to guarantee success in any field. The Aztecs tied turquoises to their weapons to make them more effective in battle. It attracts new friends, brings joy and increases beauty. As a gift, it bestows wealth and happiness on the receiver.

a ceremony for success

Use an orange candle for your ritual, because orange is the colour of ambition, goals and success. It has the power to draw good things to it and to change luck. Anoint the candle with oil to charge it with your personal vibrations and make the ceremony more effective. Using a few drops of bergamot essential oil, wipe the candle from the base to the middle and then from the wick to the middle – concentrate on your desire as you do this so that it is transmitted to the candle, and hold the candle so that you make the strokes towards your body, expressing drawing success towards you.

Place the candle in the centre of the altar. Arrange basil leaves around its base like the rays of the sun, and use cloves to make a spiral pattern around the candle, symbolizing growth and energy. (Knocking anything over on the altar might make you feel less confident of success, so avoid this mischance by arranging everything carefully.)

As you stand before the altar and light the candle, focus all your thoughts on achieving the result you desire. You can also write down your wish on a piece of paper, fold it twice and leave it under the candle. Or burn the paper in the candle flame so that the wish is carried away on the smoke, all the time thinking clearly about what you want. Empowered by your magical efforts, you can follow them up with practical strategies to achieve the right outcome.

An altar to the sun

The sun is a central symbol of creative energy, and has been an object of worship since the earliest times. The ancients recognized that without the sun, there would be no life. It is the giver of light, heat and fire: as light, it symbolizes knowledge and truth, and as heat and fire it stands for vitality and passion. In Celtic belief, fire was thought to have been brought to earth from the sun by a sacred bird – a swallow, swift or wren.

The sun provides the rhythmic structure of life on earth. It governs the seasons' annual cycle and controls our biological rhythms as we wake and sleep each day. We are creatures of the light. Even in the modern world where we can switch on artificial light and heat whenever we need it, we still

▽ Use herbs and spices that reflect and evoke heat on your solar altar.

△ Gold is the colour and metal of the male in its purest form and is offered to all sun deities.

suffer both physically and mentally if we are deprived of natural daylight for any length of time. When we talk of having a place in the sun, we are describing an enviable position where we can develop and grow, just as plants flourish in the sunlight.

deities of the sun

In most traditions, the sun is associated with the male principle, though in archaic times it was perceived as an aspect of the great mother goddess. One example of a surviving female sun deity is the beautiful sun goddess of Shintoism, Amaterasu-o-mi-kami, ruler of the high plains of heaven, who wove the fabric of the universe in her sacred weaving hall. The Arunta people of Australia recount the myth of the sun woman Yhi. Germanic and Norse tribes revered Sunna, and the Celtic sun goddess

CATS IN THE SUN

The Egyptian goddess Bastet, the daughter of Re, was first worshipped as a solar deity who represented the sun's life-giving warmth. After about 1000 BC she was portrayed with the head of a cat, perhaps because of that animal's fondness for basking in sunshine. Bastet was generally a benevolent and protective goddess of love and fertility, and cats were venerated in her name.

The whole cat family is identified with the sun and the element of fire. Michael, the angel of the sun, can be called upon if a cat is in need of help. If you have a cat, you may notice it responding to the energy of your altar, and sleeping there.

Sul was adopted by the Romans, who dedicated altars over the sacred spring at Bath to Sulis Minerva.

In patriarchal societies, the sun became a male deity. Re, the Egyptian sun god, was revered as the creator of the world, whose tears engendered humanity. The Egyptians believed that Re would one day tire of his creation and return the world to chaos; therefore he had to be placated by their worship to safeguard the future of the cosmos. But they also looked to him for fatherly protection, and his regular daily progress across the sky was evidence of the celestial order that kept them safe.

The rayed sun-disc is an important symbol in many religions, and is related to the wheel of existence. For Zoroastrians, the winged sun-disc is the manifestation of Ahura Mazda, the supreme embodiment of light and goodness. In Christian imagery, a halo of golden rays surrounds the heads of the blessed, and Jesus is described as the 'light of the world'. In the Roman Empire, Jesus inherited the role of Mithras, god of light and emblem of invincible resurrection.

solar symbols

An altar dedicated to the blessings of light and the fiery energy of the sun needs to stand in the southern quarter of a room. Dress it with the colours of sunlight: a sparkling golden cloth, orange and yellow flowers and citrus fruits. Sunday is the day of the sun, and the ideal time for a special ritual is on this day, at noon, when the sun is at its zenith. Kneel in front of your altar, raise your arms in a salute to the sun at the height of its cycle and draw in its energy and power. This is a time for vigour and self-reliance, and for fostering creative energy.

On every day of the week, light a gold or orange candle each morning to represent the light of the divine presence, and make offerings of saffron, turmeric and rosemary. You may choose to call on the power of a sun deity: Apollo for creativity and harmony, or Vishnu, the protector of the world. Or ask for the intercession of the Archangel Michael, the prince of the sun.

▷ **To invoke the power of the sun into yourself is to draw in the light of life.**

The element of water

Water is the element of love and the emotions, because it is as fluid as our feelings. It rules friendship and marriage. It also relates to the subconscious mind, constantly shifting and active beneath the surface, and this element therefore governs intuition. It influences sleep and dreaming, as we sink down into the swirling depths of the subconscious to discover our deepest desires.

The moon tugs at the oceans of the world to create the tides, which follow her

▽ The moon is the ruler of the water element, creating the tides and influencing human moods.

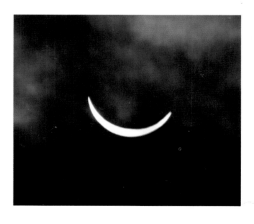

ever-changing cycle. She exerts the same pull on the fluids in our bodies, affecting our emotions, menstrual cycles and health. Thus the ebb and flow of water is mirrored in the cycles of our own lives.

The energy of water is feminine and receptive. It rules the west, the direction of the setting sun. Water is an element of purification and healing: this can take the form of healing counsel leading to emotional release, sweeping away stale feelings and inducing us to face the truth about ourselves. People dominated by water are sensitive and spiritual. It is cleansing and essential to life, and our own lives begin in water. The element is thus symbolized by the womb and is related to fertility.

Areas of the home ruled by water are the bathroom and the kitchen sink. Because it presides over friendship and relationships, it also governs the living room, the arena of social interaction. In its cleansing and healing role water is also the element of medical rooms and hospitals. In the natural world its places are seas, lakes, rivers, marshes, pools, wells and rain-drenched lands.

△ Water may be cleansing and soothing, but it also possesses frightening, unstoppable power.

▽ Though fluid and changeable, water has the power to overcome obstacles in its path. Over time it carves its way through the hardest rock.

◁ **Like ripples on a calm pond, our moods and emotions spread out to affect those around us.**

Neptune, the Roman god of the sea, was revered by seafarers whom he generally protected, but they feared his temper: his mood could change in an instant, giving rise to perilous ocean storms. Venus, the archetype of love and beauty, was said to have been created from the foam of the sea, and to have been carried on a sea shell to Cyprus. As she stepped from the sea, drops of water that fell from her body turned into pearls at her feet. The goddess had the power to calm the sea and ensure safe voyages, just as she could bring balance and harmony to human instincts and emotions.

Epona was a Celtic horse goddess worshipped during the period of the Roman Empire. She was portrayed carrying fruit or corn to show her connection with fertility and the earth's abundance. She was also a goddess of water and healing, and was the presiding deity of healing springs.

Invoke these deities to bless an altar with the energy of water.

WATER CORRESPONDENCES

DIRECTION: west.
SEASON: autumn.
TIME: dusk.
MOON PHASE: full.
PLANETS: moon, Neptune, Venus.
GENDER: feminine.
COLOURS: blue and orange.
SENSE: taste.
MAGICAL TOOLS: chalice, cauldron, mirror.
INSTRUMENTS: cymbals and bells.
CREATURES: cat, frog, turtle, dolphin, whale, otter, seal, fish.
NATURAL SYMBOLS: shells, water, river plants, watercress.
TREES: willow, alder, ash.
HERBS: chamomile, hops, lemon balm, orris, seaweeds, yarrow.
INCENSE: jasmine, rose.
MINERALS: silver, copper, amethyst, aquamarine, turquoise, tourmaline, opal, jade, pearl, sapphire, moonstone.
SIGNS: Cancer, Scorpio, Pisces.
ARCHANGEL: Gabriel.

gods and goddesses of water

Deities associated with water are Tiamat, Venus, Neptune and Epona. Tiamat represents chaos and the raw energy of the salt ocean. In Mesopotamian mythology, she was the primeval mother whose waters mingled with the fresh water of Apsu to initiate the creation of the gods.

▽ **The dolphin is an animal of the water element, and symbolizes understanding and awareness.**

An altar for healing

The home altar can be a source of healing for physical, emotional or spiritual problems. If you are in need of healing, call on the divine spirit to help you focus healing energies on yourself. Seek the wisdom to listen to your body and work in harmony with it to restore it to wholeness. If another person who is dear to you is suffering in some way, ask for help on their behalf.

Enlist the aid of the cleansing energy of water by setting an altar for healing in the west, and stand facing west to make your offerings or to say prayers. Make the altar a vision of pure watery beauty, fresh with the colour blue and decorated with flowers such as jasmine, lilies, lotus, iris or poppies, or with water-smoothed pebbles, shells, seaweed or watercress. Choose sandalwood incense, which is associated with purification and healing, or the cool, cleansing scents of camphor or eucalyptus.

If someone is receiving treatment in hospital, a small altar can be very comforting. You can simply arrange a blue shawl or scarf on a windowsill or side table, where it can be seen easily from the bed. Place on it images of wholeness and health, perhaps with some beautiful white flowers or other natural forms that speak of the vibrancy of the world that waits outside to be enjoyed.

A healing ceremony will be most effective during the time of a waning moon – particularly in the four days following the full moon. This is the time when things can be cast away or released, including grief and anger. To perform a healing ceremony on behalf of someone who is ill, light two blue candles on the altar and present a bowl of clear spring water as an offering.

Ask for the healing help of Archangel Gabriel, or Ceridwen, the white goddess of the Celts, or appeal to the compassion of

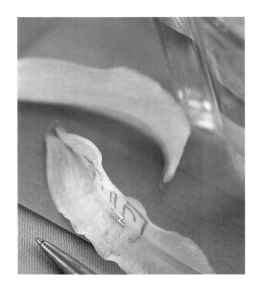

△ Write the names of people to whom you wish to send healing on the petals of white flowers.

▽ Set up a healing altar by someone's bedside to offer solace and beauty when spirits are low.

▷ When you are sending healing thoughts,

HEALING CRYSTALS

AMBER: relieves depression.

AMETHYST: protects against weakness of the immune system, calms fear and defeats insomnia.

AVENTURINE: soothes the emotions and promotes balance and well being.

BLOODSTONE: calms in threatening situations; detoxifies the blood.

CARNELIAN: increases physical energy and power.

CHRYSOCOLLA: assists in the release of grief, worry and pain.

CHRYSOPRASE: helps to relieve tension and stress.

CLEAR QUARTZ: a powerful talisman for healing, known in many cultures as the 'all-healer'. It guards against loss of vitality and strength and draws out pain, raises self-esteem, balances emotions and increases insight.

GARNET: protects against depression; boosts sexuality and fertility.

HEMATITE: protects against negativity, may be helpful for jet lag.

JET: dispels irrational fear and guards against illness.

LABRADORITE: heals co-dependence and instils courage and clarity.

LODESTONE/MAGNETITE: balances the body, relieves the pain of arthritis.

MALACHITE: releases trauma, relieves depression, acts against negativity.

ROSE QUARTZ: comforts and heals, enhances cardiovascular health.

TOURMALINE: relieves stress.

Kuanyin, the Buddhist goddess of mercy. Using a silver pen, write the name of the person and their ailment on white paper or white flower petals, and float them on the water. Place a clear quartz crystal in the water, and hold a second crystal in your hands while voicing your prayer, so that it transmits the healing power. Visualize the ailment being lifted out of the sufferer and give thanks for their recovery.

THE GODDESS OF COMPASSION

Chinese worshippers flock to the shrines of Kuanyin to seek her favour, because they believe she can cure almost every sickness and alleviate every distress. Her image stands on many family altars in the East.

Kuanyin's name means 'One who sees and hears the cries of the whole world'. She carries a vial containing the dew of compassion, and cures the seriously ill by sprinkling a few drops on their heads. While the birthdays of the gods are usually celebrated with firecrackers to ward off evil, there are no explosions for Kuanyin because she is so pure that no evil would dare approach her.

◁ Place a quartz crystal in a bowl of water and hold another while you are sending your prayers: the crystal will transmit the healing.

A lunar altar

The moon presides over the deep mysteries of our inner world, and is especially the guardian of women. As the appearance of the moon changes from crescent, full and waning to dark, it exerts its gravitational force on the waters of the earth, creating the tides and affecting the pattern of the weather. We, who are creatures of water, are also subject to its sway. The moon has always been an object of wonder.

In the moon's periodic growth and decay, the ancients saw an echo of the seasonal patterns of their lives. As it seemed to be reborn each month, the moon was widely believed to be the abode of human souls awaiting rebirth. But while the sun, rising each morning without fail, represented the stability of the cosmos, the moon appeared changeable and dangerous. It ruled the weather and could raise floods and storms,

PHASES OF MOON MAGIC

NEW/CRESCENT MOON (days 1–2): new opportunities, health and personal growth.

1st quarter

WAXING PHASE (days 1–7, active time, days 3–7): expansion, development and motivation; associated with Artemis.

2nd quarter

HALF TO FULL MOON (days 8–14, active time, days 12–14): fertility, abundance, illumination; associated with Isis, Selene, Arianrhod.

3rd quarter

WANING PHASE (days 15–21, active time, days 15–18): release, insight, wisdom, healing; associated with Hecate, Angel Gabriel.

4th quarter

DARK PHASE (days 22–29/30): meditation and preparation, time of no action; associated with Hecate, Cybele, Ceridwen.

△ Use lunar gemstones, clear crystals and lunar images to dedicate your altar to the moon.

but it also brought life-giving rain: it was both creative and destructive, and lunar deities shared this duality. The Mayan goddess Ixchel, for instance, was a vengeful goddess of storms, but also a protector of women in childbirth.

phases of the moon

Each phase of the moon's cycle came to be personified distinctly, as aspects of the 'triple goddess' or 'great mother' – maiden, mother and crone (or wise elder). The Greeks, for example, worshipped Artemis as the new moon, Selene as the full moon and Hecate as the waning and dark moon. These archetypal figures have appeared in the pantheons

▷ Blue and orange are the colours of the water element, ruled by the moon.

▷ Your lunar altar will help you to connect with the energy of moon deities, as you light a candle in their honour.

LUNAR GODDESSES

ARIANRHOD: the Celtic mother goddess and keeper of the silver wheel of stars, symbolizing time and fate.

ARTEMIS: the Greek goddess of the waxing moon and of wild places, defender of women; invoked by women in childbirth. Her Roman equivalent is Diana.

CERIDWEN: the Welsh mother, moon and grain goddess whose cauldron contains a potion for the gifts of inspiration and knowledge.

SELENE: the Greek goddess of the full moon, who rides in a chariot pulled by two white horses and presides over magic. Her Roman equivalent is Luna.

HECATE: the powerful three-headed Greek goddess of the waning moon, who rules magic, sorcery, death and the underworld.

ISIS: the Egyptian mother goddess, who governs magic, fertility and regeneration.

SOPHIA: the female representation of the holy spirit who stands for divine knowledge and wisdom.

CYBELE: the Phrygian dark moon goddess who governs nature, wild beasts and dark magic.

of many cultures, as their characteristics have been adapted and absorbed.

Although the Gregorian calendar is based on solar time, older calendars are calculated according to lunar cycles, and the moon determines the dates of many major religious festivals. The lunar cycle is celebrated by pagans at ceremonies known as 'full moon esbats', which celebrate the Goddess in all her forms.

lunar ceremonies

The full moon is the time for ceremonies to 'draw down the moon', connecting with the energy of the deity to empower wishes and ask for blessings for others. Write your wishes for them with a silver pen and burn them in a candle flame.

Setting up an altar to the full moon can help with emotional balance, bringing peace and harmony in your relationships. Decorate the altar with a light blue cloth and images of the moon or her deities. Use silver or light blue candles, jasmine, lilies or water-loving flowers, and burn jasmine or sandalwood incense. Moonstones, pearls, aquamarine and clear crystals are all associated with the moon, and will help to focus lunar energy on your altar.

TOTEM ANIMALS OF THE MOON

BEAR: sacred to Diana, goddess of the new moon, and connected with dreams, meditation and intuition.

CAT: associated with the night and the lunar goddess Artemis, it represents the mystery of the moon.

COW: sacred to Isis, who is crowned with her horns; milk is considered to be one of the gifts of the moon.

FROG: brings cleansing rain and is also a lunar fertility symbol.

HARE: represents the cycles of the moon and is associated with fertility. Indian and Chinese myths tell of the 'hare in the moon' and Eostre, the Anglo-Saxon goddess of fertility, was depicted with the head of a hare.

OWL: considered to be a harbinger of death, it is associated with the wisdom of Hecate, goddess of the dark moon. Its hooting is most often heard when the moon is full during the winter months.

WOLF: bays at the full moon, and stands for the psychic aspects of moon wisdom.

The element of earth

Earth is the element of all physical and material things, and its energy is grounding. It is our nurturing mother, and is related to health and prosperity. It is the densest of all the elements, whether it is represented by hard rock or fertile, moist soil, and it stands for stability. It is the solid foundation over which the other elements move.

People in whom the earth element is dominant are home-loving, dependable and loyal, and happiest when surrounded by their family. Earth's energy is receptive. It teaches patience and self-sufficiency, and helps us to recognize and accept our own characters – both their limitations and their potential. It shows us how to take responsibility for our lives and our destiny. Its symbol is the wise elder.

Earth's season is winter and its direction is north, where in the winter darkness the shifting, moving waters are frozen into immobility. In the natural environment, earth's place is a cave, the primal symbol of

△ **The immobility of ice represents the earth element, whose season is winter.**

▽ **Earth is the stable foundation under our feet, but it can also be massive and awe-inspiring.**

shelter. The cave's womb-like image makes it a symbol of birth and rebirth, where oracles speak and enlightenment is achieved. Forests, valleys and fields are other places of the earth element. In the home, earth governs areas of physical needs – the dining room and loo – and practical tasks: the workshop, greenhouse and garden. It is the element of buildings and their construction, and presides over financial institutions.

Earth is the element of ceremony and ritual, through which we regain our connection with the spiritual wisdom of nature. It shows us the way home.

earth gods and goddesses

Some of the deities associated with earth are Gaia, Pan and the Horned God. Gaia is the ancient Greek earth goddess whose name has been given in modern times to the life force of the earth. The daughter of Chaos, she gave birth to Uranus, the sky, and Pontus, the sea. Gaia's union with Uranus produced

EARTH CORRESPONDENCES

DIRECTION: north.
SEASON: winter.
TIME: midnight.
MOON PHASE: dark.
PLANETS: Earth, Saturn.
GENDER: Feminine.
COLOURS: citrine, brown, black, olive green, sometimes white.
SENSE: touch.
MAGICAL TOOL: pentacle.
INSTRUMENTS: percussion.
CREATURES: ox, dog, wolf, goat, stag.
NATURAL SYMBOLS: fossils, stones, grains and seeds, salt, earth.
TREES: cypress, pine.
HERBS: pennyroyal, lovage, sage.
INCENSE: myrrh, patchouli.
MINERALS: lead, emerald, aventurine, pyrites, coal, onyx.
SIGNS: Taurus, Virgo, Capricorn.
ARCHANGEL: Auriel.

▽ The wolf is a creature of the earth element, and represents loyalty and family ties.

the Titans, or giants, including Cronos (Time), the father of Zeus. Gaia was the pre-eminent prophetess, the first deity of the great oracle at Delphi. Even the other gods and immortals were subject to her law. The Greeks worshipped her as the giver of life and the giver of dreams, and the nourisher of plants and children.

In Greek mythology Pan was a shepherd, and his name is believed to be derived from a word meaning 'pasture'. He was easy-going, lazy, sensual and unpredictable, and represents the spirit of untamed nature. He was usually said to be the son of Hermes, and was portrayed with the hind legs and horns of a goat (one of the first animals to be domesticated). Pan was a very ancient

△ Earth's energy is fertile and abundant, seen in the growth of all living things.

god of wild things, and his importance gradually increased until he came to be worshipped as the 'Great God', and father of all living things.

The pagan Horned God, who is related to the Celtic fertility deity Cernunnos, represents sexuality and vitality. He is the consort of the Triple Goddess. Like Pan, he is represented as half-man, half-animal. As lord of the woods he is the hunter, but he is also identified with the hunted or sacrificial animal.

Invoke these deities to bless an altar with the energy of earth.

THE PENTACLE

This five-pointed star may be created from clay, wood, wax or metal. It is a protective symbol of positive power (represented by a circle which often encloses it). The five points represent air, fire, water, earth and spirit.

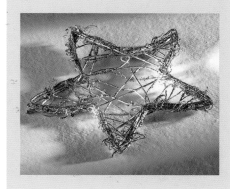

An altar for abundance

The laden altar of the harvest festival is a traditional manifestation of abundance. Corn, bread, fruits and vegetables are brought to the altar as offerings – to give thanks for the bounty of nature – but the mass of produce also acts as a visual re-assurance to members of the community: a reminder of both natural abundance and of their own abilities to harness earth's energy when they grow their food. The sight is an enriching one, expanding hearts and minds: it helps everyone to concentrate on all the good things they have, putting aside thoughts of what they lack.

Dedicating an altar to abundance is about tuning in to the blessings of life, shifting emphasis away from personal limitations and all that we lack, and opening ourselves to new and prosperous possibilities. Prosperity is not only a matter of material possessions, but an attitude of mind that includes spiritual and emotional riches. The altar can be

△ **An altar of abundance dedicated to Lakshmi, should reflect earth colours and scents.**

INCENSE FOR PROSPERITY

1 part cassia bark or cinnamon
1 part grated nutmeg
1 part finely grated orange rind
1 part star anise
Few drops orange essential oil
2 parts frankincense grains

Pound the first four ingredients using a pestle and mortar, bind with the oil and mix in the frankincense grains. Burn on a charcoal block.

a manifestation of that attitude and also a focus for meditations that build up inner abundance – the greatest wealth of all.

Use warm earthy colours such as russet, deep yellow, rich browns and olive greens. Add spicy scents to warm your soul and attract prosperity, such as patchouli, star anise, clove and cinnamon – or make up some prosperity incense mix. Make an offering of some silver coins. Think of all the things that already enrich your life and represent them on the altar to create a positive reminder of your spiritual wealth, and to express your gratitude. The more thankful you are, the more you will find greater abundance being drawn into your life.

the goddess of prosperity

An appropriate deity for this altar would be the Hindu goddess Lakshmi, who is the personification of abundance, wealth and harmony. Deepavali, which is the third day of Diwali, the festival of lights, is dedicated to her worship: lamps are lit inside every home to welcome her and fireworks are exploded in her honour.

Lakshmi is portrayed as a beautiful woman seated on a sacred lotus throne. With two of her four hands she offers blessings of love and joy, while gold coins fall from the other two into the ocean of life. She is a symbol of everything that is fortunate, and it is the nature of good fortune that it is distributed randomly. But the elephant-headed god Ganesha, the lord of obstacles, helps to clear the path of anything that stands in the way of good fortune, therefore his presence on the altar can also help to bring abundance into your home.

CHAI SHEN, THE GOD OF WEALTH

Chinese families have for generations set up an altar outside their homes on the eve of the Lunar New Year to receive the blessings of Chai Shen, the god of wealth, for the coming year. The god arrives from a different direction each year and this must be carefully calculated in case the altar is wrongly placed and welcomes the god of evil instead.

All the family members say prayers and make offerings that symbolize abundance and good fortune, including sweets, fruit and wine. Everyone writes their wishes for the year on red paper, which is burned with offerings of incense. Last year's portrait of Chai Shen is burnt and firecrackers are set off. After the ceremony, the god's portrait is carried inside to watch over the household for the next year.

▽ Be careful what level of prosperity you wish for – greed will not be rewarded.

a prosperity box

To focus on what you want to bring into your life, choose a box to be your 'prosperity box'. Using black ink, write a list of what you wish for. Then write another list using energy-enhancing orange ink: this list should contain all the things you are prepared to do in order to achieve your desires. Fold the pieces of paper and place both lists in the prosperity box, together with a handful of prosperity incense, a few silver coins and a small piece of jade to attract prosperity. Keep the box on your altar. When you receive a gift, leave that too on the altar for a while and always remember to give thanks for what you have, to sustain the flow of abundant energy.

▷ Prosperity boxes can also be filled with wishes for others and with offerings to the wish-granting powers you are calling upon.

An altar for exploring wisdom

The inner journey is a quest for understanding and insight. Regardless of how much is known or learnt, no information can be of true benefit until we have understood how to make the best use of it, and this ability is defined as wisdom. It is an alignment of thought, feeling and experience, and it is only in the light of life experiences that we acquire it.

Wisdom is represented in the person of the sage, or wise elder – someone who has lived long enough to gain experience. If a child or young person seems wise, it is said that they are 'old before their time'. Yet we accrue wisdom throughout life, gaining insight through periods of reflection in solitude and with other people, when experience can be pooled and we can benefit from the learning processes, achievements and errors of others. With wisdom, we can apply knowledge to make sound decisions.

A vast body of traditional 'wisdom literature' has been handed down by ancient sages who spent their lives pondering the eternal truths of life and humanity's place

▽ Sage placed in a shell increases a connection with the Goddess, to whom shells are sacred.

in the universe. In the Judaeo-Christian tradition, for example, these revered texts include many books making up the Bible, Islam is embodied in the Koran, as revealed to the Prophet Muhammed. Hindu wisdom is set out in the Upanishads and the Bhagavadgita, while Buddhists study the Sutras to learn the teachings of Gautama Buddha, and Taoists find wisdom in the Tao Teh Ching and the I Ching. Classical texts of wisdom include the works of Aristotle and Plato.

Aristotle defined two aspects of wisdom. The first concerns the meaning of life – the 'big picture' – which can be sought through meditation and spiritual practices. The second is a more practical kind of wisdom

△ Juno Lucina, the light-bearer, is an ideal deity to invoke for wisdom and illumination.

SOPHIA

In the Hellenistic, Jewish and early Christian traditions, Sophia (the Greek word for 'wisdom') was acknowledged as the female aspect of the divine, and the eternal mother of all. According to the Gnostics, Sophia was born from silence before the beginning of creation. Her greatest shrine was the church of Hagia Sophia, built in Constantinople during the 6th century.

▷ Touch each sage leaf to the candle flame and then drop it into a heatproof bowl to burn and release its sanctifying smoke.

which might almost be described as common sense: the ability to look at things afresh to find ways around everyday problems. In both respects, our exploration of wisdom can lead to a greater perception and acceptance of the connectedness of all things, and an awareness that this wholeness or integrity – the order of the cosmos – includes ourselves. By learning detachment from the individual and particular, we rise above the concept of a separate self to reach a higher level of consciousness that is at one with the universe.

Wisdom can lead us along the right course in our individual lives, but even more important is its role in the wider world, where only the integrating vision of true wisdom can move society towards a more equitable state.

an altar to the Goddess

In the iconography of the Triple Goddess, the third manifestation of the deity is the crone, or wise elder. Her wisdom stems from long experience and she is associated with old age, the closing of the year and the evening of the day, when thoughts turn inwards to memories of the past and visions of the future. She is personified as Hecate

or Cybele, deities of the waning and dark moon, which is the time when insights can be gained. In the darkness of the winter night, the images of the mind's eye lead towards enlightenment.

To evoke the wisdom of the Goddess, dress an altar in purple, the priestly colour of inspiration and spiritual strength. An inspirational figure for its centrepiece could be the Goddess herself, or an image of a wise man or woman whose vision you particularly respect. A figure of an animal that represents an aspect of earth's wisdom could act as an ally in your quest for insight. Focus your thoughts with an amethyst, which brings spiritual peace and good judgement, and aids meditation.

Burn white sage in your ceremony at the altar. Sacred to the Romans, sage was also

◁ Think of the wisest grandparent figure you can imagine when you burn sage, and allow its fragrance to permeate your mind.

used in native American shamanic rites to cleanse and sanctify, and is known as 'grandfather sage' because it represents wisdom. It clears the head and promotes insight. Hold each sage leaf in the flame of a violet candle before dropping it into a shell or bowl to burn, and let its cleansing smoke awaken your wisdom.

ANIMAL TOTEMS
BEAR: going within to find wisdom.
CAT: intuition.
JAGUAR: focused power.
OWL: inner wisdom, vision, the unconscious.
RAVEN: mystery, secrets, memory and thought.
TORTOISE: ancient wisdom, experience, endurance.
WHITE BUFFALO: generosity, selflessness, spirituality.

Correspondence charts

THE SYMBOLISM OF COLOURS

Red: blood, passion, the life essence, power, physical energy, courage, bringing change in difficult circumstances. Associated with Mars, battle, the element of Fire, the south, projective energy

Pink: love and kindness, reconciliation, peace and harmony, compassion, gentle emotions; associated with family, children and friendship, receptive energy

Orange: abundance, fertility, health, joy, attraction, luck; marks the boundary between the self and others; associated with the sun, projective energy

Yellow: communication, the intellect, learning, concentration, also movement, travel and change; associated with Mercury, the element of Air, the east, projective energy

Green: the heart and emotions, love, also nature, gardens and growth, money and prosperity, employment; associated with the Earth element.

Blue: wisdom, patience, possibility, the healing of the spirit, idealism, truth and justice; associated with the moon, the element of Water, the west

Purple: royal and priestly colour, a link with the higher dimension, wisdom, inspiration, magic, religion and spiritual strength; associated with Osiris

Violet: temperance, spirituality, repentance, transition from life to death

Brown: Earth and Earth spirits, instinctive wisdom, the natural world; practical and financial matters, the home, stability, old people, animals; a protective force.

Grey: compromise and adaptability, psychic protection and secrecy

White: divinity, potential, the life-force, energy, purity; contains all other colours; associated with the sun; helpful for new beginnings, clear vision and originality

Black: death and regeneration; conclusions that lead to new beginnings, marking a boundary with the past, banishing and releasing negativity, shedding guilt and regret; associated with Saturn, the Roman god of limitations, suffering and transformation

Gold: worldly achievement, wealth, long life and ambition, confidence and understanding; associated with solar deities.

Silver: dreams, visions, intuition, hidden potential; associated with the moon and lunar deities

THE SYMBOLISM OF CRYSTALS

Agate: good for grounding and protection

Amber: good luck stone, draws out disease and clears negativity and depression

Amethyst: peace, protection and spirituality; promotes harmony and balance in the home, clears negativity; disperses electro-magnetic emissions from electrical appliances; heals at all levels; helps with meditation and peaceful sleep, can inspire dreams

Angelite: heals anger, restores harmony, helpful in telepathic communication, connecting with angels and spirits

Aventurine: healing at all levels, dissolves blockages, balances the emotions, green aventurine attracts good fortune and increases perception; pink aventurine heals relationships

Azurite: mental clarity and renewal

Black onyx: protects against negative energy, helps emotional stability, encourages connection with reality

Carnelian: aids creative flow, grounds in the present, inspires confidence, courage and motivation

Chrysocolla: soothes and calms, eases fear and guilt, attracts luck

Chrysoprase: emotionally uplifting, attracts abundance and success, spiritual energy

Citrine: prevents nightmares, enhances self-esteem and mental clarity, brings abundance and material well-being; useful for areas where bookkeeping is done

Clear quartz: amplifies energy, spiritually and emotionally healing and empowering, aids meditation; can be used to dispel negative energy and harmful emissions from electrical appliances

Emerald: physically healing and protective, lends insight and security in love

Garnet: stimulates energy, aids expression, strengthens love and friendship

Hematite: aids concentration, reasoning, memory and self-discipline; healing and protective

Herkimer diamond: releases energy blockages, helps with dream recall

Jade: promotes clarity and wisdom; balances the emotions, facilitates peaceful sleep, attracts prosperity

Jet: lifts depression and wards off nightmares; brings wisdom, health and long life

Lapis lazuli: strengthens will, awareness, integrity in relationships; aids the release of emotional wounds

Malachite: healing, absorbs negativity, stimulates creativity

and strengthens intuition; useful for work areas

Moonstone: wishes, intuition and new beginnings; restores harmony in relationships, calms emotions and induces lucid dreaming

Moss agate: connects with earth spirits, brings abundance and self-confidence

Obsidian: place in a room for protection and grounding; dissolves anger and fear; snowflake obsidian has a softer effect, restores balance and clarity

Opal: visionary, attracts inspiration and insight

Pearl: enhances purity, clarity and grace

Peridot: warm and friendly, heals wounded self-esteem

Pyrites: provides protection and defence against negative energies; harnesses creative thinking and practicality

Red jasper: connects with earth energy, emotionally calming

Rhodonite: fosters patience, selflessness

Rose quartz: heals emotional wounds, restores love of self and others; brings peace and calm; can be placed at an entrance to "greet" visitors; keeps the atmosphere positive

Ruby: amplifies emotions, releases and dissolves anger, attracts loyalty, awakens passion

Rutilated quartz: releases energy blockages

Sapphire: symbolizes peace, gives protection and prophetic wisdom

Smoky quartz: lightly grounding and balancing, counteract hyperactivity, fosters self-acceptance and awareness of divine protection

Tiger's eye: creates order and harmony, stability, attracts beauty and abundance

Topaz: symbolizes light and warmth, heals and absorbs tension, attracts love and creativity

Tourmaline: grounding, healing and protective, absorbs negativity and brings discernment and vitality; green tourmaline for success; pink tourmaline for peaceful sleep; watermelon tourmaline for sexual energy; yellow tourmaline for wisdom and understanding

Turquoise: symbolizes protection, blessing and partnership

Zircon: aids healing and sleep

THE SYMBOLISM OF PLANTS AND HERBS

Angelica: burn dried leaves for protection and healing

Anise: keeps away nightmares

Apple blossom: for love and friendship

Basil: gives protection, repels negativity and brings wealth

Bay: guardian of the house, protection against illness; burn leaves to induce visions

Bergamot: attracts success and prosperity

Blessed thistle: brings spiritual and financial blessings; if fresh, brings strengthening energy to a sickroom

Boneset: drives away evil

Cabbage: brings good luck

Catnip: encourages a psychic bond with cats, attracts luck and happiness

Chamomile: for meditation and relaxation; use in prosperity charms to draw money

Chickweed: for attracting love or maintaining a relationship

Chilli: assures fidelity and love

Cinnamon: aphrodisiac; draws money, protection and success

Clove: banishes hostile or negative forces and helps to gain what is sought; burn in incense to stop others gossiping

Clover: for love and fidelity

Coltsfoot: brings love, wealth and peace

Comfrey: for safety when travelling

Cyclamen: for love and truth

Dandelion: enhances dreams and prophetic power

Eucalyptus: healing and purifying

Fennel: protects from curses: hang round doors and windows

Gardenia: for peace and healing

Garlic: for magical healing, protection and exorcism; especially protective in new homes

Ginger: for success and empowerment

Grape: for fertility and garden magic; attracts money

Hibiscus: attracts love and aids divination and dreams

Honeysuckle: strengthens the memory, helps in letting go of the past

Hops: improves health and induces sleep

Hyacinth: for love and protection

Hyssop: purification; hang up in the home to dispel negativity

Jasmine: brings good fortune in love, friendship and wealth; raises self-esteem; induces lucid dreams

Juniper: calms and brings good health; berries are burned to ward off evil

Lavender: purifying; brings peace and happiness, love and sweet dreams

Lemon: attracts happiness, relieves stress

Lettuce: induces sleep, assists in divination

Lily of the valley: brings peace, harmony and love

Lime: increases energy, encourages loyalty

Lotus: emblem of enlightenment, elevates and protects

Magnolia: assures fidelity

Marigold: enhances visions and dreams; renews personal energy

Mistletoe: for protection, love and visionary ability; hang on the bedpost for beautiful dreams

Mugwort: for clairvoyance, scrying and dream interpretation

Mullein: gives courage, keeps away nightmares

Nettle: wards off curses, allays fear

Olive: brings peace of mind and fidelity in love, fruitfulness and security

Orange: attracts peace, power and luck

Orris: attracts love and romance

Passion flower: fosters friendship; brings peace and understanding

Pennyroyal: increases alertness and brainpower; brings peace between partners

Pine: grounding and cleansing; use for a fresh start

Rice: attracts fertility and money

Rose: blesses love, domestic peace, generosity and beauty

Rosemary: protects the home; brings mental clarity and sharpens memory

Sage: brings wisdom, fertility, healing and long life

St John's wort: burn leaves to cleanse and protect

Strawberry: for love and luck

Sweet pea: for friendship and courage

Thyme: for courage and confidence

Tuberose: for eroticism and romance

Valerian: brings love and harmony, helps fighting couples to find peace

Vervain: attracts money, protection; transforms enemies into friends; brings inner strength and peace

Violet: contentment and love

Willow: use leaves and bark for healing and to empower wishes

GODS AND ANGELS

Agni: Hindu god of fire

Amaterasu: Shinto sun goddess

Aphrodite: Greek goddess of love and beauty

Apollo: Greek god of the sun, medicine and music; patron of the Muses

Arianrhod: Celtic mother goddess, keeper of time and fate

Artemis: Greek goddess of the waxing moon, protector of women

Athene: Greek goddess of war, wisdom and the arts

Auriel: archangel, earth

Bastet: Egyptian goddess of love and fertility; represented with the head of a cat

Brigid: Celtic triple goddess, fire deity and patron of the hearth, healing, prophecy and inspiration

Cassiel: angel who assists with overcoming obstacles

Ceres: Roman goddess of earth and agriculture

Ceridwen: Welsh mother, moon and grain goddess

Cernunnos: The Celtic horned god of fertility

Cybele: Phrygian dark moon goddess who governs nature, wild beasts and dark magic

Demeter: Greek goddess of the earth, corn and vegetation; represents abundance and love

Diana: Roman goddess of hunting and the moon; represents chastity, protects women in childbirth

Epona: Celtic horse-goddess of fertility and healing

Freya: Norse mother goddess of love, marriage and fertility

Gabriel: archangel of the moon; associated with the west

Gaia: primeval Greek earth deity, prophetess of Delphi, goddess of dreams

Ganesha: elephant-headed Hindu god of wisdom and literature, patron of business

Haniel: archangel of divine love and harmony, beauty and the creative arts

Hathor: Egyptian sky-deity, goddess of love, joy and dance, usually represented as a cow

Hecate: three-headed Greek goddess of the waning moon, who rules magic, sorcery, death and the underworld

Hermes: Greek messenger god; represents consciousness, transition and exchange

Hestia: Greek goddess of the hearth and stability

Indra: Hindu god of war; associated with weather

Ishtar: Mesopotamian goddess of sexual love, fertility and war

Isis: Egyptian mother-goddess, wife of Osiris; represents life, loyalty, fertility and magic

Ixchel: Mayan goddess of storms and protector of women in childbirth

Janus: Roman guardian of the entrance and god of transition

Jizo: Japanese protector of children and travellers

Kali: destructive aspect of the Hindu mother-goddess

Kuanyin: Chinese goddess of compassion

Lakshmi: Hindu goddess of abundance, wealth and harmony

Lugh: Celtic sky-god; associated with the arts

Luna: Roman goddess of the full moon

Maat: Egyptian goddess of truth, justice and order

Mercury: Roman messenger god; associated with speech, breath, wind and magic

Michael: archangel of the sun; associated with rulership, marriage, music

Minerva: Roman goddess of wisdom

Mithras: Roman god of light

Nephthys: sister of Isis, guardian of the dead Osiris

Neptune: Roman god of the sea

Osiris: Egyptian god, judge of the dead, husband of Isis; symbolizes regeneration of nature

Pan: Greek horned god of wild things; half man, half animal

Parvati: Hindu mother-goddess, consort of Shiva

Raphael: archangel of the air element; associated with communication and business

Re: Egyptian sun god and creator

Sachiel: angel ruling justice and financial matters

Samael: protective archangel; helps with matters that require courage or perseverance

Selene: Greek goddess of the full moon

Shang Ti: Chinese supreme god

Shiva: Hindu creator god, whose meditation sustains the world

Sophia: divine knowledge and wisdom

Sul: Celtic sun goddess

Sunna: Norse sun goddess

Surya: Hindu sun god

Tara: Tibetan goddess of wisdom and compassion

Thoth: Egyptian god of wisdom and the moon

Tsao-chun: Taoist kitchen god

Uriel: archangel of high magic

Venus: Roman goddess of love and beauty

Vesta: Roman goddess of the hearth

Vishnu: Hindu protector of the world

Zeus: Greek supreme god

Index

Picture Acknowledgements

The publishers would like to thank the following picture libraries for the use of their pictures.
Abode UK: 103br; 110t; 111tl.
A-Z Botanical Collection ltd.:43br(Mike Vardy).
The Garden Picture Library: 43bl (Morley Read).
Robert Harding Picture Library: 107tl (IPC Magazines); 109tl (IPC Magazines); 110b (IPD Magazines); 111bl (IPC Magazines).
Houses and Interiors: 42tr (Roger Brooks); 50bl (Roger Brooks), tr (Roger Brooks); 54tr (Mark Bolton); 55bl (Mark Bolton); 58tr (Roger Brooks); 87l (Verne); 90bl (Mark Bolton); 100tr; 116tr (Mark Bolton), bl (Mark Bolton).
Hutchinson Library: 10br (Robert Francis); 12tr (Merilyn Thorold); 15tr (Melanie Friend); 28bl (T. Moser), br (Lesley Nelson); 29tl (F. Horner); 30t (Edward Parker), bl (Sarah Errington), r (John G Egan); 31bl (Tony Souter); 36tr (Pern.), r (P.W. Rippon), bl (Robert Francis); 37tl (Tony Souter), bl (Carlos Freire), tr (G. Griffiths-Jones); 44t; 45tl (Phillip Wolmuth), t (L. Taylor), t, m, br (Andrew Sole); 70b (Sarah Murray); 71tl (Lesley Nelson); 73t (N. Durrell McKenna); 122bl (N.Durrell).
Images Colour Library:; 13b; 14b; 15bl, bl; 16tr; 17no. 2, no. 5; 27br; 31tr.
The Interior Archive: 10tl (Schulenburg); 11tr (Schulenburg); 46tr (Schulenburg); 50r (C. Simon Sykes); 56bl (Schulenburg); 57t (Schulenburg); 69tr (Henry Wilson); 76 (Schulenburg); 78tr (Schulenburg); 79tl (Schulenburg); 82bl (Schulenburg), t (Simon Upton); 86bl (Schulenburg); 86b (Schulenburg); 89tr (Schulenburg); 91bl (Schulenburg); 92br (Henry Wilson); 94t (Tim Beddow); 96bl (Schulenburg); 99r (Schulenburg); 102tr (Schulenburg),b (Schulenburg); 104l (Schulen-burg); 107tr (Schulenburg);108bl (Schulenburg); 112tr (Henry Wilson), bl (Schulenburg); 113bl (Schulenburg), br (Schulenburg); 115tl (Schulen-burg), br (Schulenburg); 121tl; 124br (Schulenburg).
The Stock Market: 16br; 17no. 1 (K. Biggs); 38tr, bl, br; 39b, t; 40tl, m; 41tl; 66t (David Lawrence); 68br; 69tl, tr; 70t; 117b;
Tony Stone: 68bl (Angus M. Mackillop).
Jessica Strang: 122r.
Superstock: 24tr, m; 25br.
View: 11m (Phillip Bier); 17no. 1 (Dennis Gilbert); 45tr (Phillip Bier); 47l (Chris Gascoigne); 56tr (Phillip Bier), br (Phillip Bier); 57bl (Phillip Bier); 67tr (Peter Cook); 90tr (Phillip Bier); 96bl (Peter Cook); 98tr (Chris Gascoigne); 101tl (Phillip Bier); 117tl (PhillipBier); 122t (Chris Gascoigne); 123l (Peter Cook);
Elizabeth Whiting Associates: 44m; 45m, tr; 46br; 50r; 62tr, bl; 63tr; 66bl; 71r, br; 72bl; 78bl, l; 79tr; 86t; 71t; 93tr; 95tl; 104br; 118tr; 119r, bl; 120t; 121tr, bl.

Bibliography

Lau, Theodora, The Handbook of Chinese Horoscopes (HarperCollins, London, 1979)
Man-Ho Kwok, Palmer, Martin & Ramsay, Jay, The Tao Te Ching (Element, London, 1997)
Ni, Hua-Ching, The Book of Changes and the Unchanging Truth (Seven Star Communications, Santa Monica, 1983)
Palmer, Martin, The Elements of Taoism (Element, Shaftesbury, 1991)
Palmer, Martin, Yin and Yang (Piatkus, London, 1997)
Walters, Derek, Chinese Astrology (Aquarian Press, London, 1992)
Walters, Derek, The Feng Shui Handbook (Aquarian Press, London, 1991)
Wong, Eva, Feng Shui (Shambhala, Boston, 1996)
Franz, Marie-Louise von, Time (Thames and Hudson, London, 1978)
Jung, Carl, Man and his Symbols (Arkana, London, 1990)
Lawlor, Anthony, The Temple in the House (G.P. Putnam's Sons, New York, 1994)
Lawlor, Robert, Sacred Geometry: Philosophy and Practice (Thames and Hudson, London, 1982)
Lindqvist, Cecilia, China: Empire of Living Symbols (Massachusetts, Reading, 1991)
Mann, A.T., Sacred Architecture (Element, Shaftesbury, 1993)
Pennick, Nigel, Earth Harmony: Places of Power, Holiness and Healing (Capall Bann, Chieveley, 1997)
Poynder, Michael, Pi in the Sky (The Collins Press, Cork, 1997)
Cowan, David & Girdlestone, Rodney, Safe as houses? Ill Health and Electro-Stress in the Home (Gateway Books, Bath, 1996)
Myers, Norman (ed), The Gaia Atlas of Planetary Management (Gaia Book Ltd., London, 1994)
Pearson, David, The New Natural House Book (Conran Octopus, London, 1989)
Thurnell-Read, Jane, Geopathic Stress (Element, Shaftesbury, 1995)
Kingston, Karen, Creating Sacred Space with Feng Shui (Piatkus, London, 1996)
Linn, Denise, Sacred Space (Rider, London, 1995)
Treacy, Declan, Clear your Desk (Century Business, 1992)